Growing into WAR

MICHAEL GILL

Foreword by
A.A. GILL

SUTTON PUBLISHING

First published in the United Kingdom in 2005 by
Sutton Publishing Limited · Phoenix Mill
Thrupp · Stroud · Gloucestershire · GL5 2BU

British Library Cataloguing in Publication Data
A catalogue record for this book is available from the British Library.

ISBN 0-7509-4285-1

Typeset in 11/14pt Garamond.
Typesetting and origination by
Sutton Publishing Limited.
Printed and bound in England by
J.H. Haynes & Co. Ltd, Sparkford.

I dedicate this book to my three children,
Adrian, Nicholas and Chloe

CONTENTS

LIST OF ILLUSTRATIONS

FOREWORD

My father never wrote at a desk. He always sat on the sofa and used a felt tip pen to write in longhand on a clipboard surrounded by books, larded with ripped-up paper bookmarks. A desk would have been too formal, too reminiscent of his father the bank manager. He didn't wear suits or ties either or go in for any of the coded trappings of probity, the Establishment or the past.

He was a man who was happy to be at home in his time. He liked contemporary things, contemporary people and ideas. I never once heard him hanker for yesterday, or ever wax nostalgic. He was a man of his age and worked in the medium that both marked and identified the age – television.

He wrote constantly: scripts, proposals, drafts, letters, chapters of books, the start of journals and for me, postcards. School breakfasts were an expectation of a card from dad. He travelled a lot filming and they'd arrive with pictures of strange cathedrals or exuberant statues and his familiar, timidly excited handwriting that seemed to be fighting its classical pre-war education to become something a little more extempore. The cards were always civilised. He had a passion for museum shops and church porch racks, and his cards were always full of information, facts and observations, wrapped up with pithy, often funny opinions. They were like scenes from a shooting script.

He never wasted time with the 'Wish you were here, weather's lovely . . . food's foreign . . .' stuff and a small but lasting part of my education came from these postcards. Not least the lesson that anything worth saying can be said both succinctly and elegantly, and that the prime purpose of writing to anyone, be it a letter, an article or a book, is not to show them how clever you are, but to leave them cleverer than they were.

When he finally finished making television programmes he settled down on the sofa with his annotated books and started to write. We'd all encouraged him to embark on a book. He has a charmingly face-to-face style, a turn of phrase that is only a voice away from listening to him; and some memoirs from the pioneering public-service age of broadcasting would have been interesting and a gift for posterity. He'd interviewed Marilyn Monroe, worked with Giacometti and plenty of other interesting people in between. We'd all lived in London during the Sixties.

So it was a surprise when he started writing the story of his childhood. It seemed very previous. When I was a child he told us stories, but they were invariably about his dog, Patch. I had only the haziest idea of his early life or our antecedants beyond my grandparents. I'd never imagined that he really thought it that important. He always seemed to have that self-contained confidence that is the consolation of the only child.

What we didn't know was that he was, already, incubating the first losses of Alzheimer's. I write about him in the past tense, though he's not dead, and I don't mean to imply that he's any less alive, or any less my dad, but dementia and the rubbing-out of words, connections and memories are a great and widening moat that separates the him on this side from the man that was on the other.

When I read this book for the first time, he'd already crossed over, and pulled up the drawbridge. It was a huge shock. I'd never heard any of it before. This life that was so vivid, so beautifully remembered and reconstructed. I would never be able to talk to him about it, ask him about this marvellous cast of characters. But as I read it I understood that that was exactly the reason and the rightness for going back. My father was as much a self-made, self-thought-up man as anyone you'll meet.

The choices we make and the courses we plot are cause and effect of where we started and who we started with. The man my father became and whom I knew wasn't so much a reaction against the world he was brought up in, but someone who felt that he and his generation had an obligation to change and improve it. I realised there is far less distance between my childhood and my children's than between mine and my father's.

There was another pressing reason to write this down. The Alzheimer's meant that it would all be lost and broken into shards of non-sequitur and nonsense. This book is Daddy committing his memories to the lifeboats, this is what got out, this is what survived and made it safely into print. Women and childhood first.

A.A Gill
London 2005

1

DISTANT RELATIONS

I

The first thought that I can recall – something that came from my own mind as opposed to feelings and reactions to outside events – this thought, powerful enough to seem still vivid over sixty years later, came to me on a summer Sunday morning in 1929.

My parents had just built a house in Herne Bay, the small town on the south-east coast of England to which we had moved. It was near the brow of a hill on what was a wheat field when we first saw it. Ours was the first house on a new concrete byroad that was built at the same time.

Every Sunday morning my father would play golf while my mother cooked the lunch. Coming from a Yorkshire farm, she was a very good cook. Often, when the roast beef was nearly ready, we would walk together over the fields to meet my father returning from the golf club in the valley.

One day she told me I could go and meet him by myself. I was nearly six years old and about to start school. I was very proud of the responsibility. She waved me goodbye from the door.

I walked up the road to where it petered out in a wilderness of nettles and thistles and took the familiar path across the fields. Rabbits scuttled away into the hedgerows. I climbed the first stile, between the pallid blooms of wild rose. This was a favourite playground: a wide breast of the hill, comfortable to lie back on and watch the occasional biplane rising and falling as it droned its way across the Channel to distant magical places. A few months before, when it had been bright with poppies, I ran straight into a lark's nest, a rough twist of grass holding four tiny eggs. Now I walked firmly forward, not even stopping to see how ripe the blackberries were. I was pleased with my independence.

When I crossed the second stile I began to falter; I would soon be entering unfamiliar territory. Then I saw my father coming into sight over the slope. I felt a tremendous wave of pleasure and excitement. I rushed up to him and banged him on the knee, explaining that I had been sent to hurry him up, as lunch was ready. (He was often a little late, if the nineteenth hole proved a long one.)

He took my hand, and told me how the match had gone. Golf was not a game I understood very well, but I liked walking beside him, having a serious conversation. When we had nearly reached our house, my mother came to the doorway.

'Look,' I shouted, 'I've brought Daddy home.'

She smiled. Throughout my life she had enveloped me with love and power. Having been away from her on this great adventurous journey, I suddenly saw her as though for the first time. She was beautiful. I felt sure that no one else would ever mean as much to me.

II

Of course, if I trawl my mind back to my earliest memories, many fragmentary images occur. One *feeling* dominates: pain. A terrible piercing pain that filled my head so that I wanted to wrench it off and throw it away. Instead, I would throw myself about and scream and scream. My head would be wrapped in scarves and laid on a hot-water bottle. This was only a temporary comfort. The pain would return, shooting triumphantly through my head in great throbbing bursts.

Though I remember nothing of it, when I was eighteen months old I was taken to Southampton Hospital and had a mastoid operation on my left ear. I have been told that this was a relatively rare and serious operation in 1925, and especially at my age. It involved chiselling through the bone of the skull. What I thought about it was expressed in my reaction to my father. He had carried me into the hospital and when, weeks later, he came to collect me from my cot, I turned my back on him. Intermittent pain and infections in my ear troubled my childhood for years. This was long before the days of antibiotics. I remember being dosed with a dark sticky medicine of indescribable bitterness.

Illness has been a recurring thread in my life. For years it was assumed by my parents that I would be fit for only the most sedentary job. Fruit farming was the general preference. At that time we lived in Kent, in a landscape jostling with apple trees. I preferred the thought of writing – though it has taken me a long time to get down to it seriously.

That all comes later. My first four years were spent in Winchester in a big half-timbered Edwardian house that my parents shared with my mother's parents. Memories from those times are like the vivid images from a film trailer. Now I can subtitle them with what my parents told me later. I recall a kindly old man with grizzled whiskers peering down at me as I lay in my pram in the garden and tickling me. I still had a bandaged head, so it must have been soon after my operation. He was Sturt, the first in a long line of benign gardeners who have weeded my paths.

Another favourite was Bailey, my grandmother's chauffeur. I was fascinated by his olive uniform with its shiny buttons and polished leather gaiters. A ride in the big upright Chrysler was a great treat. It had a silver vase attached to the dividing panel, always with a fresh cut rose in it, and a yellow corded speaking-tube. The glossy fur rug to put over our knees I imagined to be a buffalo skin that had come, like the car, from America. The huge head of a real buffalo that had been shot on the Great Plains by my great-grandfather adorned the wall of the local museum in Batley, Yorkshire. My mother's family had been mill owners there for generations. We often went back to Yorkshire for Christmas or summer holidays to stay at the family farm – now run by my mother's elder brother, Tom. He was said to have been a wonderful horseman in his early days. Lean and bow-legged, he had the look of a rider.

I have another reason to remember his legs. On my third Christmas I was given the game of Snakes and Ladders. The board was illustrated by Mabel Lucie Attwell and showed a mustachioed policeman pursuing a plump little dog that had stolen a string of sausages. If you landed on the sausages you slid back down the board; land on a ladder and you would climb up to where the policeman was brandishing his warning truncheon. I was greatly taken by the power this truncheon demonstrated. One morning I went into the kitchen and 'borrowed' the rolling pin. I ran along the narrow corridors and steep stairs, from the dairy to the music room, brandishing my new authority at all I met. Eventually I reached the bathroom. My uncle was shaving with his usual care. (He had a different cut-throat razor for every day of the week.) His long, bony legs, bare between shirt-tails and garters, were just on my eyeline.

'Unc,' I shouted, 'I'm a policeman.'

And, in proof, I whacked him on the shin with all my strength. The dent was visible decades later.

Equally memorable was our return to Winchester at the end of that holiday. Much of England seemed to be flooded. Men carrying red flags diverted us down winding lanes where the water lay like glass on every side. It was nightfall before Bailey's careful driving brought us in a snow blizzard into Hampshire. I dozed on my grandmother's knee waking to a succession of snow palaces glittering in the headlights. I doubt if I had ever been driven at night before. To my sleepy mind it seemed as though we were entering a magic world.

Eventually I woke with a start to realise the car had stopped, it was pitch dark and Bailey was lifting me out onto his shoulder. I couldn't tell where we were, but Bailey explained that we were on the last stretch of the road home when the Chrysler stuck in a snowdrift. Sometimes he was up to his waist in the fine powdery stuff. I didn't mind. I would have liked every homecoming to have been as exciting.

There was still a further surprise. Instead of only my grandparents' cook waiting to welcome us, the kitchen was crowded with dark-skinned people hugging round them a mixture of colourful rags and our blankets. Their strange chatter was hushed as Bailey carried me through to my nursery. He knew them, of course. They were the gypsies who lived in two caravans over the hill. Lacking any heat except peat fires, they had been given shelter from the blizzard by our kindly cook.

This bastion of caring, cheerful servants peoples my memories of Winchester. They came to us, as did the big house itself, through the generosity of my uncle in Detroit. My mother's families, the Taylors and the Thomases, had started emigrating to the States in the 1830s. Each generation sent over a fresh wave. My mother's favourite brother, Clifford, went to join *his* uncle when he was sixteen. He returned to lose a leg fighting at the Somme. This had not impeded his financial success as a stockbroker. His business acumen was no doubt aided by his personal friendships with Detroit car builders such as Edsel Ford. He never gave up his British citizenship or forgot to share his good fortune with his parents in the old country.

By contrast, my father's family was solidly working class. Both my grandfather and my great-grandfather spent their lives in the noisy dusty caverns connected with the clothing industry.

The mill owners, like my grandfather's family, the Taylors, built big houses for themselves on the hilltops. The factories were down by the fast-running stream, and on the steep slopes between were the long rows of workers' cottages. We used to visit my grandfather George Gill when we were staying at the Taylor farm. My grandfather was a stocky man with a heavy beer belly. He smoked a pipe and when he bent to kiss me his moustache smelt of tea and tobacco. I liked him, though I thought his house much too small. There were only two rooms, one on each floor. The front door opened straight in from the street. There was room for a couple of shabby armchairs. Then the room changed into the kitchen with a long coal-fired range that included an oven and heated the water and the cottage itself. A sink, a table, two wooden chairs and a larder completed the downstairs furnishings. The narrow stairs ran up the side wall. The upper room had a double bed and a smaller bed in which my father and his elder brother slept through their childhood. A blanket pinned to the ceiling divided the generations. What would they have done if they had had a son and a daughter?

Out the back there was a water tap (this was a recent luxury; beforehand they had had to use a pump at the end of the terrace); a clothes line, a heap of coal (part of my grandfather's wages was a sack of coal a week) and a shed housing an outside lavatory shared with the neighbours.

Reviewing it, I'm struck by how efficiently it covered the bare necessities. No radio, no TV, no CD. No supermarket range of goods. My grandfather had one week's holiday a year. He always spent it with us in Kent. While with us, he and my father would take a day trip to Calais or Boulogne. He would send French postcards to all his cronies in Dewsbury. It was the high point of the year.

I cannot remember my grandfather losing his temper, or seeming discontented with his lot. I never met his wife, my grandmother. She was said to be highly strung and to adore her clever younger son Arnold, my father. During the First World War she received an official telegram informing her of his death in action. It was untrue – he was not even wounded – but she suffered a stroke from which she never recovered.

My grandfather accepted this loss with the resignation that he showed in so many different ways. He had a consolation. He was a brilliant wood-carver. He could make cabinets and bed tables and chests of drawers of a perfection that made it a pleasure to touch them. I still have a bed table he made for me in my years of illness and a smoothly articulated tool chest. And, as often with a skilful craftsman, he acquired a companion to compensate for the long lingering death of his wife. Because of this unmarried woman friend I was never allowed to spend as much time with him as I would have liked.

III

A mouse robbed me of a sister. Running across the kitchen floor, it so startled my pregnant mother that she jumped on a chair and had a miscarriage that evening. At the time I was three and a half and knew nothing of such things. I missed my mother at breakfast (she went on a recuperative cruise to the Canaries with my Aunt Mabel). In compensation I saw more of my grandparents.

I was in awe of my grandfather, William Taylor. He was very kind, but he often seemed far away. His white imperial beard made him look like the King (I sometimes mixed them up). There was no mistaking my grandmother.

Emily Ann Thomas was handsome rather than beautiful, dark and vivid. In her youth she looked Spanish, her eyes deep pools in the powerful angles of her face. She was always very trim and erect. In her thirties, when she had spent some eight years married to her cousin William Taylor, a charming but improvident farmer, she looked quite different. A wild defiant gaze must have reflected the pains and disappointments of life with an alcoholic. It was her inheritance that kept the farm going.

The money came from the piano factory that my great-grandfather had set up in Kilburn in the 1860s. A skilled craftsman in furniture, he made the casing while his German partner provided the musical parts. When my grandmother was in her late teens she was entrusted with collecting the weekly wages for the factory hands. She carried this considerable sum of money in a leather briefcase that was chained to her wrist. One Friday she was walking back from the bank along the busy Kilburn High Road. A man darted out of an alleyway and grabbed the bag. He nearly dislocated her arm, but was unable to break the chain. She resisted as best she could, but was dragged further and further down the deserted alley. None of the hurrying passers-by took the least notice. She was thrown from side to side and retaliated by beating at the man's head with her free hand. He was quite a small fellow, she remembered, when she told me half a century later.

'Didn't you call out?' I asked.

'No, that was the strange part. We neither of us said a word.'

When she felt her strength was nearly gone, a policeman appeared at the end of the alley. Her assailant ran, leaving her with a bruised and torn arm.

'Did you carry the money the next week?'

'Yes, but one of the bigger factory workers came with me.'

That was my grandmother. She would not let a small misadventure put her off carrying out her duty. Brought up in a mid-Victorian house in London, where music was played and German spoken as a second language, where there were regular visits every few years from relatives across the Atlantic, she acquired a sophistication and poise she never lost. Even though I knew her only in the last few years of her life, I was aware of the close relationship she had with her only daughter, my mother. My grandmother's strength of character was always a support for her gentle, inherently shy and sensitive child. My mother also visited America, first when she was twelve and then she spent a whole year there when she was eighteen, but she preferred the moorlands of the Brontë country to the hustle of the New World. That might have been all right for my mother, but for my grandmother a small farm in Yorkshire was not a good exchange for a mansion in Kilburn.

Why did my grandmother throw herself away on her fecklessly charming country cousin? He was the youngest son of the Taylor whose factory processing shoddy or woollen waste was one of the many polluting the atmosphere of Dewsbury. There was nothing for William to inherit but the farm, which his father had acquired only as a hobby.

My grandmother with her sharp business sense must have realised it was never going to make an adequate return. Why did she not insist that William follow the example of her own brothers, who were doing extremely well in the booming Midwest? William had no ambition; he liked the country life and the chummy drinking bouts that followed the local cricket matches. There was no cricket in America. He himself had been an elegant batsman. Perhaps it was his physicality that kept the unlikely couple together.

My grandmother had had many other admirers in her youth. One was still with us in Winchester. Henry Talbot had fallen for her when she first appeared in Yorkshire society some forty years before. His devotion never flagged. He never married and lived with a spinster sister on a small inheritance. He and William used to go up to London to watch the test matches, staying in Henry Talbot's club. When his sister, his only close relative, died, it seemed the natural thing for him to move into a spare room in the farm and later into Pitt Corner. In Winchester, he had his own bedsitting room and bathroom. I took his presence entirely for granted. He would take me for walks.

We would go to a big pond in a hollow and throw the ducks scraps of bread. I was probably not a very accurate thrower. The ducks would come clamouring out of the water and once I was bitten by an importunate drake. I can still remember how curious it felt; like being slapped with wet rubber. Climbing out of the hollow, I would take Mr Talbot – Tor as I called him – by the hand. In it would be a boiled sweet wrapped up in paper. Nothing would be said, but when I had finished it another would miraculously appear.

These satisfactory excursions cannot have lasted long. Tor vanished out of my life with no more explanation than went with the appearance of the sweets. Years later I was told that he had been arrested strolling down Winchester High Street in his shoes and spats. He was always a meticulous dresser, but on this occasion he was wearing nothing else. Shortly after he had a brain haemorrhage and died.

His old drinking companion soon followed him. I knew my grandfather was ill. Even on the warmest days he would sit wrapped in a rug in a sheltered corner of the garden. I would take advantage of his somnolence to creep up close and study every aspect of his appearance. I was particularly fascinated by his hands. Long and slender, his fingers lying on the rug seemed almost transparent, as fragile as our best-quality china, which I was always being warned not to drop when it was brought out for Sunday tea.

2

A FRIEND FOR LIFE

I

The Scottish soldier sat at the entrance to his tent. He was a blaze of health and colour: scarlet jacket, scarlet and green kilt, fair moustache, pink cheeks, pink knees, a dirk sticking in his fat stockings. His Indian servant stood at his elbow, impassive and attentive in immaculate white. Beneath their feet the grass was bright green. Behind them, I imagined, loomed the gloomy defiles of the Khyber Pass and beyond, glittering peak on peak, the Himalayas. I had to imagine that, because what I actually saw were the upraised noses of the Bisto Kids, sniffing appreciatively at the cardboard steam. There were other cut-outs in the window of the village shop: a prancing golliwog advertising marmalade, the gleaming teeth of the Eno's girl; but it was this big central group for liquid coffee that held my attention when I first passed by in my baby chair.

I still got whoever was pushing me to stop. It was a sort of indulgence, because now I was eight years old and could read in *Wizard* the adventures of King of the Khyber Pass and his squat servant, who cracked the heads of recalcitrant tribesmen with his battered cricket bat, Clicky-ba, and in *The Times* of the bombing of villages in the region by the RAF. It seemed there was always trouble on the Frontier. My father thought they should send T.E. Lawrence to deal with it. Would he grow a beard and carry two long curved knives like King? Was he really needed? Surely nothing could be more imposing than the Scottish soldier. I would have looked longer, but my dog, Patch, grew impatient and jerked at his lead. It was tied to a spring of the spinal chair and the bouncing told me it was time to move. Patch was lifted onto my lap and I stroked him quiet. He was small and fluffy and a wire-haired fox terrier. He had replaced Teddy, my bear, as my closest companion.

Illness had grown imperceptibly from a temperature, which would not return to normal after a cold. I was moved into my parents' bedroom. The flower patterns on the wallpaper took on strange shapes, fluctuating and twisting. I watched them from the end of a long tunnel, infinitely receding. Just to be lifted up while the sheets were straightened was exhausting. One day the doctor stood with my parents upside down on the ceiling at the foot of the bed and told me I must hang on. The voice that answered did not seem to be my own. For some time I existed on lemon ice cubes and vitamins fed through a tube rectally. It was an odd, soothing sensation and used to send me to sleep. Eventually, wrapped in blankets, I was taken to London to see a famous children's doctor. He looked like the photograph of J.M. Barrie in my *Peter Pan* book. His name was Sir Frederick Still. I sat on his knee and he probed me with gentle, bony fingers. It was decided I had a disease from milk, bovine tuberculosis, with complications. The treatment was rest. I rested – altogether for five years. The first three I was mostly flat on my back.

I did not regard this as an imposition, except during the ferocious attacks of vomiting which were among the complications. Indeed, especially after the first few months when I could be pushed out in the long wickerwork spinal chair, I thought of myself as singularly privileged. I knew I got more attention than the ordinary boy. So many interesting people would come up and talk to me. An only child, I did not miss the company of children. How many enjoyed the friendship of a talking raven? He would join us near the village shop, and pace alongside the carriage like a black hunchback, causing Patch to retreat between the wheels, growling quietly. Occasionally the raven would hop onto the wickerwork side of the carriage and utter a cry so wild and desolate that it prickled my hair. His actual conversation was more mundane. He could say 'How d'ee do' and 'What's your name?' over and over again in a tiny mechanical voice. Often he refused to say anything. He was the pet of an old bachelor with a straggling moustache and watery eyes. He persuaded me to read *Bevis: The Story of a Boy*, by Richard Jefferies, and Kenneth Grahame's *The Golden Age*. I think now this must have been a form of inverted pity, as both were stories of active youth. I found them very boring.

Much more to my taste were the anecdotes of a couple who lived on the edge of the village. They often came out and invited me into their big old house. The carriage crunched over the drive between dark pine trees and neglected flower beds, bumped up the stone steps, eased through the door and into a world of dusty marvels. Lion and leopard skins, the head of a rhinoceros, the heads of deer with twisted horns, barbaric masks, shields, spears and lumpish clubs crowded the walls. Huge tusks stood in racks in the corners, there was carved ivory from Zanzibar, knobkerries from Zululand, drums covered in monkey skin and tufted with the beards of gnu. The man had been a district officer in Africa in Edwardian times. Plump now and a little moth-eaten like his trophies, he told terrible things in a kindly way. He would let me finger the gnarled surface of the thirty-foot-long rhinoceros-hide whip. One flick could lift a strip of skin 'as thick as your finger' off the back of a recalcitrant servant.

He pointed out the grains of greyish powder in the grooving of a spear.

'Deadly poison.'

'Would it still work?'

'Oh, I expect so.'

I fingered the dry, almost weightless, skin of a mamba, the coarse hide of a zebra, the bristles of a wart hog, and touched the sharp barbs of a fishing spear. I learnt how the lightest tap could set a drum vibrating, and how it was speed of impact rather than force that could send the sound ringing round the ceiling.

They were a childless couple and they never seemed to mind lifting things off the walls, or bringing them down from the attic, so that I could touch that hot dusty continent that had dried them and weathered them and finally exiled them to this untidy house in Kent. They had been friends of Cherry Kearton, the writer and lecturer on wildlife. At his suggestion the wife had taken up photography. She had mounted her pictures in many albums and would point out the exciting ones.

'That elephant is about to charge the camera; see how he's spread his ears and put his tail up.'

'Did you take the picture?'

'Yes.'

'What happened?'

'Frank shot him.' Small and practical, her hands flicked through the sepia pages.

'Those are Watusi; they're over six feet tall and they never wear a stitch of clothing.'

'That crocodile has caught a pigmy deer.'

'Beastly things, crocodiles,' said her husband. 'Used to give me the willies.'

'What about snakes?'

'Oh snakes are all right. A snake won't hurt you unless you hurt him.'

Since then I have met other couples that sufficiently reminded me of them to make me think they are a type that endures in harsh and alien environments: modest, quiet, bound together by mutual loyalties, too lacking in self-regard to notice the idiosyncrasy of their enthusiasms; commonplace in every way, really, except in what they expected of themselves and of each other. At the time I hardly thought of them at all. I was occupied with the world they showed me.

In bed at night I would remember some photograph of an expedition weaving its way through tall grasses and baobab trees, Frank in front, pith helmet on his head, rifle across his shoulder, and behind the line of bearers, half-naked, anonymous, black skins gleaming. Travelling with them along that twisting trail, the heat sweating my back, stumbling past roots and vines, caressed by hot winds, wrapped in dark rich smells, inhaling the aroma of exotic flowers and nameless beasts, entranced by the flutter of vivid wings, I felt the fear of unknown danger. Would I be the one who caught the flicker of velvet skin stalking through the yellow grass? Over thirty years later, as the jet circled down to the landing field and I saw for the first time such paths crisscrossing the bush and the bright splashes of colour of the women's djellabas as they went in groups to the waterholes, it was then that I thought of Frank and his wife.

Our house stood on a hill. On top was the village; below, the small seaside resort of Herne Bay. Sometimes my parents would push me to a tea-shop there. It was run by a friend of my father's. He was a thin sallow man who had lived for years in China as the agent of a tea company. His café was full of bric-a-brac from his stay — red pagodas, and huge blue and white jars and tiny model gardens, perfect in every detail. The man himself interested me most.

'Show me, go on, show me.'

He would glance at my parents and then with a deprecatory laugh, bend towards me, lifting the grey hair from his ear. But there was no ear; only a dull red hole.

'Now show *it* to me.' He went to a lacquer-work desk beyond the potted palms and brought back a small cardboard box. He offered it to me.

'You sure you want to see? You open it then.'

'Ugh, no I couldn't.'

'It won't bite you know.' Lying on cotton wool, it looked like a piece of dark brown rubber. It felt rather like rubber, too, when I could bring myself to touch it; something as difficult to do as stroking the back of a pet toad — fascinating and disgusting at the same time. He had lost it during the Boxer Rebellion in 1900. Bandits had taken advantage of the unquiet times to kidnap him. They had held him to ransom for months in a cave in the mountains. Growing impatient, they had sent down an ear as proof of his captivity.

'Didn't it hurt?'

'I suppose it did. I was really more worried they were going to cut off my head.'

Eventually the ransom was paid, and a friend returned the severed ear. He had kept it with him ever since. Oddly enough, I found this the most disturbing part of the story: to live with your ear, but separate from it, all those years.

This old China hand upset our family in a more concrete way. Occasionally he would sell a piece from his collection and my father bought a Buddha. It was about two feet high in gleaming highly coloured ceramic. My father put it on a table in the hall. Obscenely fat with shiny bald head and wide smile, it immediately commanded the space around. It even dominated the grandfather clock, the oldest member of the household, which had been with my mother's family for nearly two hundred years. It was not only that it seemed incongruous among those familiar sober furnishings. It introduced an alien presence into the house. You could feel it as far away as upstairs, silently gathering power. A mysterious realignment of forces was in progress. The hall was no longer our hall, but its shrine. The next morning my mother announced that it must go. She had experienced horrible nightmares and she knew it was a nasty wicked thing. We did not disagree. My father wrapped it up carefully and took it back. The clock resumed its old peaceful dominance of the hall, as it was to continue in other halls, ticking away, the metronome of my parents' lives, and later of my own.

II

About the time he bought the Buddha, my father took up Pelmanism, joined the Freemasons and attempted, unsuccessfully, to record in short stories his experiences in the First World War. My mother had just prohibited him from playing golf, a game of which he was very fond. He was a natural games player; had been in the Tank Corps rugby team at the end of the war, and played tennis well. My mother had also enjoyed tennis in her youth, but she never played in my lifetime and disliked any activities that kept them apart.

That same summer there was an occasion when my mother ran round the room after my father, dodging tables and chairs until she caught him and tickled him so unmercifully that they both fell to the ground, rolling about and laughing. Such physical exuberance was rare. For over forty years my parents were obsessively devoted to each other. They almost never spent a night apart. Yet sexual matters were unmentionable and also, my mother inferred, disgusting and unclean. She was very fastidious, and would actually shiver at any account of drunkenness or coarse behaviour. Perversely she had a number of such stories to tell, because her family had contained some notable drinkers. This was hard on my father, who liked a convivial pint. She often subtly discomfited him.

My father won a scholarship to the local grammar school, became head boy and wanted to be a doctor, but his father, the factory worker, thought it safer to put him in a bank. Even as a very small child I knew my mother was superior – though it is hard to define precisely how I knew. My father was the more intelligent of the two and outwardly took all the important decisions. He was very patient. I cannot remember him making a critical or unkind remark about anybody. As a young bank clerk he had taught in a non-Conformist Sunday School and though he never went to church after the First World War, I think of him as a morally good man.

My mother had taken on his job as a bank cashier as war service. When my father returned after the war and they met for the first time, she was suffering from a great loss. In 1914 she had become engaged to the dashing, well-to-do son of a mill owner. I know he was handsome because, years later, she showed me his photograph, taken that last summer of peace on the beach at Scarborough. He never came back, of course; though by an irony of fate he died after the war was over, on the North-West Frontier of India. In her sorrow my mother came to rely on the serious dependable young tank officer, two years her junior. It was a long time before they married, and I doubt if my father ever took the place in her heart of her first love. But she trusted him and he always did what she wanted.

Their relationship withstood some harsh and bitter times. They were unlucky in that, meeting under the receding shadow of a terrible war, another even more devastating conflict dismembered their middle years, and in between they had the anxieties of bringing up a chronically sick child. That first winter of my TB fever, my grandmother was also ill with terminal cancer. At one period there were two full-time nurses in the house. In the midst of my ochre and magenta dreams I would hear my grandmother's groans of protest at being turned over in bed in the next room. My hold on reality was so unstable that I sometimes thought it was another part of me that had split away and was moaning to return. It must have seemed to my parents an awful (and expensive) burden to bear. Yet they were never other than kind, loving and considerate. My father had come to regard my grandmother almost as highly as my mother did. Crisis steeled their reliance on each other.

They grew together so that, over the years, even their writing came to look alike. Yet there was something stultifying in their affection. Outwardly so contented and inwardly so close, they fed on each other. They did not dare to look far aside. She was a woman of deep but narrow feelings, centred on the home and her immediate family. I remember thinking how dull their lives were when I was very small. Because of what I intuited from her I tended to look down on my father (though I loved him, too). I think I must subconsciously have wanted him to make more of a stand against her, but he never did. As I grew older I came to understand him better and admire him more. Then I threw the blame on my mother; not difficult to do as she looked at the outer world with a mixture of fear and gentle snobbery. Now I feel there was a tragic inevitability in their relationship. Once, later, when we were living in Canterbury and had a car, my mother slipped on the wet gravel drive as she was getting in and fell. My father, running round the bonnet to help her, slipped and fell as well. Neither was hurt, and watching, safely tucked up in rugs on the back seat, I thought, with the cruelty of childhood, that it was a funny sight. It was also symbolic; they were paralysed by their mutual concern.

III

So my father gave up golf, and eventually found in gardening the ideal activity he could share with my mother. He was an instinctively hard worker. Though he had never wanted to be in a bank, he stuck at it and became, at 33, the youngest manager in the Midland at that time. Banking was something my parents had in common. Her wartime experience as a cashier had given my mother a lively appreciation of money, and every evening they would discuss the problems and people he had encountered that day.

Herne Bay was under two hours by train from London's Cannon Street and in the 1930s was a growing dormitory area. Whole estates of flimsy bungalows, of mock-Tudor semi-detacheds, sprawled along the cliffs and grew over the fields that had once crowded so close to the town. 'Jerry building' was a phrase with which I was familiar long before I knew what it meant. There was something gimcrack and depressing about those characterless suburbs, where the gardens were still raw earth and weeds and the concrete ribbon roads had begun to slip and shift almost before they were dry, so that the wheels of my spinal chair would bounce over the asphalt strips that joined the sections.

Each evening on a weekday the owners of these new mansions would return from their labours in the City. Sometimes in summer I would be pushed out to watch them. At 7.15 the train would come in and dozens of sallow-faced men would pour out of the station. Dark-suited, bowler-hatted, each clutching an umbrella and a rolled-up copy of the *Evening Standard*, they seemed like a macabre army as they fanned out down the side streets, hurrying without a sideways glance towards 'Mon Repos', 'Sea View', 'Uplands' and their supper. Some residents were less prosaic. At least three of our neighbours went to prison for embezzlement – a term I understood as little as 'appeasement' and 'sanctions', which were soon to be in the wind.

The London evening paper was dramatically responsible for increasing my knowledge of the world. You could buy the afternoon edition at Herne Bay station and in May 1930 my father bought it every day. A unique journey was under way. Amy Johnson was flying to Australia. Alone. Without radio. In a second-hand little plane with an open cockpit that had already flown thirty-five thousand miles. Amy herself had been flying for only eighteen months. In photographs she looked more sturdy than her Gypsy Moth.

No woman had ever made such a journey. Each day the paper published a map showing where she had got to. I began to understand that the world was much bigger than I could imagine, when the distance between my fingers was over a thousand miles. Amy Johnson, with her pleasant North Country voice, seemed, as all those lone flyers of the 1930s were to seem, an augury of the future – a symptom that this great big world which I was being introduced to day by day in the paper was going to be encompassed. If an ordinary young woman could do it, others would. Perhaps I might one day. (When the wings of her plane were pierced by bamboo spikes in a forced landing in Java, she mended the holes with sticking plaster. What an adventure!)

Occasionally, even in Herne Bay, I would catch a glimpse of someone whom I heard described as a real adventuress: a beautiful young woman with startling blonde hair and a big fur coat coming out of a shop would give me a smile or bend to pat Patch with jewelled hands. My mother would look flustered, her pace would quicken and her lips compress.

'Why don't you like her?'

I never got a satisfactory answer, but later I knew. She was a local girl who had become a fan dancer in a London nightclub. There she caught the eye of a maharajah who had installed her with her parents in one of the new bungalows on the sea front. He appeared only occasionally, racing through the High Street in a white Lagonda, but he constantly embroidered the dreams and anecdotes of the town. Envy and spite were not my mother's vices, but distaste for sex was another matter. I was never allowed a long conversation with the Scarlet Lady, but I remember her kindly glance and vivid appearance, so out of keeping in those dowdy streets. What was the mystery about her? Something ominous that grown-ups knew and I did not; yet even lying in my spinal chair I was beginning to feel its stirrings.

On Sundays my parents would often push me to the end of the pier. At three-quarters of a mile it was the second longest in Britain. I liked the alteration of sound once the land was left behind: the echoing clank of my parents' feet on the slats; at first the cheerful cries of children playing on the beach coming up from below; the hum of land traffic fading under the approaching wash of the sea, endlessly varied as it broke on the metal struts and pillars; the reverberating passage of one of the two trams that ran up and down the pier, grinding slowly along to the insistent clang of a bell; finally to feel enveloped by the murmur of the ocean, the screech of gulls, the occasional hiss of an angler's line. Peeping over the edge of my chair I could look directly down at the water through the gaps in the slats. Swirling, green, foaming and opaque, always racing forward and retreating, it seemed the opposite of the motionless world I inhabited. Away it stretched to a limitless horizon, fading into the blue of the sky. Beyond there was France, but those smudges heading west down the Channel would be going to more distant places, Brazil and Africa and Mandalay, unimaginable coasts and tropic shores. A bottle thrown with a message in it might float all the way to Treasure Island. It was as if the world were a vast drum of which the skin was the sea; sitting on the edge, were I to tap it the reverberations would go on forever. Crouching on my rug, Patch would snuff the salt wind and sneeze.

Walking back along the front, past the Edwardian bandstand and the 1920s Pavilion where the Fol-de-Rols played in the summer, my parents would stop at the Italian ice-cream shop for a coffee. It came from a huge bubbling and hissing machine, very newfangled then. The proprietor was as cheerful as his brightly painted furniture. He seemed an innocent contrast to the ambiguous ruler of his country, about whom, I gathered, opinion was divided. People said he had drained the Pontine Marshes, a feat reminiscent of Thor's in drinking up the sea. My friend the milkman said he should stick to his spaghetti – he looked as if he'd eaten plenty – and stop going on about them poor natives. These views didn't affect custom at the ice-cream shop, even though the proprietor had pinned up a newspaper photograph of Mussolini skiing bare-chested in the snow. Tactfully he put it below the large framed photograph of our own old King that occupied the centre of the wall.

I was allowed an orange water ice and my father would go to the paper shop next door for the *Sunday Express*, the *Sunday Times* and a comic for me. My favourite was *Boys' Magazine*. I preferred it to *Magnet* and *Gem* – the schoolboy antics of Billy Bunter, Bob Cherry and Harry Wharton were as remote from my experience as life on the North-West Frontier and much less exciting. *Boys' Magazine* was running a serial about a return to a lost world of giant animals, capitalising on the current success of *King Kong*.

In the stories of my favourite writer, John Hunter, there was a recurring note of horror and pain, beyond the general bombast of such comics as *Wizard*. The arch-criminals would often employ evil demons, fit for a medieval fresco, that would spirit the drugged hero from his bed and flit with him held in giant claws, high above sleeping London, to a remote mountain eyrie, there to face interrogation, torture and death. Death never came to the hero, of course, but tortures were many, ingenious, described in detail and only escaped with agony. A typical example would have the naked hero, tied hand and foot, and weighted with corks, placed on his back in an empty bath. (Though this was being done by masked, chanting monks in Tibet, I imagined the bath to be exactly like mine at home.) A red hot grill was placed over the bath, which was slowly filled with icy water, straight from the Himalayas, lifting our hero inexorably towards the glowing bars. Would he first freeze or burn? Read next week's thrilling instalment. It was those painful episodes that made me read *Boys' Magazine* so avidly.

The prevalence of such themes in boys' literature suggest they fulfil some need. I doubt if girls have a similar taste. And in my case there were additional reasons. Decades later, in a general surgical ward, I noticed the most popular books were the novels of Ian Fleming. Their many accounts of torture and unpleasant death would seem inappropriate relaxation for advanced cancer patients, yet the opposite seemed to be the case. Perhaps it was a relief to read of miseries worse than one's own, and to identify with a hero who, though apparently helpless, was usually able to master his dangers by his physical and mental adroitness. Perhaps; though what I remember of the long afternoons when I would lie resting in my spinal chair in the garden, was the pleasurable dwelling on the torments themselves and not how the hero might avoid them in the next episode. Maybe it was a way of communing with my own condition and making my weak, trapped, unnatural life more acceptable. Consciously I did not, of course, regard it in this light. I knew myself to be extremely fortunate to have such an unusual existence. Perhaps my unconscious was having its own back, seeping subversive thoughts into me through the icy water trickling along the back of the hero in the bath. I had given considerable thought, too, as to which part of his anatomy would first come into contact with the red hot metal. I had no doubt which it was and that added to the uncomfortable guilty pleasure.

IV

My parents employed a genteel maiden lady called Ruby Arnsby to take me for walks during the week. She was in her forties and lived with her invalid mother. For some reason her heavy application of powder, the cloying wafts of sweet scent which preceded her into the room, and the cooing way in which she would correct my homework, infuriated me. One day I showed her a series of drawings I had done. At this time I filled sketch pads with the adventures of heroes such as Tarzan drawn in comic-strip style. I told her this batch were of Odysseus on his voyages. Actually they showed a naked bearded man having awful things done to his penis. In one it had been hooked onto a pulley and line and he was being hauled towards the ceiling, though weighted down by a heavy stone. In another, he was strapped to the ground while a whole tug-of-war team hauled on a rope attached to the unfortunate part. In every case the effect was the same: enormous extension. I must have meant to shock her and I succeeded. My parents never referred to the incident, but Miss Arnsby was replaced by a young man.

Jack Packham was the son of neighbours. A stills photographer with a film company in London, he had taken pictures of the young Gracie Fields, but lost his job in one of the endemic slumps in British films. He was twenty-nine, unmarried, a shy, gentle, melancholy person, and an indefatigable walker. Every morning he would call for me at nine o'clock and push me eight or nine miles before lunchtime. Sometimes we would go up through the village of Beltinge and along country lanes to the ruins of Reculver. Originally a marshy five miles inland, they now stood on a mound above the encroaching sea. Two gaunt towers with only a few coastguard cottages nearby, they were desolate and forbidding even in summer. The actual towers were of medieval flint, but some of the broken walls were Roman. Jack showed me how to identify the narrow bricks. The gloomy atmosphere had no effect on Patch, who went bounding across the stones and over the fields after the rabbits.

This part of north-east Kent was mostly sheep land and quite empty. There were few private cars; once in a while a delivery van would go by. Very occasionally a pony and trap would jingle past; already a rare sight. Once we watched three men and a dog catching rabbits at a warren beside the lane. One of the men took a ferret out of his pocket and pushed it down a hole. Then they waited with concentrated intent. After a few moments a rabbit bobbed out of an entirely different hole. The dog was on it like a flash; it was knocked on the head and popped in a sack. The ferret made its sinuous appearance from the original hole and was pushed down another one. There was something malevolent in the rapidity and silence of the whole operation. Sometimes there was no rabbit, and the ferret would come out wrinkling its whiskers and blinking sulkily.

Often in winter we would see no one the whole morning. Jack would enliven the time by telling me stories. *The Speckled Band*, *The Hound of the Baskervilles*: he must have gone through all the Sherlock Holmes œuvre. He told me historical romances, too; I remember *The White Company* and Stanley Weyman's *Under the Red Robe* and *The Viper of Milan* by Marjorie Bowen. The longer stories would take several days. He told them very well; quietly, with a sharp choice of phrase and dramatic pauses at moments of tension. He ransacked the local library for suitable material. Often he would embroider his narration with details appropriate to the countryside we were passing through.

One gloomy morning he told me the story of the Mummy. We were on a concrete road that ran straight, mile after mile, between flat waterlogged fields. The new coastal road, as it was then called, was quite deserted. There was no sound except the strange resonant call of a bittern, the scamper of Patch's feet and Jack's compelling voice. The Mummy was brought to England and resuscitated. It was sent to hunt down the hero, who, by an unpleasant coincidence, was walking along a straight empty road in winter twilight. When Jack told how he heard behind him a patter like the falling of dry leaves in autumn, I could hardly breathe with fright. There, far down the road, bent almost double, but trotting on remorselessly, the Mummy was on his trail. And there was nowhere to hide or escape; only the straight road and the waterlogged fields on either side. At the end of his tether the hero saw a lone house in the distance. He reached the door as the Mummy turned in the gate. Was anyone in? Would they answer his frantic knocking in time? The steps were puttering right behind him as he threw himself through the opening door and slammed it shut. Something fell against it with a thud like a rolled-up newspaper. Eventually the Mummy was burnt, crackling away like dried tinder, but he haunted my nightmares for a long time.

Was it wise to tell a nine year old, with an imagination presumably inflamed by a constant high temperature, quite so many frightening stories? I always asked for more, accepting the real terror at night as the price of the pleasurable fear in the telling. I suppose they were a sort of drug: I was addicted. I often saw phantoms. They would creep on all fours round my half-open door when I lay sleepless watching by the light of my Osglim lamp. Dim figures with faceless faces, they would even come rustling through the flower beds into the corner of my eye when I was lying outside in the hot summer afternoons. Then Patch would pant out of the bushes, notice me and come bounding over, and I would remember the long-ago days before my illness when he was a puppy and I had hunted him round the garden.

V

We seemed to have a special affinity from the first. My parents had decided to give me a dog when I was seven. We had gone to a house in the country where fox terriers were bred. At the back there was a wire-fenced run and the puppies were let out in turn. They were about eight weeks old and most just rushed about, happy for the chance to stretch their legs. Patch came straight across and jumped up at the wire. I knew I wanted him right away. He was a very good-natured dog. It's hard not to sentimentalise a childhood relationship with a pet. Patch would never have won a prize at Crufts. His nose was too square, his front legs too short, his hair too fluffy, his whole shape too dumpy. But his very defects were part of his appeal. He never really lost his puppy-like look. When we were out together, perfect strangers, old ladies in particular, would rush to embrace him with cries of praise. Even the milkman, a sallow young man with a sardonic tongue, was moved to draw a pastel portrait of him, which he gave me on my ninth birthday. I liked the milkman – he used to tell me funny involved stories, which I did not always understand but was flattered to hear; nevertheless for a member of his trade to look with favour on a dog must be rare.

Patch never bit anybody, but he could have done. When we were walking through the neighbouring village of Herne, a rat ran out of the gutter in front of us. Almost before we had seen it, Patch had it by the back of the neck and threw it in the air with an expert flick which broke its back. He was tremendously pleased with himself over this exploit, and for several days had especially excited dreams, uttering faint barks and twitching his legs.

He could be naughty and so could I. When he was still a puppy, I was told by my mother one afternoon to come inside and get on with my homework. I objected, argued and lost. Approaching the house in anger, I gave a token kick to the French window. To my amazement, the bottom pane dissolved with hardly a tinkle, leaving a single ragged shard of glass in the frame. My mother had gone upstairs and I was too frightened to tell her immediately. Instead I went inside, quietly closed the door and got out my books. Patch came gambolling across the garden and jumped at the door to be let in. Petrified, as in a slow-motion film, I saw his left front leg come through the broken pane and slice open all along its length in a deep gash that revealed the bone. The vet put twenty-two stitches in it. Patch nearly died from the loss of blood. He lay very quiet and dignified in his basket accepting teaspoons of brandy from my father. For three or four weeks he hopped around with his leg neatly taped around a splint. When it was taken off, he was so excited that, rushing round the garden, he split the wound open again. Eventually he recovered completely, though you could always see the scar if you looked beneath his fur and, when he was very tired, he would limp slightly. Sensibly, my parents did not punish me for the broken window.

Though I felt deeply guilty, Patch never bore any grudges. Sometimes I made him play a game I called wolves and bears. To make him more like a wolf, I wrapped him in a couple of old fox furs my mother had once had as a stole. I was the bear and when I approached on all fours, covered in a black fur rug, bellowing hoarsely through the wickerwork wastepaper basket that encased my head, he got terribly excited. He would bark furiously and then rush forward and take a quick sniff to make sure the odd contraption really was me.

Whatever I did, he never got angry or vicious. Occasionally he would grab an unsuitable bone, such as a lamb chop, from the kitchen dustbin and retire under a bed with it, growling and gnawing. No one else could get near him, but I would crawl straight under the bed and seize the bone. He always gave it up immediately and licked my hand. When illness altered my life, he accepted the modification to his own without fuss. He would sit for hours curled up on my bed, listening with apparent interest while I told him interminable stories that could not have had much appeal to a dog. On our country walks he often shared the spinal chair with me. He had that amazing empathy of a close animal companion, the ability to reflect and take part in whatever mood was dominant. Often he seemed able to anticipate them. Once, lying in bed in the early days of my illness, I felt a sudden wave of depression. It was just physical weakness no doubt. I made no move, but at that moment Patch, who had been lying by the fire, got up and licked my hand. Looking in his trustful brown eyes, how could I feel lonely?

VI

Patch was one of the audience of two for the plays, battles and sporting events that I arranged. My paternal grandfather, the skilled carpenter, had made me a bed table, which became the centre of my activities.

Sometimes it was a theatre, at other times a war ground or playing field. I had been given some wooden articulated circus animals and performers. They were each about eight inches high and dressed in real clothes that could be taken off. I had a ringmaster, moustached, with a top hat and red coat, white breeches and boots; two clowns, one with a white face and red nose, the other a tramp; a lady rider with frilly skirt; a dappled horse; a mule; a baby elephant; a seal; and a lion. There were also various props – ladders, tubs, boxes and chairs. They were beautiful toys and came, I think, from Germany. I have never seen anything like them since. My plays tended to be violent and derivative, involving magicians and dragons and comic elderly characters. I acted all the voices and liked to do plenty of squeaking and roaring.

Battles involved many more characters and on a much smaller scale. There was a shop in Burlington Arcade, which sold boxes of flat metal soldiers made in France. They were about one inch or so high and painted in exquisite detail and variety. About eighty came in a box, which in those days cost 8s 6d. They were my favourite toys and my father brought back a set every time he went to London. I had Joan of Arc leading a charge of French knights against the English archers; the Crusaders fighting the Saracens in the Third Crusade; a battle in the American Revolution with Indians and French and buckskinned colonials shooting down the Redcoats; Roman legions struggling with horn-helmeted Gauls. Best of all was the Battle of Waterloo with Bonaparte and Wellington surveying the charge of the Scots Greys. Unlike the much larger lead soldiers made by William Britain, almost every figure was different and allowed endless variation of action, ambush, charge, defence. I had a tiny cannon which would fire bits of matchstick just powerful enough to knock them down.

Cricket matches were less realistic. I threw two dice and evolved an elaborate set of rules: double one meant clean bowled, four and three caught, and so on. I usually played for both sides and took a lot of care in choosing my teams. I often opposed real cricketers, such as Bradman and Hammond, to a team of poets. I would open with E. Spenser and W. Wordsworth, whom I'm sorry to say I characterised as safe, but dull batsmen. W. Shakespeare was not only captain, but the best all-rounder and would go in number three. Very sound and capable of long hours of concentrated play, J. Milton was number four. My spirits perked up when they were out and in came my favourite, Lord Byron, a dashingly brilliant attacking batsman, able to rattle up a big score quickly. Less reliable, but with some attractive strokes, P.B. Shelley and J. Keats were numbers six and seven. A safe wicket-keeper, but stodgy bat, M. Arnold was number eight. Then we were into the tail proper. Lord Tennyson, demon fast bowler, might occasionally hit a flashing four, but the googly expert, A. Pope, and the slow left-hander, S.T. Coleridge, rarely hit anything.

I would play cricket for days on end, keeping all the scores and arranging the hazards to favour the better batsmen (unless I had decided it was a rain-affected wicket, in which case I doubled the difficulties for everybody). But for the plays I wanted an audience, and, as well as Patch, I could call on Dorothy, our maid. The daughter of a shepherd, from near Faversham, she had come to us when she was sixteen and stayed until she went into factory work during the war. Even when my parents considered they were not well-off enough to run a motor-car, they always had a living-in maid. These country girls, with big raw-boned hands and shy manners, would wear plain blue or brown uniforms during the morning, cleaning out the fires, pounding the clothes during the weekly wash in the scullery, blacking the oven, polishing the brass and helping with the cooking. In the afternoon they would change into a frilly cap and apron and serve afternoon tea to my mother and her women friends, with the cakes on little lace doilies. They had one afternoon off a week, a back room of their own and a salary of £35 per year. (My father at this time as bank manager was probably earning about £400 per year.) All the neat three- or four-bedroom houses of my parents' contemporaries had such maids. Their total disappearance from middle-class homes with the advent of the war was one of the most striking social changes of my lifetime.

Dorothy was a kindly and undemanding audience. Seated beside my bed in the evenings, she never complained about the incoherent plots in which I involved my circus performers, or about the repetitious slapstick with which I sought to enliven them. But she must have preferred the great event of the month – the film show. My parents had bought a film projector and a small silver screen, and on the first weekend of the month it was rigged up in the living-room and, wrapped in blankets, I was carried down and put on the sofa to watch a magic programme of my own choosing.

Kodak ran a library of silent movies and from their catalogue I selected the items for the next showing: a one-reel cartoon, a two-reel comedy (usually Chaplin), and a five- to seven-reel feature. The cartoon was often one of the adventures of Felix the Cat, though it could be the other silent series, *Out of the Inkwell*; the feature might be a relatively well-known film such as *The Lost World*, made in 1925 with Bessie Love and William Gargan, or one featuring Rin-Tin-Tin, but generally I chose a Western. Far and away my favourite star was Ken Maynard. His cheerful good-looks, his striking black outfits complete with silver twin-holstered gun belt, his beautiful and intelligent palomino horse, Tarzan, capable of feigning dead, attacking an enemy or unpicking his captive master's bonds with his teeth: all were irresistible. Maynard's brilliant trick riding, the sheer attack of energy and violence that unfolded on the flickering screen, carried me into a drugged ecstasy.

Ken Maynard was the first tangible object of my hero-worship. I put up photographs of him in my room and would have viewed his films over and over again had I been able to do so. Recently I was gratified to read in an American study of the Western that these late silent films of Maynard's were considered among the best examples of the genre ever made. Had they been categorised among the worst, it would not have altered my affectionate memory of them one iota. I suppose this cowboy film star (who was to die alcoholic and forgotten in a home for poor people) filled for me the need that, had I been a normally fit child, I would have projected onto a sportsmaster or athletic senior schoolboy. Bed-bound as I was, how much more overwhelming was the impact of his physical daring and masculine energy.

VII

Despite my obsession with Ken Maynard, I spent a lot of time each month selecting the items for the next show. I read the Kodak library catalogue from cover to cover and through it became familiar with the plots of a great many silent films. This led me to start writing my own imaginary screenplays. I had dictated stories, which my father had written down, before I could write. The earliest to survive, probably from the age of six, is called 'The Blue Wizard'. It begins, predictably enough: 'Once upon a time there was a Blue Wizard . . .'. Within a couple of years I was writing of buffalo hunters on the Great Plains, and British slaves forced to fight in the Roman arena; all derivative stuff from my reading of the time. My interest in the cinema led to more interesting adaptations: from the novels of Zane Grey (by the age of nine I had over twenty of them in the two-shilling Hodder and Stoughton edition), from P.C. Wren and the Martian stories of Edgar Rice Burroughs, and, most ambitiously a few years later, Shakespeare's *Anthony and Cleopatra*. I still think that would make a marvellous movie. I went so far as to cast my version. Michael Redgrave (whom by this time I had seen in *The Lady Vanishes*) was to play Anthony, and Ralph Richardson (I had seen *him* in *Q Planes*) Enobarbus.

Another of my writing experiments was a monthly magazine, the *Highfields Gazette* (Highfields was the name of our house). My mother was forced to contribute a cookery page, which she hated, not believing that she had any talent with the pen, although, in fact, she was a lively letter-writer. Among her first entries were recipes for steak and kidney

pie and roly-poly pudding, two of my favourites. I got my father to write
his war memoirs, which I serialised as 'Memories of a Tank Officer'. (I
had been reading Siegfried Sassoon.) Privately, I found them very
disappointing. My father could recount in vivid and dreadful detail his
experiences, but when he came to write they became very pedestrian and
long-winded, despite my ruthless editing. I dunned the more racy of his
business friends for funny stories to use as fillers. I myself wrote the
fiction serial (more about brave young British chiefs fighting the
Romans) and the political leader. One of the first was titled 'The Decline
and Fall of a Great Empire'. I had become acquainted with Gibbon
through the serialisation of extracts in *John O'London's Weekly*. It was my
first contact with serious history, and I found it enthralling. From it I
drew the conclusion that the British Empire was also in peril. This must
have been in the summer of 1935, and I was eleven years old. I had not
much personal experience to go on, but what leader writer has? I knew
there was still trouble in India (Gandhi had recently organised the Great
Salt March and the Civil Disobedience movement was at its height), and
Mussolini was threatening Abyssinia. I predicted that there would be
another Big War and that in it the Empire, which was already showing
the symptoms of dissolution and decay, would be dismembered. My
father thought this was much too alarmist, but said an editor had a right
to print whatever opinions he liked so long as they didn't hurt anybody.

I got my views from reading the *Daily Mail*; I found our other
newspaper, *The Times*, too indigestible. Much more came from listening
to the wireless. I had begun with *Toy Town* and the Children's Hour plays
of L. du Garde Peach, *The Castles of England* and *The Roads of England*. I
was hooked on them by the comically pathetic voice of Richard Goolden,
who played the little Everyman, continually put down and always
bobbing up again like an indestructible penny. He was also a staunch
Mole in the radio adaptation of *The Wind in the Willows*, for years my
favourite book. But, by this time, I was listening to everything: news and
plays and talks and documentaries. The wireless provided the variety of

conversation and attitudes that my life lacked; friends who joined me at breakfast and often were heard last thing when I was tucked up for the night. One of these late listenings introduced me to an entirely new dimension of experience: this was *The March of the '45* by D.G. Bridson, an evocation of Bonnie Prince Charlie's rebellion, in words, music, song and trenchant effects. Its sounds still live in my memory.

Slowly my health improved. This year, 1935, I took my first steps across the garden. I had been three years in my spinal chair and even a brief walk, supported on both sides, was very difficult. A big chunky masseuse came down three afternoons a week from Canterbury to pummel a response from my sticklike limbs. Gradually they grew stronger and I emerged upright, a weedy youth, bespectacled as the result of the years of reading in trying circumstances. I did not immediately appreciate my new condition. I had learned the pleasures to be extracted from illness; it took longer to accommodate to the joys of health. And I was still precluded from many of the normal pursuits of my age: school, sports, the rowdy horseplay of other boys, few of whom I knew.

Of course, there were compensations. In May was the old king's Jubilee. I was driven through the flag-decked streets to the cinema. The film was *The Lives of a Bengal Lancer* with Gary Cooper. It confirmed my lifelong affection for the movies. My father had bought his first car: a Humber. How sleek and modern it looked compared to the upright old Chrysler. This summer of flags and local jollification, we drove round the many pleasure resorts that crowded the south-east corner of England. I was well enough to play cricket with my father on the sands. Cricket seemed another example of the continuity and stability of the kingdom that reached its principal manifestation in the person of the old king.

Yet, unbeknown to us, a wind of change was rising that would blow through every corner of the globe. Its voice could already be heard in Germany, snarling and screeching in that language that seems so suited to invective. In our deceptively peaceful island it was still far away. More immediately shocking was the loss of those unique tones that sounded more like a border farmer than a monarch. 'The King's life is drawing peacefully to its close'; I heard that unforgettable announcement not in the bedroom where I had experienced so much sickness, but in a new house smelling of fresh paint and virgin dampness. We had moved in only the day before. My father had been transferred to Canterbury at short notice to replace a manager who was to go to prison for embezzlement (despite which he ended the Second World War a general).

There was one companion who did not come with us to Canterbury. On the evening before my eleventh birthday Patch was run over by the local fire engine. That year my last two grandparents had died, but nothing had prepared me for such an agony of loss. A devoted friend was gone, who could never be replaced. Later I was to have two other dogs, but neither meant anything to me. You are lucky to have such companionship once in your life.

3

EXPECTATIONS OF LOVE

I

From our house in Herne Bay we could look down across the sloping fields to the clustered streets of the small town below, and beyond to the distant shimmer of the English Channel. It was appropriately named Highfields. It was the first house on that particular hill. (When I went back a few years ago I counted 276 houses on a checkerboard of new roads that covered the slopes.) It was right to be facing the sea, because Herne Bay was only just growing from a fishing village to a dormitory area for distant London.

Our new house in Canterbury (it took about five months to build) was also appropriately named – Green Gates. The gates were green and they were overshadowed by a huge and ancient elm that curved protectively above them. There was a big beech tree with a swing in the back garden and lines of trees on both sides of the road. It was called the New Dover Road and it ran, straight as an arrow shot, from Dover, some twelve miles away, past our house, through Canterbury and on the sixty-five miles to London. It was the A2, the second most important road in Britain (the A1 was the Great North Road that linked London with Edinburgh). The Romans built it, hence its straightness. Despite its name, the New Dover Road had been there a very long time, as shown by the noble proportions of the trees. Many of the houses were massive Victorian or Edwardian mansions, largely masked by the surrounding foliage (this was to be an unexpected blessing later).

When we sat down to breakfast, our dining-room faced onto the road. I looked forward to a daily performance by our neighbour opposite. At 8.05 a.m. precisely he would come down his gravel drive at a brisk pace. At the exact same spot between his gate posts he would turn and hold his rolled-up copy of *The Times* aloft in a gesture of romantic salute. A handkerchief would flutter from a first-floor window. The paper tucked once more under his arm, our neighbour would swing round and plunge rapidly down the road to catch the 8.30 to the City. Day after day, week after week, month after month, year after year, this ritual continued. We could time our watches by his appearance, check the weather by his preference of overcoat or Burberry. So much of Canterbury appeared timeless and unchanging, there seemed no reason not to think the same of this sprightly social gesture. But it was not to be so: neither our neighbour, nor his house, nor the ancient city of Canterbury itself was to continue as they were for much longer.

Looking back with all the benefit of hindsight at the three houses that contained my childhood, there seems an appropriate shift in perspective between each of them. Furthest away, largest and most mythical, is The House at Pitt Corner, Winchester, peopled by kindly deities like Bailey with his brass buttons and leather gaiters, but also by strange troglodytes such as the gypsies from over the hill. Everything was unexpected, answering to patterns that I did not fully understand.

With Highfields there was a great increase in vision. The world looked at from that vantage place had a recognisable shape, though the humans in the scene were mostly far away. I had no companions of my own age. Books, invented games, my dog, occupied the foreground of my days. My illness made it necessary for me to be content with myself and I was.

Green Gates brought me back into contact with a town that had been a centre of human endeavour for close on two thousand years. I was fit enough now to be a part of it, just as our house was. If I walked down our short gravel drive to the gate and looked left past the massive trunk of the elm, I looked directly at a magnetic centre that had drawn travellers from all over the world. For hundreds of years they had summoned fresh energy to complete their pilgrimage with the sight of the great tower that loomed above the line of trees that bordered the Dover Road. It was about half a mile from where I stood. Was it the rustle and flutter of the leaves that gave the pinnacles the illusion of floating like a stone flag above the earthly foliage?

From whatever direction you approached Canterbury, the cathedral dominated your view. Far to the south it rose like a rock in the distance through the flowery foam of blossoming apple trees. Coming out of Blean Woods to the north, you looked down the steep slopes of St Stephen's Hill to where it basked like a stone leviathan above the twisting clutter of the town. Wherever you walked in those narrow streets a turning would reveal a further dramatic perspective. Finally, the twin towers of Christ Church Gate, their newly painted angels displaying the heraldry of visiting kings, led you out of the tea-shop bustle of the marketplace into the calm of the Precincts. There the whole cathedral (of which you had seen many snatches) unfolded before you. How many times, feeling tired or impatient with the speed of my recovery, I limped to a seat and drank in the confident energy of those vaunting towers.

You could feel the aches and anxieties of every day ironed away in their splendid confidence in human destiny made visible. Angels, saints, gods and devils, pinnacles and buttresses, spires and crenellations blended into a harmony which enveloped you as it reached out to absorb the whole town. For eight hundred years the cathedral had been a finger pointing the town towards God. The town had grown in its shadow. Many of its half-timbered houses, with their bulging upper floors almost meeting across the streets, were older than the cathedral's Bell Harry Tower. The cattle market held twice weekly under the city wall, bringing its flocks and herds bleating and bellowing and befouling the High Street, probably went back before Christian times. On several occasions the cathedral was desecrated and burnt by the Vikings; yet it grew greater and more potent, despite the threat of Reformation and levelling priests.

They had their descendants. A familiar figure striding down Butchery Lane on spindly gaitered legs, with a mane of white hair framing his nutcracker face, was the formidable Dr Hewlett Johnson. He looked every inch a Renaissance prelate, but his political predilections had made him known the world over as the Red Dean. Even more scandalous to the prurient citizens than his embracing Communism was his ability to enfold a new wife less than half his age and to produce a covey of beautiful daughters in his seventies. Brushing past him in the street gave the giggly thrill of touching a star.

Sacred and profane were always mixed in this city of God. Walking along Broad Street in mid-morning you could be swept aside by the clangour of marching feet: three soldiers and a corporal of the Buffs marching to the cathedral as had the four knights of old looking for Becket. These military were not bringing death, but commemorating it; every day turning a page in the Book of Remembrance in their chapel and reading out the names of those who had fallen from Inkerman to Malplaquet, Rorke's Drift to the Somme.

Someone else who died a violent death when young, but not likely to be honoured in the cathedral, was the Elizabethan poet Christopher Marlowe. He is said to have been born just south of the cathedral, in the densely crowded area of Burgate Street. His atheist views were probably too much even for those free-thinking days and may have led to his death, apparently in a tavern brawl, while still in his twenties. So I was told by the owners of a beautiful bookshop in Burgate. Two middle-aged ladies, Miss Carver and Miss Stanyforth, ran the shop, which sprawled onto several floors and across the road. This second shop, mostly novels and continental books, was the domain of Miss Carver. An impressive and somewhat formidable lady, upright, dark and handsome, she would often stand like a caryatid in her open door cupping a lighted cigarette in her slightly shaky hand. The third partner, Mr Adams, sitting by the desk under the stairs surrounded by order forms, would also be smoking, a curved meerschaum pipe. Heavily built, dark suited with a watch chain across his waistcoat and a gold chain drooping from his pince-nez, I found him difficult to converse with. Someone told me he was a cynic; someone else that he was in love with Miss Carver. I was not particularly interested in either proposition. What held me were rooms full of intriguing second-hand volumes at amazingly cheap prices.

I find it difficult to explain how important this bookshop was to me. For about three years, the darkest period of my life, it was an anchor to civilisation. Buffeted and despairing of ever making contact with my peers, half-an-hour's immersion in those dusty shelves would revive my hopes for life. It was not only the books. The ladies, especially little Miss Stanyforth with her wisps of hair that kept escaping from their bun, her gentle good humour and self-deprecatory laughter, always treated me, a gangling awkward schoolboy, as someone worth a serious conversation.

For privileged customers there was a small back room with wickerwork armchairs where you could spend an hour engrossed in the conquest of Peru, before deciding it really wasn't worth your half-crown. It was a good time for books. I remember going in one day and finding the whole window given over to some small orange-covered books. They were only sixpence each, but I didn't like the uniformity of the Penguin covers. Miss Stanyforth explained it was a real breakthrough; that new books would be much cheaper. 'But you have lots of hard-cover books that are only sixpence,' I pointed out. 'But these will be *new* books.' Would that make the difference? I was not convinced; but I bought *Ariel*, André Maurois's biography of Shelley (though I did not read it for many years).

A book I both read and reread over half a century was Jacob Burckhardt's *Civilisation of the Renaissance in Italy*. Phaidon had, I believe, just started to publish in England when this illustrated edition came out. I wanted it immediately; its brilliantly chosen pictures introduced me to a dazzling new world of beauty and vitality that I ached to join. It cost

7s 6d and was eventually given to me as a birthday present by my father in 1937. The range of its illustrations was to prove useful many times in my life, not least in filling in the gaps in the 1969 television series *Civilisation*, which I co-produced and directed, and in an earlier series on *People of the Renaissance*, which I produced under the guidance of Professor Leopold Ettlinger in 1960.

II

The year 1936 not only brought us a new environment, it also gave me a new tutor and new physical challenges. I was not yet thought fit enough to go to school, but some crack-pot persuaded my parents that I needed toughening up. So I was to ride and swim: two activities I never properly mastered, and hence did not enjoy (and still don't). Hill-walking I did like, but there were few hills in east Kent. There were some fine woods. I could easily have been lured onto botany trails, but they were not within the interests of Mr Goldfinch, my new teacher. Female biology was more his line. With curly dark hair and bouncy charm, he preferred to while away our mornings with accounts of his nights; a subject grotesquely unsuitable for a feeble, feverish twelve year old, privately wrestling with the first stirring of his own sexuality. I felt as excluded and alarmed by Mr Goldfinch's smirking exploits as by the nervy prancing of the sixteen-hand-high hunter I was supposed to mount.

Fortunately, my American uncle and his wife came to visit us that summer, bringing with them their bewitching nine-year-old daughter, Carolyn. The contrast of this sparkling, freckled, wickedly cool, funny and sympathetic breath of Midwestern air to the lip-licking lubricity I got every day from my tutor was more than I could cope with. One morning I ran into my mother's room when she was dressing, burst into tears and said I never wanted to see Mr Goldfinch again. I never did.

What must have been a shocking surprise for my parents would have been alleviated by the practical judgements from my mother's favourite brother. Clifford had a zestful enjoyment of life that was capable of lifting his sister out of her timid doubts about her own abilities. Rapidly moving with a powerful swing of the wooden leg he had acquired in the war, forthright in his opinions and profoundly fond of his little sister, he was well balanced by his wife Harriet. Elegant and sophisticated, with a long ivory cigarette-holder, Harriet had three times sailed around the world by the age of twenty-five. Unruffled in temperament, she was the most worldly-wise person I had met.

Once Mr Goldfinch had been disposed of, it was probably at my uncle's suggestion that my parents found a young working-class intellectual who had won a scholarship to Oxford. His poetry had already been published by Tambimuttu. He was a tremendous influence on me in all sorts of ways. So, more indirectly, but possibly even more deeply, was Carolyn.

That summer, when war began in Spain, when our young and glamorous king, Edward VIII, visited the moribund pits in Wales and came away saying something must be done, when Jesse Owens dominated the Olympic Games as Hitler did the rest of Germany, when we sat and listened to the wireless dedication of the Canadian war memorial at Vimy Ridge with our fathers, both of whom had been so marred and changed by that war and were stirred to feel it might be going to begin again: that momentous summer was made incomparably more momentous by the discovery of companionship. It was as though all twelve years of my life had been spent on a desert island. Longing for company, I had lit metaphorical fires whenever a ship passed, but none had ever responded. Was my whole life to be passed alone? Then suddenly fate had produced this captivating Girl Friday. She was no savage, but infinitely more travelled and sophisticated than me, a native of that dazzling film fairyland, America.

We spent hours and hours talking about every subject under the sun. Even her turn of speech, her choice of words, were piquantly different from mine. And, of course, though I could hardly see it, she felt much the same about the way I expressed myself and about the ancient walled city where I lived, the rolling landscape of fruit trees, woods and craggy white cliffs and red-sailed fishing boats. 'Gee, it's all like a movie,' she would often say.

So wrapped in mutual glamour the summer passed; rounders replaced cricket as the beach game. How did we move from childish knock-about to passionate embraces? I cannot remember, but we certainly did. We would lie, seemingly for hours on end, eye to eye, nose to nose, mouth to mouth. After a life of austere loneliness I was wallowing in riches I could hardly understand. At the time it seemed inconceivable that our parents would not have sensed the change in us. How we walked everywhere hand in hand. How on trips in the car she would curl up on my lap, or lean her feather-light head on my shoulder. I consulted no one, but blundered from peak to peak. Decades later I asked her if she had told her parents. 'Yeah, I told my mother.' 'And what did she say?' 'Keep your clothes on.' Sound advice from a woman who came to maturity in the twinkle-toed twenties. I should also point out, what I have no doubt had been in Harriet's mind, that undressed I would not have known what to do anyway.

Kissing seemed the dazzling height of sensuous pleasure; capable of infinite subtle modifications. Most precious of all was the enwrapping tenderness of another youthful body, slender, taut and silky-smooth, loving and adventurous, gentle and trusting. This year I was reading much more poetry and these lines by Byron seemed appropriate for my feeling for Carolyn, even though she was only nine years old:

> She walks in beauty like the night
> Of cloudless climes and starry skies;
> And all that's best of dark and bright
> Meet in her aspect and her eyes:
> Thus mellow'd to that tender night
> Which heaven to gaudy day denies.

·   ·   ·   ·   ·

And on that cheek, and o'er that brow,
So soft, so calm, yet eloquent,
The smiles that win, the tints that glow,
But tell of days in goodness spent,
A mind at peace with all below,
A heart whose love is innocent!

That second verse certainly applies to my Carolyn. For many years my memories of those days of happiness coloured my hopeful expectations of love. Perhaps they have never entirely left me, rekindling with each fresh flame a memory of those days 'in goodness spent', and the love of the innocent heart.

III

My new tutor, Stephen Coltham, greatly extended my grasp of the world of books. From the novels of Walter Scott and G.A. Henty to Dickens – *Great Expectations*, *Oliver Twist* and *Nicholas Nickleby* – to the science-fiction stories and social humour of H.G. Wells and Aldous Huxley. In poetry I had long liked the rhythmic ballads of Macauley; Stephen brought me the harsher, more sensuous medieval romances of William Morris. They suited the bittersweet memories I had of that last summer.

I was half mad with beauty on that day,
And went without my ladies all alone,
In a quiet garden walled round every way;

.   .   .   .   .

Came Lancelot walking; this is true, the kiss
Wherewith we kissed in meeting that spring day,
I scarce dare talk of the remember'd bliss,

44

When both our mouths went wandering in one way,
And aching sorely, met among the leaves;
Our hands being left behind strained far away.

Much of adolescence seems to consist of a sort of formless longing; a daydream of the unknown. Lyrical poetry can help to focus the questing senses and so to universalise what can seem a very lonely period.

Stephen introduced me to T.S. Eliot, and not only the invocations of London fog and genteel tea parties, but 'Ash Wednesday' and *The Waste Land*. I admired their mastery of language, but found them too cool and austere for my taste. I preferred the early Irish lyrics of W.B. Yeats. He was the first poet I heard reading his poetry on the wireless, probably in 1939. He read very fast, in an incantatory monotone. By that time I was under the spell of W.H. Auden and a poet I admired even more (probably because Stephen did): Stephen Spender. The Civil War in Spain came to occupy the emotions of my tutor's generation. For me it was too far away. It was as hard to visualise violent death as passionate love.

One poet I found very easy to resist was Shakespeare. Without the possibility of group reading, the theatrical language seemed ornate and difficult to follow. All that changed at Easter 1937 when my parents took me to London for a long weekend. We went to the British Museum, where I was greatly confused by the multiple endowments of the classical reclining figures of hermaphrodites. But there was no confusion in recognising the mastery of Laurence Olivier on the stage of the Old Vic in *Coriolanus*. His power, vanity, impatience and arrogance were overwhelming. I had never seen a great acting performance before; the human presence was a revelation. At the end, Olivier appeared haranguing a crowd of enemy Volscians from a balcony at the top of a double flight of stairs. Two of his enemies grasped his arms, while a third came up behind and stabbed him in the back. Olivier stiffened and then fell forward as the Volscians let him go. He crashed down both flights of stairs in the clangour of his golden armour, ending at the bottom completely covered in his scarlet cloak. A spectacular moment of theatre of the sort for which he was already famous.

The other holiday treat was *Snow White and the Seven Dwarfs*. The cinema in Regent Street had been transformed into the magic wood, the ticket office had been turned into a thatched cottage. Dwarfs took you to your seat. As to the performance, it would be a surprise if whoever is reading this hasn't seen it. It was the first of Disney's feature-length cartoons and remains one of the most tuneful.

Equally unchanging is the restaurant where we had our final lunch of the holidays: the Criterion in Piccadilly. It was a favourite with my parents. When I visited it sixty years later, time had done nothing to dim the glamour of its gold mosaic arches. Perhaps its splendour was a little too much for me. The golds and greens and blues, the hurrying trays piled high, the gurgle of pouring wine and cheerful chatter of family parties swam together into an unexpected sob: 'Just going back to school, is he?' said the friendly, but observant waiter. I could not tell him that I was not going back, but about to start.

How to educate me must have been a continuing problem for my parents. They never talked about it with me. In the summer of 1937 we visited Wootton Court Preparatory School. I remember the huge rhododendron bushes making splashes of purple on the lawn of what seemed a very grand house. It had been converted into a boarding school. I was to be the only day boy. This was a mistake. I might not have been strong enough to survive the rigours of sleeping away from home, but I had an even harsher adjustment to make in withstanding the animosity of over a hundred of my peers; envious of my (unsought) privileges and gloatingly able to exploit my all too obvious physical weaknesses.

The year I spent at Wootton Court and the following two at St Edmund's School, Canterbury were the most unhappy of my life. They coincided with an ominous darkening of the world scene. Though the focus of events might seem as far away as Spain or Africa or Asia, the repercussions could stir the stones in a small school in Kent. Many of the pupils at Wootton Court were no doubt undergoing this expensive private education (the headmaster had taught King George VI mathematics at Dartmouth Naval College) in order to get enough learning to enter a reputable public school. Some had been trying for several years. They were well into their teens, bored, loutish and discontented with their lot.

I don't remember being physically molested, although there was the threat of having your head pushed down the lavatory. Teasing was carried to a fine art and included complicated dares. The most common involved sexual display while the class was in progress. The erect penis was used to flip ink-filled pellets at another pupil. Or the desk lid would be slammed down on the victim's organ. Some of the more daring boys would actually masturbate to an orgasm and toss the sticky emission at the victim. I never remember anyone being caught doing this sort of prank.

That summer a new element was included. Two young men in their late teens were put in the top class. Ostensibly this was for thirteen year olds, but these youths were much bigger. And they were Italian. They had come (it was said) to learn English. The British press had published stories of the Italian air force having sprayed mustard gas on Abyssinian tribesmen. We never had the opportunity to find out the Italian youths' attitude to this. The British bullies acted as though our Italians had done the spraying personally. They began throwing stones. Not immediately very violently, but it quickly got worse. In two days the boys had to leave.

A few weeks later my parents and I were in a crowd of tourists being shown the splendours of Windsor Castle. Pacing alone and slowly along the battlements, wrapped in a romantic dark cloak, was an unmistakable figure. How had His Most Exalted Majesty, the King of Kings, the Chosen One of God, the Emperor Haile Selassie, Lion of Judah, Defender of the Faithful, got to be walking by himself on the battlements of Windsor Castle? There was no question it was him. Even my mother recognised him. We knew him and his picturesque titles (there were at least twenty more), because he had had to flee from Abyssinia recently when Italy completed the conquest of his homeland (with barbaric cruelty, the papers said). That was the reason why my schoolfellows had wanted to stone the Italians. If they had been told that the Lion of Judah had been just as brutal, slicing up the poor young Eyeties, they would have been equally delighted to stone him. Perhaps more so, because he looked so small and fragile that even a well-aimed pebble would have knocked him for six.

Why had he chosen chilly England as his place of exile? I don't know, but perhaps because he was a Christian (Coptic) emperor, the English king might have offered him accommodation in one of his grace-and-favour houses. There are a number of such medieval dwellings at Windsor, facing St George's Chapel. This would have been an appropriate home as one of Haile Selassie's ancestors – the euphoniously named Prince Alemayehu – is buried in the Chapel. He died while undergoing the rigours of English public school life at Rugby in 1879. The Abyssinian royal family, of course, claims direct descent from King Solomon and the Queen of Sheba.

Later, I think the Emperor went to live at one of those sunny south-coast resorts beloved by deposed royalty: Bognor or Bournemouth or Brighton. One of the results of his sojourn was that we all got to recognise the Abyssinian national anthem. Every Sunday evening at 9 o'clock, during the early days of the war, while we were waiting to hear the latest heartening homily from Mr J.B. Priestley, the BBC played on the Home Service all the national anthems of our defeated allies. By mid-1941 this was a considerable concert honouring Poland, Denmark, Norway, France, Belgium, Holland, Czechoslovakia, Greece, Albania, Hungary . . . Did it include Hungary at this early stage? At any event, some pundit decided to put in Abyssinia, because it looked as if we might be about to liberate it. It had, I remember, a very boisterous Sousa-like march, which turned into a romantic melody rather like *Some Enchanted Evening*. It did not at all evoke our tall leather-cloaked spear-carrying allies, but it did get the often rather mournful collection off to a rousing start. And the pundit was right: quite soon the small expeditionary force (which included my wife Georgina's father, and my friend Joanna Drew's father, and Laurens van der Post) had defeated a much larger Italian force. Its leader, the Duke of Aosta, was hiding in a cave in the mountains, and the Emperor was driving in triumph into Addis Ababa in an open staff car.

This was later; when we saw the Emperor at Windsor he looked as fragile and bereft as I often felt. Growing up alone with very protective parents had made me not only a coward, but a prig. Qualities I have not completely lost. I made one useful discovery at Wootton Court. For weeks I was shadowed everywhere by a cheeky lad who mirrored whatever I did. Often he would repeat something I had said over and over again until I thought I would go mad. Others would come and join in, making a taunting chorus that accompanied my attempts to find out what was our homework or some such essential part of school routine. Masters must have known this sort of thing went on, but condoned it as a part of life's hazards. It gave 'character' to have to learn how to cope.

I was so unused to ragging of this kind that I was a victim far longer than I need have been. Eventually my tormentor, getting bored with his role as echo, came close to me and whispered mocking and unpleasant thoughts right into my ear. Perhaps it was his proximity that did it. Though thin and bony I was taller than him. Without any warning I took a step backwards and hit him as hard as I possibly could on the face with my open hand. The sound of the smack resounded down the corridor. He stopped in mid-sentence, looked at me for what seemed a long time, then ran away. I had no more trouble from him. This worked only because I was bigger than him. It would not have been advisable conduct to use against the gangling louts who had so far failed in life. As with the stoning of the Italian youths, they often worked in groups.

They were responsible for the most unpleasant incident that happened in my year at Wootton Court. A number of boys had parents who lived overseas, many of them in the colonial service. Some of the unhappiest boys in the school were the youngsters of six or eight who saw their families only on their home leave every two years. Perhaps as a protection against the pain of such a loss there was an unwritten rule that parents when they did appear should look as dowdy and undistinguished as possible. One family completely ignored this sartorial convention. They would drive into the quadrangle in a canary yellow Rolls-Royce, mother in a silver fox fur, father in an astrakhan overcoat, chauffeur in yellow and black. Darling Roger, an ungainly lad of about eleven, would be whisked away for a chocolate cake tea on the Leas at Folkestone. This happened several weekends in succession.

The first period on Monday was physical education. The whole school exercised in the gym to the Coriolanus-like ranting of the sports master. The standard attire was grey flannel shorts. After a cold shower we would all change back into uniform grey blazers and slacks. All that is except for Roger on this occasion. When he went to his locker it was empty. Even the shorts he had discarded before showering had vanished. The changing-room was next to the gym, which was a couple of hundred yards of open asphalt away from the main school house with its dormitories and clothes cupboards. No one had any spare clothes to offer Roger. He refused to run the gauntlet, but when matron and the assistant headmaster went down to the gym with his spare uniform, he had gone. Someone said they thought they had seen him lurking near the pavilion on the cricket pitch. Someone else could swear he had seen him flashing on the flat roof of the science block. Several others said it stood to reason he would be out on the main road thumbing a lift home to Golders Green. 'Thumbing a lift? You mean waving a branch.' 'Waving something.' 'Nonsense, he'd be arrested for indecent exposure.' 'He's too young.' 'It's not the age, it's the size that counts.' 'Well that's all right then; he's been circumcised.'

One thing was clear: there would be no more school until Roger had been found. The sports master divided us into seven groups, each under a different master or janitor; even the lady music teacher had a party. I was with the assistant headmaster. He had rowed three years for Oxford in the boat race. He had shoulders like a barn door and two Irish setters that went bounding ahead of us into the wood. We were supposed to be keeping a long line just in sight of each other. The ground was so rough and the underbrush so thick that we were continually getting bunched up. In our raincoats and jackets we were finding it very hard going. I quickly became convinced that it would have been impossible for a naked Roger to have gone that way. At that very moment I saw him hiding behind a bush not more than twenty yards ahead of us. The dogs barked and dashed forward; we all shouted; Roger leaped away like an ungainly naked frog. We rushed after him. Regrettably, it was most exciting.

It did not last long. Another group cut off his retreat. He was wrapped in a blanket, and matron doctored the myriad scratches and bruises he had got in the wood. That evening the yellow Rolls-Royce came for the last time to collect him.

IV

The year 1936, which began with the death of an old king, ended with the departure of a young one. Our American relatives had sent us clippings from *Time* and other journals about King Edward VIII's affair with Mrs Simpson. Twice divorced, she was no beauty. That at least was the opinion of one who until recently had been having a hot romance with an American young lady. Admittedly she was about forty years younger than Mrs Simpson: so much the worse the luck of the King. I heard him make his abdication speech on my bedside wireless. It was on my thirteenth birthday.

I don't remember there being anything like the publicity which accompanied Prince Charles's marital difficulties some sixty years later. Of course, television brought the protagonists into every household and would presumably have revealed the monumental stuffiness of the Duke of Windsor that was so immediately apparent when he was interviewed on TV in the 1950s.

Most of the controversy at the time turned on the behaviour of Stanley Baldwin, the Prime Minister, and Cosmo Lang, the Archbishop of Canterbury. They had been determined to reduce the scandal by hustling off the King as quickly as possible and immediately bringing out his younger brother to replace him. The purpose of the King's speech was to prepare us for that scenario. Unfortunately, Edward VIII (David) was rather a good speaker and gave his statement considerable passion. His successor, George VI (Bertie), suffered from a most debilitating stammer. His preoccupation with getting out the words meant there was no room for nuance or inflection. Over the years he became more adept at rolling with the impediment, but it remained a painful experience to listen through one of his radio broadcasts: like seeing a man playing hockey from a power-operated wheelchair.

The new king also, though he could not know it at the time, walked into one of the most difficult of all reigns: six years of war followed by six years of austerity and then an early death. Yet he did his duty. He was widely admired and he showed the nation the face of fortitude and resolution which was expected of it. As a role model he had an enormous advantage over his wayward brother: his wife, Lady Elizabeth Bowes-Lyon. Scottish, she was the first non-royal queen since Edward IV had fallen in love with Elizabeth Woodville. Her charm, humour and courage were noticeable even to self-centred youths like myself.

She was to outlive her husband by many decades. We know now that she blamed his death on David's selfishness. He, after all, had been trained from childhood for kingship. If only he had never been beguiled by that awful Mrs Simpson.

But Mrs Simpson may have done the nation a great service by diverting David from the throne. His leaning towards fascism, his vapid upper-class friends, his failure to find an appropriate consort, and hence his inability to give his country a stable family image for it to live up to in this time of trial, made him an inadequate figurehead. Appropriately, he and the title invented for him – Duke of Windsor – survive in the style he used for tying his tie. As for Mrs Simpson, she was embodied in many rude limericks and children's songs:

> Hark the herald angels sing
> Mrs Simpson's pinched our King.

Some of those blue verses were aimed at the Archbishop of Canterbury. He looked a figure of princely authority of the sort invariably questioned by the English northerner. Two years later I had the opportunity to judge him for myself. The motto of St Edmund's School was 'Sons of the Church'. It had been founded at the end of the eighteenth century to give a classical education to the sons of impoverished clergy. Over the years the link with the church had grown more tenuous, but it was a rule that all the boys had to be communicants of the Church of England. Every year, in December, the reigning Archbishop came to school personally to confirm the new boys, usually as in my case, at the beginning of their second year.

Until my arrival at St Edmund's in autumn 1938 I had not taken any active role in church ritual. Religion had no part in our family life. I have no memory of my parents ever going to a service. Nor did my grandparents. Now I had to attend every Sunday morning in term time. The school chapel was a handsome neo-Gothic building with beautiful stained-glass windows. I didn't particularly mind the service, though I had been prohibited from ever singing at my first choir practice. The combination of my voice breaking and total tone deafness made the choirmaster and other clergy blanch.

I didn't think it was any more ludicrous than some of the sermons we had to sit through. One visiting missionary began by making a direct appeal: 'Stand with me' – the whole school stood; 'Stand with me on the banks of the Ganges,' he went on hastily.

Attendance at such services was not sufficient preparation for the solemn act that was to commit me to God. I had to learn large chunks of the catechism. Worse than that, I had to recite them to our headmaster, Canon Henry Balmforth. He was a cold, prickly man with pale sandy hair and pale blue eyes that lurked behind gold-rimmed pince-nez. He expected perfection from his pupils. One reason for his being a Christian would have been that it allowed him to contemplate the most perfect being and hold Him up as a model for his erring students. One of his books was called *The Christ of God*. Such an intellectual – one might say aesthetic – approach to religion was very hard for boys to take at a time when living together through radical changes in their physical development. Their introduction to morality was largely through the ethics of the sports field: rough and ready, but real. It was easier to see God as the great games captain in the sky than as an all-pervading searchlight probing every aspect of your life. Take the headmaster's two final sessions in my catechism, labelled personal hygiene. Was he going to recommend cold baths or demand to see that I had washed behind my ears?

It was more painful than I could have imagined. Those meetings were held once a week on a Friday afternoon in the headmaster's study. No one else was present. On this occasion he produced a twenty-page pamphlet, murmured in his pinched voice: 'Read this. I'm sure you'll want to talk it over,' and sank back behind the opened pages of *The Times*. Clever chap: he had covered himself in approximately three feet of heavy protective newsprint. I had only six inches or so of his miserable little pamphlet. And it was the cause of my confusion.

What I had to read in front of him were detailed descriptions of all the unmentionable things that were happening to me when I retired to bed. Things that I knew were happening to all my school contemporaries. Yet things that must never be mentioned, because adults never did talk about them in polite society. And such things certainly could not be discussed with this desiccated, dried-up shrimp of painful intent. I must not even let him know by a change of breathing that I was responding to the descriptions in his horrid pamphlet.

I got to the end as quickly as I could and put it down firmly on the small table between us. Simultaneously Canon Balmforth looked over the top of his newspaper like a rat in a store house.

'Well?' he said sharply.

'Well, I've read it; thank you very much, sir.'

'So what are your main problems?'

'Problems? Oh I don't have any.'

'But haven't some of the things described there happened to you?'

'Oh no sir, not at all sir, never.' I made my voice as firm as possible. If only it didn't go up into a squeak at the end of a sentence.

The Canon folded up his newspaper, the better to look at me.

'You mean you haven't experienced any one of those symptoms?'

'Oh no, absolutely not.'

'If you look at page two – please look at page two – if you look there, you'll see that the findings are based on a sample of over three thousand Scandinavian students, 98 per cent of whom displayed some of the sexual symptoms described.'

'Ah well, but I've never been to Scandinavia.' That seemed the best line to follow.

'The facts apply universally. It doesn't matter where you are domiciled. As you'll see 94 per cent of young males masturbate with a bar of soap or some such. Has this really never happened to you?'

'Oh no, certainly not, never.'

'Well, perhaps proximity; friends all showering together?'

There was the way out. 'I don't have any friends,' I said firmly and truthfully.

The pupils at St Edmund's were very unlike those at Wootton Court. For a start they went in age up to elegant young men of nineteen. On Saturday, when they were allowed out into town, they wore cutaway jackets and top hats and carried canes. The junior forms – the Remove and the Lower Fifth, where I languished – looked quite different. Everything you wore was designed to make you sweaty and uncomfortable: stiff white Eton collars, blue-and-white flannel shirts, woollen underwear, heavy worsted suits and straw boaters that were a perpetual incitement to attack from our neighbours, Kent College. They were lucky enough to wear plebeian caps, easy to stuff in your pocket in a scrimmage.

Some of the St Edmund's boys would undoubtedly have made good friends if I had had the opportunity to know them better. Being the only day boy in the school was an insuperable barrier. The young boarders of my level had nowhere to go in the evening except to sit in their smelly grubby classroom. The older boys had a big common room with armchairs and piano. They also had tiny cubicles with bed and desk in which to carry out their own studies. The younger boys had no privacy, only the inside door of their work-locker on which to express their personality, usually with a glossy pin-up of a film star, but occasionally a favourite dog or pony.

Their life seemed to me a fair representation of hell. Every Monday night, huddled up on the wooden benches of their classroom prison, they would hear an ominous thunder overhead. It was the grand piano being pushed back into a corner. No master at St Edmund's was allowed to cane a boy, but the prefects were. It was they, the elected representatives of the sixth formers, who maintained school discipline. Bad behaviour got penalty marks. Enough of those earned a caning. This was delivered on Monday evening and covered the marks of the previous week. The canes were the whippy smart objects that the sixth-formers slapped their legs with when lining up the classes on speech day and for every morning service. When used as a punishment, the cane was not allowed to be raised above waist height. Hence the rolling away of the piano, allowing the prefect a long run to gather momentum before delivering the stroke.

I was never caned, but many boys regularly got eight to ten strokes a week. When their names were sent down, they would go up to the common room with an affected swagger. On their return they would show the crisscross of weals on their palms with an attempt at bravado. But, even with those who were regularly punished, I sensed a shock that was near to tears. I found the whole concept of an internal hierarchy maintained by pain deeply disturbing. It seemed to me entirely wrong that older boys should be bribed by special privileges to punish their juniors.

Though I never fathomed it at the time, I feel sure that this closeness of punishment, which was condoned and accepted by the real authority, the teachers, and carried out by the oldest and most physically developed boys, often on the most youthfully pretty, was deeply involved in the massive sexual prohibitions needed to control the urges of so many suppressed youths. Pain became a substitute for love. Or, perhaps even more common: masochistic love became the most pleasurable.

Something of this we all knew. On the morning when we were going to be confirmed, one of our number, a freckle-faced Scots lad, went around saying over and over all the dirty jokes and blasphemous expressions that he knew. He did this, he said, because once the Holy Ghost had come into him there would be no room for anything like that.

'There won't?' said one of our fellows. 'So you're going to leave school straightaway then?'

When it came to my turn to kneel before the splendidly robed prelate, I felt no sudden flash of illumination. Instead, the pressure of the Archbishop's hands on my head was surprisingly forceful. Perhaps that was appropriate for such a worldly priest – physically pushing out the Devil.

Afterwards we all went with our parents to have tea in the school library and I was introduced to the Archbishop. What did we talk about? I think it must have been the novel *The Cloister and the Hearth*, which I had just been reading. The subject, the choice of religion or art, was sort of appropriate, though I actually thought it long and rather dull (I would never have said that, of course).

I do remember the Archbishop talked in a glittering, sophisticated way, with a gently teasing manner which alleviated the faintest trace of condescension. He carried himself with the conscious grace of a Renaissance cardinal. It was no coincidence that his brother was the romantic actor Matheson Lang. I had seen him play Dick Turpin in an old silent film we had on our home movie projector a few years before. It was Cosmo Lang's relationship with a film star that most impressed me (though I naturally would not have said that either).

Years later he said something I thought memorable enough to keep. On his resignation from the see of Canterbury in March 1942, he said: 'Of all the sorrows of parting, I think the saddest is parting from this holy and beautiful House of God.'

I agree. What I miss most from childhood is the sight and the sound of the sea, our garden at Highfields, the companionship of my dog Patch, and coming out of the bustle of narrow little Chancery Lane into the serene calm of the cathedral close.

V

Just round the corner from our house on the New Dover Road was the county cricket ground. It is one of the most charming of cricket fields; not grandly beautiful like Worcester, where the ground seems the ideal frame for a splendid view of the cathedral across the river, but friendly and – like Canterbury itself – full of history. It is the only ground I know that has a magnificent tree in full foliage on the pitch itself. And during the August Cricket Week, a military band in scarlet and gold, provided by the Buffs, marches up and down playing in the lunch break. Lunch could be an event in itself, for all around the edge of the field were tents with comfortable deck chairs from which to watch the game and shaded bars and lunch tables in the tents themselves.

My father had access to one of these tents – probably he was a member of Rotary. He was able to invite me to join him in the Cricket Week at the beginning of August 1938. I had never thought much of live cricket till then. I was quite bowled over. The conditions were ideal. The sun shone every day. When the game ran into a dull patch I could buy an ice cream choc bar from the light refreshment centre.

But the real stroke of luck was that I was able to see Frank Woolley bat five or six times in this, his last season. How to describe this experience to someone who has never seen Woolley play and probably only has a confused idea about the rules of cricket? Well, it was like having a privileged close-up view of Torvill and Dean ice-skating when they were at their peak, or Margot Fonteyn and Rudolf Nureyev dancing a pas de deux in a ballet by Tchaikovsky. The physical perfection is right, but the element of partnership is not. The batsman is alone playing against eleven men who are seeking to bring about his downfall. There is in every serious cricket match the spirit of contest distilled through many tactical choices and nuances. The wonder of cricket is that it is in some ways like a three-dimensional chess game to which all twenty-two players are contributing, and yet each team has a captain who, like a conductor, has to bring out the best in his team. And it is also like war – war between rival platoons. So, hold the analogy of the chess game with its infinite potential of alternative strategies, and superimpose on it the formality of the dance. And then give to that discipline the individual choice of movement and stroke play which a great actor gives to his interpretation of a major role in Shakespeare – say Vanessa Redgrave in her first youthful portrayal of Rosalind in *As You Like It*.

It is not surprising that the greatest English cricket captain of the post-war years, Mike Brearley, is a psychoanalyst. And equally not surprising that he was not in the absolute top class as a performer. Through the history of cricket runs the conflict between rational control and instinctive physical response. This has drawn to it the most unlikely admirers – Samuel Beckett, Mick Jagger, the philosopher A.J. Ayer, Imran Khan. All have agreed that Frank Woolley was a unique genius.

Even I, watching my first matches of first-class cricket, could see that Woolley, aged fifty-two now, was playing on a different level from everyone else. And I was watching some of the greatest players of the century. They included Len Hutton, the twenty-three-year-old Yorkshireman who had just made the highest score in test-match cricket, 364 against Australia, and the captain of the Australians Don Bradman, the great run-making machine himself. No batsman has ever been so ruthlessly, remorselessly successful. You could tell that all he cared about was making runs, and he started the moment he got in: a quick push down the wicket and he was off with a scoring stroke off the very first ball he received. And he went on like that prodding, pushing, flicking the ball just where the fieldsmen were not. It seemed inevitable that he was going to make a big score, and there was no particular reason why he would ever be out.

Woolley, on the other hand, looked as though he might be out at any moment. At six foot four inches tall and beautifully proportioned, he, too, played to score off every ball. But, whereas Bradman achieved his ends by grafting and a marvellous command at placing the ball exactly where he wanted, Woolley played with an imperial flow and elegance that was like looking at a painting by Tiepolo: effortless brilliance of execution made everything seem possible, yet anything could happen.

By this time you will be thinking this is the infatuation of youth. All right, take some other evidence. Here is what one of his contemporary players, Sir Pelham Warner, said of Woolley: 'His method of play is an almost unique combination of ease, grace, style and power and, above all, of correctness, the foundation of the art of batting.' The foremost historian of cricket, H.S. Altham, wrote: 'Technically one can review any stroke Woolley ever made and discover that every ingredient is perfect . . . I will always regard the brief innings of 41 with which he opened the Lords Test of 1930 as the most perfect piece of cricket I have ever seen.' And the greatest writer on cricket, Neville Cardus:

Cricket belongs entirely to summer every time that Woolley bats an innings . . . The bloom of the year is on it, making for sweetness. And the brevity of summer is in it, too, making for loveliness. The brevity in Woolley's batting is a thing of pulse or spirit not to be checked by clocks . . . An innings by Woolley begins from the raw material of cricket and goes far beyond. We remember it long after we have forgotten the competitive occasion which prompted the making of it . . .

That must be true of all great sporting achievements. But the lonely elegance of cricket, of one against eleven, sets it apart from other games. Each individual batsman, sensing this, gives it his own interpretation in the innings he plays.

It was my great good fortune that I saw its peak achievement through a famous innings of 81 that Woolley created in 1938, the last occasion when he played against the Australians. And it was not only Woolley, the supreme embodiment of the transient essence of this most subtle and profound of all team games, who was about to leave the field for the last time. The very game of cricket was undergoing one of its fundamental changes. In the early nineteenth century cricket was a rich man's whim. He would pit his team of champions against other star players. Out of this evolved the county side with its mixture of gentlemen and players. The gentlemen were given their initials on the scorecard and entered the pitch through a different gate from the players who were simply recorded by their surnames. It was a typically Edwardian demonstration of class hierarchy and continued up to the Second World War. Teams chosen from the best of the county players voyaged every four years across the oceans to the far reaches of the Empire: Australia, South Africa, New Zealand. They were bringing England's greatest game, with its lessons of sportsmanship and team spirit, to all the lands where the Union Jack flew. Ultimately, the sport was also taken up by the lesser breeds without the law: the ex-slaves of the West Indies, the crowded millions of India and Pakistan.

There was an unforeseen result. In the 1970s, the tough media tycoons in Australia saw the game as an exploitable event. It had to be jazzed up, compressed into a series of single-day contests, played by floodlight at night, the players squeezed into new colourful and distinctive outfits (which had enough space on them to advertise the names of the sponsors of the show). Teams went all over the globe and there were endless World Series, as though it was baseball or netball.

At the opposite end of the sports authority, the more conventional matches between the various countries took on an increased competitiveness. Test matches (as they were called) grew to be five days long. Winning them was an important gesture of national feeling and rejoicing. A potent weapon in achieving victory was the fast bowler. So lethal became his deliveries that the batsman had to wear an increasing amount of body armour, helmet and visors. Broken bones were commonplace. Standing up to this sort of battering often reduced the game to a dogged survival. The glory of stroke play, which had particularly graced the carefree brilliance of a side like Kent (under the visible influence of players such as Woolley), was no more. Of course, there were occasional players of such genius that they could still transfigure the experience of watching the game. And many such were from the ex-Dominions. England was no longer the dominant partner in the cricketing league. It had fed into cricket a unique mixture of top professional skills, largely from the mining and industrial areas of northern England, and amateur elegance, bred by the public schools.

St Edmund's produced its best-ever player in the brief years while I was a student. In 1938 G.P. Bayliss scored seven centuries against other schools and averaged over 70 per match. That was an unprecedented figure in a side where the next player averaged 16. I remember Greville Bayliss as standing out in the line of prefects for his dark, casual good looks and Irish charm, which extended to jollying on the small fry. He went up to Cambridge for a year or so and played in one of those unofficial varsity games that reflected the absence of so many students at war. I heard of him only occasionally after that. He was commissioned in the Irish Guards. After the war he went into the City and married a well-known beauty, the actress and television presenter Katie Boyle. Her real name was Caterina Irene Elena Maria Imperial di Francavilla, and she is perhaps best remembered for the years in which she introduced the Eurovision Song Contest.

Greville Bayliss died tragically and suddenly in 1976, but remained a powerful influence on his widow. She was convinced he continued to guide and protect her. In a newspaper interview she said: 'I'm tremendously psychic and get this extraordinary sense of being guided, nudged in certain directions.' His adeptness at striking the ball between hostile fieldsmen in his cricketing life has continued in the afterlife in finding free parking meters for Katie Boyle. 'Grev's wonderful with parking meters. I know perfectly well that when there is a drama, he will be there to help.' Does he return to the scenes of his boyhood cricketing triumphs to help guide the successors to his old teams?

We should remember that the greatest of all poems about cricket concerns ghosts:

> For the field is full of shades as I near the shadowy coast,
> And a ghostly batsman plays to the bowling of a ghost,
> And I look through my tears on a soundless-clapping host
> As the run-stealers flicker to and fro,
> To and fro:
> O my Hornby and my Barlow long ago!

They were real enough once. They opened the batting for Lancashire in the 1870s. The amateur A.N. Hornby was famous for taking short runs. The professional Barlow said of him: 'First he runs you out of breath, then he runs you out, and then he gives you a sovereign.'

For two summers, 1938 and 1939, I watched first-class cricket wherever it was being played in Kent: Gravesend, Canterbury, Folkestone, Dover. The last game I saw was at Dover at the end of the county season in the last days of August 1939. Kent was playing Yorkshire. This was always a tense match. The two teams represented the opposite ends of the philosophy of the game: Yorkshire calculated, cautious, dour and relentless; Kent freewheeling, adventurous, opportunist and pleasure-seeking.

There could not have been a more dramatic ground for this clash of temperaments. Dover is a harbour built between cliffs and hills. The county cricket ground occupies the flat summit of one of these hills. From it you could look down to the embracing arms of the harbour and beyond to the corrugated rhythms of the grey Straits of Dover. And beyond them lay the endless flat plains of northern Europe where a very different conflict was coming to a boil. We would not escape it, as was acknowledged by the frequent parade around the ground of men carrying billboards with messages blocked out in hasty capitals: 'All Air Force officers to report to RAF Manston,' 'Members of the Buffs on parade at 2 o'clock,' 'Naval personnel return to ship,' 'Flight-Lieutenant Brown to contact his commanding officer,' 'RNVR officers meet at Naval HQ Dover Castle.'

Yet the game went on, developing its ruthless rhythms, as Yorkshire, a superlative bowling side, relentlessly screwed the nails in the coffin of cavalier Kent. Not without struggle. Two players dominated this final day. Hedley Verity, the Yorkshire slow bowler, showed his quiet, undemonstrative skill in spin and accuracy. Only one Kent player, the captain Gerry Chalk, was able to master Verity. Going in first, Chalk batted throughout the innings while wickets fell unceasingly at the other end. At the close he was left not out 115, a worthy conclusion to a cricket career which seemed hardly to have begun. Nor was Verity to play first-class cricket any further. He fell, mortally wounded, while taking part in the Allied invasion of Italy. In the same year, 1943, Chalk was shot down in his fighter plane over northern France. His body, still in the cockpit of his Spitfire, was found in the 1980s and given a proper funeral attended by the two or three ageing survivors of that faraway team of the 1930s. They, too, are dead now. For so long he was a lonely victim of war; time has rejoined him with his old teammates.

> For the field is full of shades as I near the shadowy coast,
> And a ghostly batsman plays to the bowling of a ghost.

4

'THE NAVY'S HERE'

I

The week after the cricket match at Dover things went on getting worse. To everyone's shock and surprise Hitler and Stalin made a non-aggression pact not to attack each other. Nazi and Communist seemed arch enemies until they made it up at Nuremburg. On 25 August 1939, the day Chalk made his masterly 100, the British Government proclaimed a formal treaty with Poland. Much good it did her. After six years of war, oppression and massacre, Poland was no better off under the boot of Stalin than she had been under Nazi Germany. On the other hand, the 'non-aggression' pact lasted less than two years and after it Germans and Russians slaughtered over fifty million of each other, the greatest bloodbath in history.

All this was in the future when we dutifully switched on the wireless at 11 o'clock on Sunday morning, 3 September. The German invasion of Poland had begun the day before. We expected we would hear a message of war, though I could not imagine what that would mean. The Prime Minister, a lugubrious loser, had been told in the House of Commons on 2 September to speak for England. And I suppose he did that, rather laboriously and with a curious accent: 'This morning the British Ambassador in Berlin handed the German government a final note stating that unless we heard from them by 11 o'clock that they were prepared at once to withdraw their troops from Poland, a state of war would exist between us. I have to tell you now that no such undertaking has been received, and that consequently this country is now at war with Chairmunny.'

It was rather like a country grocer demanding payment of an overdue account from Bonnie and Clyde. Five minutes later a strange ululating wailing grew and filled the air. It seemed as if the Valkyries, the Germanic war maidens, had been summoned forth by Hitler to chastise his enemies, though now they had grown old and their singing had turned into a rusty screeching. That's what it *seemed* like. We knew what it really was: it was the air-raid warning. It had been demonstrated in Canterbury only a few days before. Every town in Britain had one and they were to be sounded only when enemy bombers were approaching. Hitler, like us, must have heard Mr Chamberlain's speech, and no doubt his reply was winging its way across our coasts at this moment. We had an idea of what it was going to be like; in the cinema newsreels we had seen the bombing of Guernica and Shanghai. That was small stuff in a civil war and in distant Asia. We were sure Hitler would be much more efficient and would send thousands of planes and darken the sky with falling bombs.

We rushed out into the garden (not the best thing to do in an air raid, but we were curious to see the form of our destruction). It was a beautiful sunny morning. The air was full, not of falling bombs, but of the dusty perfumes of late summer. From two gardens away came the rhythmic creak of the nine-year-old daughter on her swing. It was as though we had stepped into a different play. All was familiar, but everything was changed. In my head I kept saying to myself: we are at war, we are at war with Germany. What could it mean? This grass growing under our feet, would it ever need to be cut again? It was one of the most crucial days of my life: nothing was the same and I, like everyone else, knew it, yet the bees buzzed as confidently as ever among the roses.

It wasn't as though war was a new idea in itself. I was born only five years after the Great War ended (it was not yet called the First World War, because we did not expect there would ever be another). My father was a member of the Ypres League that met every year to keep the memory of those terrible trenches alive. Every year of my life at 11 o'clock on 11 November we observed the two-minute silence in tribute to the dead. Wherever they were, everybody stood still. You could hear the silence spreading along the streets, across the fields and valleys. It was moving, because it was heartfelt. There must never be another war like that one.

That didn't mean that there might not be a minor war such as the one in Spain. When Mr Chamberlain came back from Munich in September 1938, waving his piece of paper and bleating about 'peace in our time', I had just started at St Edmund's School. Our class of twelve to fourteen year olds debated the crisis. We all believed there would be a war and that we would all be in it. But it was one thing to indulge in a bit of corporate gloom in the classroom and another to grasp that it was really happening. At this very minute people were being blasted and maimed on the plains of Poland just as my uncle had been maimed on the Somme. That thought brought some consolation. It could not be as bad as the Great War. How wrong I was. The war that was beginning was a truly global conflict. It would last six years not four, and the casualties worldwide would be four times as great. Nor was it – as the First World War had been – largely confined in its depredations to young males. This war set a precedent that later minor wars have followed. Everyone was to suffer, young and old, halt and lame, infants and octogenarians, mothers and children, healthy and insane.

Luckily I could not imagine anything like that. In a few minutes there was the soothing hoot of the all clear. People said that the new radio direction finding station on the cliffs near Dover had mistaken a flock of birds for Hitler's bombers. We were spared his wrath for another day.

II

Now there followed a most curious winter. It was as though we were allowed a trip through Purgatory before entering the Inferno towards which we were inevitably heading. Each nation followed a path characteristic of its own soul. Thus Hitler blitzkrieged Poland into extinction in under a month. France showed a film of its wonderful new defences, the Maginot Line (I remember endless shots of heavy metal doors opening and closing automatically like a vast refrigeration plant, but in the end it failed to save France's bacon: Hitler bypassed it). England continued to call up and train a citizen's army without possessing enough First World War rifles to arm them, it was rumoured. Russia enigmatically followed up the terms of its pact with Germany and swallowed the other half of Poland. Watching from the far side of the Atlantic, America's twice-elected President Franklin Roosevelt seemed to be friendly to us. Our family's hundred-year link with the States made us hope they would eventually come down on our side as they had in the First World War.

In the meantime, there had been no major air attack on Britain. The cover of the *Boy's Own Paper* for November showed a heroic young soldier guarding the White Cliffs of Dover. But those early months of war were most brought home to us, as so often in wars in the past, by naval action. On 14 October a U-boat penetrated the so-called impenetrable defences of Scapa Flow, the huge natural bay in the Orkneys that was the northern anchorage of the British fleet. A British battleship, HMS *Royal Oak*, was torpedoed and sank immediately with the loss of 786 officers and men. Such dreadful casualties sustained in what was believed a safe anchorage brought home the horrors of war.

We had not only U-boats to fear. The Germans had built three fast, heavily armed warships to maraud British merchant convoys. One of these pocket battleships was intercepted by three British cruisers off South America on 13 December. Though outranged and outgunned, the British flotilla drove the *Graf Spee* into Montevideo harbour. The German captain scuttled his ship and shot himself. The companion German auxiliary vessel, the *Altmark*, temporarily escaped carrying over two hundred British sailors captive in her holds. Two months later she was cornered off the coast of Norway by a British destroyer, HMS *Cossack*. The *Altmark* was boarded in Nelsonian style. After a hand-to-hand struggle, the 299 prisoners were released to the cry 'The Navy's here'.

These distant echoes of ancient sea wars defined the hopes and fears of the early uncertain months, like the songs we schoolchildren sang: 'We're Going to Hang Out Our Washing on the Siegfried Line' and 'Run Rabbit Run'. No one less like a rabbit than the foamy-spittled Hitler could be imagined. Now the pain and idiocy of the terrible conflict we were about to embark on seems only too clear. How little we knew then. We look back at 1939 across a vast abyss of impending horror: total war, saturation bombing, the concentration camps, mass executions, the London Blitz, Pearl Harbor, the fall of Singapore, the siege of Leningrad, the Burma Road, Stalingrad, D-Day, Dresden, the atomic bomb, Hiroshima, Nagasaki . . . We could go on through the ethnic, tribal, religious, colonial and territorial wars that have continued to strew atrocity across our path.

War or no war, I went back to school that September. The only noticeable change was the deep trench the senior boys were digging in the quadrangle. It was to be an air-raid shelter. Its wet and muddy depths were among the few images I saw in the Second World War that reminded me of photographs from the First. Another was my father's tin hat. This flattish circle of metal hardly seemed to have changed since Agincourt. It looked much less effective in protecting the brain than the German coal scuttle version. My father acquired it because he had volunteered to be an ARP warden. He was forty-five and, as the manager of the local bank, beyond calling-up age. But all able-bodied men were expected to contribute to the war effort. As an air-raid warden he had to patrol the local streets three nights a week checking that every house was adequately blacked out.

The blackout was a disagreeable and unexpected consequence of the war. The government rightly foresaw that enemy bombers would follow street lights and would be helped to concentrate their night attacks by the lit windows of houses and shops. So for six years our cities, towns and villages, down to the remotest farmhouse, had to show not a chink of light; all street lamps were doused, car lights were reduced by 60 per cent, even hand torches had to be masked so that they gave only a feeble glow around your feet. Unless the moon was out, the hapless pedestrian was reduced to a stumbling shuffle with many a bruising encounter with an invisible lamp-post. After the first year, petrol was so severely rationed that most civilians like my father took their cars off the road for the duration. This menacing darkness, which you tried to avoid entering unless you had to, was one of the enduring miseries of the war. At first, when there were no major air raids on Britain, it seemed an unnecessary discomfort.

Sometimes I went with my father on one of his nightly patrols under the mistaken expectation that it might be exciting. The glamour of darkness quickly wore off. What greatly increased was my admiration for my father. His main patrol area included a new estate a little further out of town. The brand new semi-detached houses had only recently been occupied. Their owners probably disliked the very idea that an air raid might damage their handsome new property. Hence they didn't want to put up the heavy black material that was required by law to cover every inch of window that might be illuminated. Often they would simply put out all their lights when my father knocked on their door. A shouting conversation would take place through their letter box.

Such arguments usually followed the same pattern. The tenant would point out that there had been no air raids, there wasn't one at the moment, when there was he would be the first to put out all his lights. My father, in the most reasonable tones, would read out the letter of the law, which required that they shroud their property, just as every hospital and palace in the land had done. He never lost his temper even when a tenant threw a bucket of potato peelings at us. Only once did he have to return with a police constable to ensure that the law was being carried out. The muddle, confusion and grudging acceptance that the war could not be denied and would affect everything; that it was likely to be nasty, tedious and boring as well as dangerous – these were facts brought home to us more by the blackout than by anything else in the early days.

They were facts even admitted by the recalcitrant householders my father had to convince on his evening patrols. I saw a side of my parent I had never had cause to witness at home: his reasonableness. I remember the excellent conversations we had, especially when a near full moon made walking easier (we had not yet had reason to call such nights 'Bombers' Moon'). My father, unruffled by abuse and potato peelings, would point out how conscientious most families were. He always saw the other side of things without being at all unctuous. I remember as I write this the lucidity and good sense that he invariably showed in the various crises of life that I brought to him. Many years after his death I found myself sitting at a wedding lunch next to the father of the bride, a man I had never met before. We discovered by chance that he had known my father. His whole appearance lightened. 'What an extraordinary man. Such sound judgement, such humanity,' he said. 'He was a really good man.' I think he was.

III

It is rare for a new human encounter to bring with it a direct insight into your own past in the way that this wedding guest gave me an assessment of my father that both confirmed and enriched my memory of him. But, of course, there are things more durable than memories: houses, photographs, furniture like my old grandfather clock. By our bedside in Kensington is a small Victorian armchair. It came originally from my grandparents' farm in Yorkshire. The many curved slats that make the back include two that are broken. For years I have intended to repair them, as I have preserved the broken sections. The sight of the damage reminds me of the first winter of the war, because that was when it happened.

My mother, knowing my difficulty in making friends at school, had suggested that I should give a Christmas party to some half-dozen of my classmates who lived in Canterbury or nearby. Notionally a good idea, it was bound to be a failure because of the frozen nature of my relationship with my peers. Even while they were busy scoffing the bloater paste sandwiches and lemonade, I knew they would be storing up fresh observations of my home life with which they could torment me. Nothing could be better fodder than the sight of how the parents of the victim behaved towards him.

But the task of being both beady-eyed and sufficiently obsequious to disarm the parents' natural reserve put quite a strain on the acting abilities of the would-be tormenters. One of them, a freckle-faced, ginger-haired youth whose name I have forgotten, squirming in embarrassment at being asked a direct question by my mother, leant so far back in the little Victorian chair that it went over and broke the two slats that I have in my hand now. This was one down for him. To be a successful tormentor you yourself must be invisible and impregnable. However, not even the breaking of the chair was sufficient to unfreeze our relationship.

So sparse were my dealings with my fellows that I can remember only two other guests at that party. They were called Reynolds and were the sons of a clergyman who had seen fit to christen his elder child Lionel Cuthbert. If that wasn't a sufficient handicap, the school added another. All boys answered to their surnames. If there were more than one with the same surname, the initials of the Christian names were added. Thus the elder Reynolds became Reynolds, L.C. Like me, he wore glasses and found life difficult. There was no escape: Elsie or Cuthbert he remained throughout his school career.

This era of my discontent was mirrored and magnified a billion or so times by the impending trials of war. Christmas could not be the season of goodwill to all men when we were preparing for the death of so many. There was a new moral dilemma to perplex us that horrible Christmas. It was The Tragedy of Brave Little Finland. It was an episode without connection to all the disasters that were about to encompass us. Yet, for a few weeks, it occupied the centre of the world's stage. Let me tell of it through the way I was reminded of it many years later.

In the spring of 1976 I was filming the graves of the English kings Henry II and Richard I in Fontevrault Abbey in France. This was for the BBC television series *Royal Heritage*, which took two years of intensive labour to prepare in time for the Queen's Silver Jubilee in 1977. Recording the towering stone arcades of the nave was a refreshing change from the pomp and circumstance of state occasions. I was surprised and not entirely pleased therefore to get a direct message from the Queen. She had heard that the entrance to Helsinki Harbour was past a series of spectacularly beautiful islets. She was about to sail there in the Royal Yacht on an official visit and wondered if I wanted to film the event.

Only a minute's reflection decided me in the affirmative. The Queen made few direct interventions in the filming, but they were always helpful. I arranged for an additional camera team to go from London to Finland, hired a local helicopter to film the arrival of the Royal Yacht from the air, and arranged that a second team and myself would board the Yacht while it was under way in the Baltic to get the Queen's eye view of the approach past the islands. The next day I boarded a Finnair passenger flight from Charles de Gaulle airport to Helsinki.

It was my first visit to the home of Sibelius. I was met by a bearded government official. He explained that before taking me to my hotel he wanted to show me the most important site in Finland. He would not tell me what it was. We drove up to a green hill overlooking the city. A simple stone entrance led to a wide perspective of rolling hillside. It was entirely covered with uniform white gravestones: a heart-stopping sight. These were the young men who had died in the Winter War with Russia.

Then I remembered. 'It was at the beginning of 1940?' It was. It lasted four months and killed more than 2 per cent of the male population. Finland's southern border was only fifteen miles north of

Leningrad. Despite the secret non-aggression pact signed by Hitler and Stalin in the summer of 1939, its actual results, the partition of Poland, brought the rival dictatorships eyeball to eyeball. Russia had always feared an attack through Finland. This tiny, unprepared and ill-armed country was invaded by the Soviet giant at the beginning of December.

At first the massed Russian forces were opposed by poorly armed men who threw bottles of flaming petrol against the caterpillar tracks of the tanks: the famous Molotov cocktails. No other nation went to the aid of the Finns, but they had a powerful ally in General Frost. They were trained for guerrilla warfare in the forest and tundra. The Russians were heavily armed, but lightly clad. The winter of 1939–40 was one of the coldest in memory. In a few days more than two hundred Soviet tanks were lost to a mixture of fire, ice and courage.

To us, reading about these things in the *Daily Express*, it seemed intolerable that this land of free-thinking independent Davids should be battered to death by the hammers and sickles of the Soviet Goliath. But whose side were the Finns on? The British arranged to sell them some out-of-date fighter planes; so did Italy, which was shortly to join Germany in the invasion of France. There was talk of an army of volunteers (on the lines of the International Brigade in Spain); it never got under way, though the French supported the idea of sending in an army of the defeated and exiled Poles.

The Soviet invasion broke Finnish resistance before there was time for the politicians of Europe to make up their minds as to how they should react. Perhaps this was just as well, not only for saving Finland from further devastation, but also for faraway Britain. Had we sent a force of 100,000 troops, as was under serious consideration, they would have faced the hug of the Russian bear, and far away in Finland there was no Dunkirk and no twenty-mile stretch of water to retreat across. If Britain had found itself at war with both Germany and the Soviet Union (in the spring of 1940 they were still allies), what would have been the outcome of the war for us?

We were lucky. Ours was the only nation which was in the war from the beginning to the end and which survived. Finland, defeated by Russia, chose to join with Germany in May 1941 in the hope of getting revenge. She only added to the stones in the graveyard: 85,000 young men died in the Winter War; 500,000 were seriously wounded; 10,000 were permanent invalids. This was the debt my government official found it intolerable to have to carry. For us, in 1939, it was a tingling premonition of what we might be facing.

5

REGIONS DOLOROUS

I

Farewell, happy fields,
Where joy for ever dwells! Hail, horrors! Hail,
Infernal world! And thou, profoundest Hell,
Receive thy new possessor! One who brings
A mind not to be changed by place or time.
The mind is its own place, and in itself
Can make a Heaven of Hell, a Hell of Heaven.

I first read, and to a considerable extent understood, Milton's *Paradise Lost* in 1940. It was to be the set poem I had to study for the London Matriculation exam. It was also a poem whose bitter inflexible stance suited the mood of the day. Just as for the Romantics its heroically evil Satan focused their feelings for Napoleon; so, in this year of destiny, its rhetoric summed up the previous vainglory of Hitler and his beer cellar braggarts.

Unfortunately there was more to both Napoleon and Hitler than clever showmanship. Leaving out the purely personal hazards of ill-health and accident, 1940 must have been the most fateful year I have lived through (though clearly close run by 1941 and 1942).

Just look at some of the dates. On 8 April Germany invaded Denmark. Resistance lasted a few hours. Sea battles off the coast of Norway followed. An Allied Expeditionary Force landed near Narvik on

22 April. It was withdrawn within a few weeks. On 10 May Holland and Belgium were invaded. The Dutch capitulated in five days. Belgium capitulated on 28 May. France capitulated on 16 June. The German army reached the Pyrenees on 27 June. In less than two months it seemed the European war was over.

This brief summary of disaster omits two important facts: on 10 May Chamberlain's government fell and Winston Churchill was asked to form a coalition government of all three parties. His message to Parliament was brief: 'I have nothing to offer but blood, toil, tears and sweat.'

At that moment the British Expeditionary Force was fighting in Belgium. Ten days later a far-sighted admiral began getting together a fleet that might be needed to bring back the retreating army. Ferries, fishing boats, pleasure steamers, Royal Navy craft of all sorts – within a week they were under way, heading for Dunkirk. Dunkirk, that was where it had to be: Calais and Boulogne had already fallen.

It wasn't only the larger ships that were involved. In a big Victorian house a few doors from us lived a widow, her four sons and a daughter, all in their twenties or late teens. They were an outstandingly handsome quintet. They, along with many, many others, vanished for a few days. They had sailed their yacht over to the bomb and shell-blasted beaches where the troops were assembled, crouching in dug-outs, waiting to be ferried out to the big ships that would carry them across the Channel to home.

It was the sort of spontaneous enterprise that the English seem able to carry out well. When it was first considered, it was hoped to evacuate a few thousand of the rapidly disintegrating Expeditionary Force. In fact, in the nine days from 27 May to 4 June, 338,226 British and Allied troops were ferried back to Dover and Ramsgate. The rear guard fought stubbornly, the RAF kept the German bombers at bay and the Royal Navy did superbly what the nation expected of it. They even brought back 800 stray French dogs that had attached themselves to the canine-loving Tommies.

Dunkirk became a myth overnight, like the defeat of the Spanish Armada 350 years earlier. But the Armada *was* defeated. This was a disaster for Britain, coupled as it was with the collapse of France and of our other European allies. Time has given it the accolade of the ultimate victory. But that was no consolation in those bewildering spring days when battle no sooner seemed to be joined than it was lost. We were expecting a return match on 1914–18: a steady slog in the mud and blood of Flanders. Instead, we were embracing a whirlwind: the Blitzkrieg entered our vocabulary. How terrible it must have seemed to that little army of professional soldiers who had probably seen service on the North-West Frontier in the 1930s. One of them wrote a book about his experiences at Dunkirk that came out that same year. Reading it at Christmas 1940 gave a clearer understanding of what we were in for:

A mile behind us, Dunkirk, as the darkness of the night closed in on it, ceased to be visible as a vast welter of black and grey smoke and became a great red, angry, glowing cinder. The pillar of cloud by day became the pillar of fire by night. Against the impenetrable ebony background of the sky it glared forth upon us like a ferocious bloodshot eye. In front, along the near horizon, a couple or so miles distant, long flashes like summer lightning played continually, orange and greenish in hue. They were the explosions of our own shells mingled with the flashes from the German artillery replying. Above this play of summer lightning, every now and then a rocket soared high into the sky, bursting into a brilliant white light. German success rockets recording the capture of some objective. They were disconcerting to watch, bursting as they did with such frequency, and in the darkness seeming to draw nearer and nearer . . .

On either side, scattered over the sand in all sorts of positions, were the dark shapes of dead and dying men, sometimes alone, sometimes in twos and threes . . . A horrible stench of blood and mutilated flesh pervaded the place. There was no escape from it . . .

'Water . . . Water . . .' groaned a voice from the ground just in front
of us. It was a wounded infantryman. He had been hit so badly that
there was no hope for him. Our water bottles had long been empty,
but by carefully draining them all into one we managed to collect a
mouthful or two. A sergeant knelt down beside the dying man and
held the bottle to his lips. . . .

Our only thoughts now, were to get on a boat. Along the entire
queue not a word was spoken . . . Heads and shoulders only
showing above the water. Fixed, immovable, as though claimed
there. It was, in fact, practically impossible to move, even from one
foot to another. The dead weight of waterlogged boots and sodden
clothes pinned one down . . .

The gunwale of the lifeboat stood three feet above the surface of
the water. Reaching up, I could just grasp it with the tips of my
fingers. When I tried to haul myself up I couldn't move an inch . . .
I might have been a sack of lead. A great dread of being left behind
seized me . . . Two powerful hands reached over the gunwale and
fastened themselves into my armpits . . . Before I had time to
realise it I was pulled up and pitched head-first into the bottom of
the boat. 'Come on, you b———. Get up and help the others in,'
shouted a sailor, as I hit the planks with a gasp.

I saw some of these others landing back in Britain. Canterbury is on
the southern toe of England. North of us was the Thames Estuary, east
was Ramsgate, south-east Dover and south Folkestone. In that last week
in May we began to realise that an amazing act of deliverance was being
played out on the narrow seas. On Saturday or Sunday 1 or 2 June my
father drove us down to the coast.

In some ways it was almost like a regatta that we looked down on
from Shakespeare Cliff. The sea was full of small boats of every
description bobbing about in the summer sunshine. Smears of black
smoke blotched the horizon. Grey forms of destroyers clashed here and

there, churning up the already turbulent water. By contrast, one of the Thames pleasure boats, a paddle steamer, came limping slowly into harbour, its decks almost awash and crowded with men.

Dover harbour was equally crowded. Men sat, or lurched about looking for their regiments, shouting out for their friends. Many appeared to be asleep on their feet. This was no army: some had bare feet wrapped in grass, some were on crutches, some clothed only in filthy blankets. Few had rifles or any other arms. The wounded were being tended by nurses on the quayside. Many sat or stood motionless: their jaws dropping, they seemed to be in the last stages of shock and fatigue.

Yet, through this filthy multitude, smart, brisk transport officers ran backwards and forwards organising the loading onto the trains that were leaving every few minutes. Uniformed members of the Women's Voluntary Service (WVS) were supervising steaming tea urns, handing out sandwiches and bars of chocolate. At another part of the harbour children were being assembled. These were not war orphans, but the children of Dover who were being evacuated. Might not Hitler follow on this defeated host? The children also had to be organised. They had all the mobility that the shell-shocked troops had lost. They dashed in pursuit of their friends, hid from them behind the soldiers. Sometimes they got genuinely lost and tearful. From time to time they burst into song. The thin wavering notes of 'There'll Always Be An England' drifted up to us on the windy cliff top.

What was it like? It was a unique event. I had never seen anything like it. I wanted to understand it by comparing it with something I knew. The only thing I could think of was that Victorian painting of a railway station. But that was too mundane. Something was missing.

The outer quay was almost clear of troops. From the deck of the now much lighter paddle steamer came shouted words of command. Another sodden and dirty group of men climbed out onto the quay. They formed up in threes; they shouldered their rifles (they still had their rifles). Then, officers and NCOs at the front, they *marched* off to the waiting train. I think they were the Scots Guards. That was the element that had been missing from the scene.

It was restated with unforgettable power in the radio speeches that our new Prime Minister, Winston Churchill, made in the next few weeks. I can still hear them ringing through my imagination:

> The whole fury and might of the enemy must very soon be turned upon us. Hitler knows that he will have to break us in this island or lose the war . . . If we fail, then the whole world, including the United States, including all that we have known and cared for, will sink into the abyss of a new Dark Age, made more sinister, and perhaps more protracted, by the lights of perverted science. Let us therefore brace ourselves to our duties, and so bear ourselves that, if the British Empire and its Commonwealth last for a thousand years, men will still say: 'This was their finest hour.'

II

A danger in this sort of retrospective assessment of a life is making it appear more patterned and organised than it seemed at the time. A disaster of such enormous magnitude might be expected to dwarf everything else. Admittedly, the resourcefulness of the Navy, the courage of the Air Force and the stubborn endurance of the Army had given us the possibility of fighting again on another day. We had saved 338,226 men. But in doing so we had lost 68,000 fighting men, killed, missing or taken prisoner. And, with them, 63,879 motor vehicles, 679 tanks and half a million tons of military stores and ammunition, 243 ships, including six destroyers, and 474 aircraft. Of course, we didn't know these dreadful figures then. We had nothing to fight Hitler with except Churchill's rhetoric.

But the war, even such devastating events as Dunkirk, remained at the periphery of my life. The foreground continued to be my home and my relations to my classmates in the Remove. I was most concerned with the ingenious verbal tormenting by the Pelly brothers and the even more disturbing violence of the English master Mr Johnson. Youthfully handsome with dark curly hair and a splendid voice, he had recently shown unexpected paroxysms of rage at the smallest demonstration of student sloth. This would usually consist of him suddenly swinging round from the blackboard and hurling his chalk at the inattentive pupil – not an uncommon teacher device when carried out a relatively slow pace, but when delivered with all the vim of a Larwood out to upset Bradman, it was quite another matter. When he graduated from the small shrapnel of chalk to the blockbuster of the wooden mounted blackboard duster we began to take bets as to who would get the first fatal injury. A few days later he went over to his desk in the middle of reciting to us Wordsworth's 'Daffodils', leant his head in his hands and burst into tears. Still sobbing, he shut his book and walked out of our life. We were most scandalised that he had left when only halfway through the lesson.

I naturally relayed this story to my parents when I was at home that evening. My father must have mentioned it to my housemaster, Mr Stephen-Jones, commonly known as The Beak because of his Punchlike nose. He was a personal friend of my father's and the principal reason that I was allowed to be a day boy at a boarding school: a dubious advantage except on occasions like this. 'You know your Mr Johnson,' said my father a few days later. 'Well, you must promise not to tell anyone, but he's suffered a bereavement.' 'A bereavement?' I wasn't sure I knew what it meant. 'Yes,' said my father. 'His wife has left him. As a matter of fact she has gone off with the music teacher at Kings School. Now you mustn't tell a soul. Promise?' It wasn't a difficult word to keep. If I'd let it out, it was such a bizarre story it would have been twisted to rebound on me.

Nor was that quite the end. On Sundays my father drove me up to the school chapel to attend the service. He would be waiting for me when we all came streaming out an hour or so later. Seeing him, Mr Stephen-Jones came over and leant in on the driver's side. He murmured too low for me to hear. I guessed it was about Mr Johnson, when I heard Mr Stephen-Jones say something, something . . . couldn't perform. So was it the music master's ability to play a tune that had won over Mrs Johnson? Something like that, said my father, but he resolutely refused to go into detail.

There was one person I could have discussed it with. This summer term of 1940 we had another weekly boarder. Like me, William Harvey was not allowed to play games; tuberculosis had left him with a weak heart. When it was time for cricket we would often go for long walks. Balanced on the spur of hillside above the town there were a number of paths that gave us splendid views of the cathedral. And if we chose the opposite direction, Blean Woods were a mass of bluebells and other wild flowers, and could hardly have changed since the days when the Canterbury pilgrims must have wandered through them.

My friendship with Harvey was a good example of how propinquity can draw together the most unlikely couples. We had hardly an interest in common. He was extremely practical: he loved tinkering with machinery and working out electrical circuits. I liked to imagine what the town would have been like when the first parties of pilgrims came over the hilltop and saw it below them. That was the sort of unanswerable speculation that cannot have appealed in the least to Harvey, but he was kind enough to enter into the spirit of the occasion by suggesting that most of the travellers would have been more concerned with getting their aching feet into a hot bath than in admiring the view. Equally, I would be incapable of understanding the ballistics that spun a revolver shot in the direction you wanted it to go, however patiently Harvey explained them. His father had kept a German Mauser automatic that he had acquired in the First World War. We were at one in believing that we would shortly have the opportunity to test its capability.

In 1939 we had expected an avalanche of bombers to devastate the English countryside immediately, but the eight months of phoney war had lulled us into a false confidence. Just as the victims of the Holocaust politely asked the German soldiers the way to go, so the inhabitants of the Kentish coast thought of ingenious means of repelling the expected invaders. A plump middle-aged friend of my mother's had arranged a line of flatirons on a window ledge above her front entrance. She was going to drop these on the heads of the Germans as they came to batter in her door. The part of this counter-attack with which she was most proud was that each iron was tied to a length of stout string attached to a clothes rail so that it could be hauled back and used again on the second wave of Jerries. The grain of truth behind this fantasy was that Hitler was indeed planning an invasion on this part of the coast. Operation Neptune would have come into force in September and Canterbury should have been taken on the second day.

We didn't know this as a fact, but it seemed a likely supposition. If it had come, would we have given up the fight immediately like the inhabitants of Brussels and Paris; or would we have fought on to the bitter end like the people of Leningrad and other Russian cities? The way we stood up to the Blitz, and later the even more terrifying flying bombs, suggests the latter. It would have been goodbye Folkestone and Dover and all those charming villages of the Weald and ancient Canterbury. And probably, not so ancient Gills.

III

Where the road to Dover dipped into a woody hollow, our car was halted. A tall young officer stepped out of the trees, his right arm cradling a Bren gun. As my father drew us to a halt beside him, other soldiers jumped onto the road. The car doors were thrown open, rifles with nasty looking bayonets on them were poked at us. It was about a week after our excursion to see the soldiers returning from Dunkirk. There had been constant air battles overhead, and I suggested we might make another trip to see what was happening at the airfield at Hawkinge near Dover.

The gleaming bayonets were a reminder that war was not an occasion to satisfy curiosity. The officer put it more sharply. We might be involved in an air raid or a parachute attack. All this coastal zone was now out of bounds to visitors without direct permission. (So it remained throughout the war; when coming on leave I had to produce evidence that my family lived in east Kent.) In June 1940 all this was an unsettling surprise.

After a stern warning the officer let us through. There were indeed changes at the airfield. The newspapers had said that a new RAF plane, the Defiant, had gone into action. Not very successfully it would seem by the wrecked fuselages that scattered the perimeter. Indeed, the Defiant was quickly taken out of the front line. It was an attempt to install a four-gun turret and gunner into the shape of a single-seater fighter such as the Spitfire. Ingenious, but too ambitious. The littered airfield was a reminder that the supreme test of our aircraft, and the quality of our pilots, and indeed the character of us all, was upon us.

At very short notice two weeks before, St Edmund's School had amalgamated with Kings Canterbury, and left for wartime exile in Cornwall. As a day boy I did not go with them. That was the end of my school life, though of course I could not know it then. What was going to happen? My parents were decided by an order my father received from head office instructing him to commandeer a lorry, put the contents of the bank vaults in it and proceed with them to an address in the Midlands. This should not be done until my father was certain that the invasion had actually begun. Would Hitler tell him my father wondered? We had heard something of the chaos that fleeing refugees had caused in the war zone in France.

The summer of 1939 my parents had taken a furnished bungalow in Morecambe. My father's brother lived in Morecambe. His son, Douglas, another only child, was about eighteen months older than myself. We seemed to get on reasonably well. Rather than waiting for Hitler to make his move, my father packed my mother and me off to the re-rented bungalow.

I spent the summer months of the Battle of Britain in a place as far removed from it as it was possible to imagine: the broad sweep of Morecambe Bay with its deceptively inviting, but treacherously quick-sanded strand, its confident north country people, out for a last summer of seaside jollity before getting down to the job of putting Hitler in his place, its raucous funfairs with big dippers and hurtling, jamming Devil's Rides, which could simulate the planes twisting and jinking in mortal combat, and the rifle ranges where Douglas and I might imagine we were getting the invaders in our sights.

Like Harvey, Douglas was an unlikely friend: heavily built, with long arms and a slouching walk that increased his somewhat simian appearance. He had an unhappy childhood to overcome. His father had an ungovernably violent temper. It was said that Douglas was the result of the only physical connection that his parents had managed to achieve. Like many women who grew up in Victorian times, his mother disliked sensuality of any kind. According to what my father told me much later, she actually developed some incurable infection of the womb. Douglas was born with asthma. This was not all my Uncle Bernard had to contend with. He had been a clever draughtsman and had advanced rapidly in the early days of aircraft design. In the slump of the late 1920s he lost his job. All that he was able to acquire was sales representative to a whisky distiller. He had to drive from pub to pub across Lancashire and the Lake District selling his firm's brand. He was paid only a commission. Other job prospects would have meant leaving Morecambe, but this his wife Phillis refused to do. The seaside air was supposed to be especially favourable for sufferers from respiratory complaints.

When all this got too much for Bernard he would find an excuse to take Douglas into the back yard and thrash him mercilessly with a leather strap. Douglas never cried, but he hated his parents with a sustaining hatred. To me, Douglas was tolerant and protective. He already demonstrated the determination to succeed that was to carry him to a directorship in ICI. I've suggested that he was far from graceful in his posture. He was bow-legged, with his feet naturally splayed apart. Yet in his teens he took up ballroom dancing and within a year had won a gold medal.

Despite his unrewarding appearance, Douglas was seldom without a girlfriend. Later in the war, when Morecambe became the centre for the initial training of women in the Air Force, there was a surfeit of lonely and frightened young women wanting comfort, but even in 1940 he had a delightful level-headed grammar school girl in tow. I was allowed to accompany them on long walks. I can still remember the thrill of helping her over a stile, because then our hands touched. It was the first opportunity I had had since my cousin Carolyn's visit four years before to probe female ways of thinking. I found them deeply attractive, stimulating and awe-inspiring – a view that has not changed much over the years.

IV

At the end of August my father came to visit us. The Battle of Britain was at its height. It was mainly fought over Kent. There was no saying when it was going to end or what would follow. Stories of escapes from casually dropped bombs were as prolific in Kent as accounts of mugging were later to be in New York. We were somewhat misled by the exaggerated figures of enemy losses that were published every day, but there was no sign of the German attacks flagging.

My parents agreed that it would not be sensible to move the family back to Canterbury. Instead, early in September my mother and I went over the Pennines to the West Riding of Yorkshire. There on the hills above the valley of the Calder my Uncle Tom Taylor had the family farm. He was my mother's elder brother. In his youth he had been a fine rider.

Drink got to him as it had with his father. Any of the villagers finding an empty bottle in a hedgerow would murmur: 'Ah, Tom Taylor's been along here.'

He was another example of an unhappy and frustrating marriage. His wife was a strong and cheerful woman. There were no children. When in the drink, Tom would sit in the stone-flagged kitchen, a loaded shotgun across his knee, threatening anyone who tried to get the whisky bottle from him. Eventually, well before my police-impersonating visit, his attacks of delirium tremens became so violent that he gave up spirits more or less entirely. He slouched gloomily over his fields, cursing his cattlemen and the fate that had brought him such an inadequate inheritance. His younger brother, Clifford, had taken up their uncle's offer of a share in their brick factory in Detroit. Tom could have gone, too, but he had no stomach for the Atlantic crossing.

Yet there were just too many Taylors in the West Riding. I have a large family photograph taken in 1893 at the wedding of my great-aunt Sarah Jane. There are more than fifty people in the photograph, all ultimately dependent on Taylor's Mills (of which there were several). Like his father, Tom had only the profits of running the farm. It was too small to support anyone except the family of the farmer himself. Tom employed a foreman, a horseman, and two cowmen. He had four magnificent shire horses, about twenty-four dairy cattle, several pigs in litter, a dozen hens, a noisy cockerel, and a pony and milk float to deliver the milk to the neighbouring hamlets. It was one of the few things that Tom did himself. I would sometimes go with him: jumping off at each cottage, dipping the measure into the churn and filling up the jugs and bottles that had been left out.

It had been decided that I should not go to a local school, but take a correspondence course that would prepare me to sit the London Matriculation examinations. One of the general examination halls where this could be done was at Wakefield. I registered there and settled into the novel business of being tutored by letter. I was taking courses in mathematics and geometry, English grammar and English literature, history, geography and French. There were a lot of books to master and a written examination every three weeks. It was not very interesting, but it filled up the time, and it gave me a goal. I had definitely decided that I wanted to go to university, thus fulfilling my father's ambition for himself.

Now I come to think of it, in the 1920s he had taken a correspondence course in banking and followed it up by being a tutor himself. Throughout my childhood in Herne Bay he would settle down to a paper-laden dining-room table and be marking and commenting for a couple of hours or so each evening. So, for the best motives, he threw me back on my own resources.

So much of my life seemed to be spent in having conversations with myself or with one other: Jack Packham, or Mr Goldfinch, or Stephen Coltham. Now that dialogue was etherealised and came floating through space to land illegibly on my breakfast table. (Most of the tutors seemed to follow the university convention of writing in as tiny a hand as possible.) Instead of the lush hills of Kent there were the bare moors of the West Riding. Walking there gave you time to dream. And to mourn.

To those taking part in it as passive victims, the Battle of Britain had no specific end. Some days the plane casualties reported (over-optimistically on both sides) were much higher than on other days. There was a general movement by the enemy towards massive night raids. Anti-aircraft defences were incapable of destroying night bombers on the scale that they could in daylight. But daylight bombing went on through the autumn. Much of it was casual and seemingly motiveless: a single German plane losing touch with its fellow, probably under attack from a Spitfire, jettisoning its bombs over any built-up area. Only, to us below, each 'built-up area' was home and loved ones for some.

Our maid Dorothy continued to look after our house in Canterbury for my father. She did the same for his second man, Mr Harding. He, too, had sent his family off to relatives in the Midlands. Every morning Dorothy went down to do his washing and tidy and clean his modest three-bedroom house on one of the estates that my father and I had inspected for blackout the year before. Dorothy was notoriously dilatory at getting anywhere on time. One day in October she was an hour late leaving Green Gates. She had not yet reached the road where Mr Harding lived, when an unexpected bomb fell and destroyed his house completely. Ten minutes later and she would have been in it. That was shocking enough, but worse was to follow.

On Friday 11 October, at about 11 o'clock, a group of Messerschmitt fighter bombers pursued by Spitfires dropped their bombs on Canterbury. The attack was a complete surprise. The first bomb scored a direct hit on the fur shop next door to my favourite bookshop. All the people in the furriers were killed; so was Miss Carver. I expect she had been standing in the doorway of her shop having a quiet smoke. My friend, Miss Stanyforth, was buried under books, but dug out alive. I wrote her a letter of condolence. It was the first really adult letter I had written. I thought of all the quiet hours I had spent reading in the back room. The charm of old Burgate, its connection with the poet Marlowe, now lost forever. And the gentle kindness of Miss Stanyforth herself. She replied, thanking me for all the support I had given the shop, and explaining that she had no heart to carry on and was going to live with relatives in the Midlands. I never saw her again.

There was a surprise casualty at the furriers. The shop had been quite crowded. One victim was identified only through a severed hand with expensive rings on it. Only the hand was recovered, but it was sufficient. The costly rings had been presents from a maharajah. The owner was that scarlet lady who had so flustered my mother when she had petted Patch on my spinal chair. No doubt she had come in from Herne Bay to get her furs spruced up for the winter. Instead, she had been relieved permanently of all such anxieties.

My mother and I had heard our first enemy bombs when we were in our reputedly safe haven of Morecambe that summer. Late one evening in July a plane passed low overhead, followed by three thumping crashes.

We both knew instantly they were bombs and not fireworks. High explosives put pressure on the atmosphere unlike any other bang. No one was hurt. No significant Nazi war aims can have been advanced by churning up the sandy soil of the quiet Lancashire suburb of Heysham. It seems surprising that such a methodical people as the Germans should have vacillated so frequently in this crucial year of the war. The daylight attacks on our airfields and across the south of England were followed by night raids on the capital. On average two hundred planes a night bombed London every night from 7 September to 3 November. Overwhelmingly, the main pressure fell on the crowded tenements and Victorian terraces of the city and the docks. They seemed undaunted; *London can take it* ran round the world.

Even Hitler, reviewing the course of the air war against England in February 1941, wrote: 'The least effect has been that upon the morale and the will to resist of the English people.' Would we have been capable of standing up to a continuing bomb attack of the kind that reduced Churchill to tears when he visited Peckham and saw the previous night's devastation? I remember each day reading the news of the previous night's blitz with a sense of anguish, like getting the latest report on a dangerously ill patient; even more, listening to the wireless news, feeling the tense ordeal that our great city was being subjected to, and wondering how long it could continue to take it.

What difference would television have made? Presumably much of the devastation would not have been shown, as it would have been useful information for the enemy. Perhaps even more in those poverty-ridden days the people had less to lose and a solidity in shared frugality. Were those days really so heroic and self-sacrificing? Radio certainly brought us together. Television might have driven us apart, for inevitably it would have shown what a relatively small part of the country was bearing the brunt of the battle.

It did seem almost a relief when Hitler turned his attention to Coventry on the night of 14 November. Other industrial centres and ports were attacked in turn. Early in December it was the West Riding. Dewsbury and Batley were the centre of the heavy woollen trade. (The Taylor family had profited greatly from the cold of the Russian winter during the Crimean War.) What possible harm in the long term could the destruction of a few bales of shoddy do to our war effort? This was total war of course.

The air-raid warning was shortly followed by the fateful moaning of the German bomber engines. They were desynchronised to throw off the efforts of the RAF sound locators to track them. The counter-effect was to inform the people of Britain when the enemy was passing overhead. We had heard them a few nights before when they were on their way to Liverpool. But this time they didn't go away. One or two anti-aircraft guns went off. (At this stage of the war, firing ack-ack guns was as effective as clapping your hands at an advancing lion.) The bombers continued to circle. Uncle Tom and I went into the yard to have a look. It was a dark cloudy night. Suddenly a stick of bombs went off. They were not particularly close, but in my experience it is such a violent noise that it almost always makes you jump with fright.

The Taylor farmhouse was built in the mid-eighteenth century and had a deep stone-lined cellar. As we had planned, Uncle Tom, Aunt Laura, my mother and I dutifully went down below. However, nothing much seemed to be happening and it was very cold in the cellar. Despite the entreaties of the women, Tom and I went outside. It was a most spectacular sight. One of the factories in Batley Carr must have been burning, though the tree-lined brow of the hill kept it from our sight. The sky, and especially the underside of the clouds, were lit by a flickering, brilliant red glow. Occasionally, something like a factory floor must have fallen in; burning fragments sailed up and even lit the windows of our farmhouse. Guns of the defenders were going off with flashes like sheet-lightning and sometimes in long lines like flaming ping-pong balls that must have been tracer bullets. I was quite entranced by these firework effects. The raid itself seemed to be rumbling off northwards towards Bradford. The next day we discovered that the nearest crater was just within our farm land, on the brow of Carlinghowe Hill, about a quarter of a mile away.

V

It was this autumn that we got acquainted with one of the most lasting and unpleasant effects of the war: rationing. It was to continue for thirteen years. The majority of groceries were still severely limited when I got married in 1952. In 1940 and 1941 there were real shortages. Aunt Laura was a good north-country cook, but there just wasn't enough. Even potatoes and beets were in short supply.

A new person appeared at the door. He would be a distant cousin or an old acquaintance of Tom's. 'Remember? We last met at Barnsley Horse Show in 1932.' He just happened to be passing and wondered if we would be interested in buying a side of bacon. Yes, he had several. Let's say the pigs met with a severe accident (wink, wink). And if that was too much, how about some choice Stilton? Of course, it wasn't cheap.

And it wasn't legal either, but the police had bigger things to deal with than black marketeers. Nor had we much money to spare for forbidden luxuries. One thing that is hard to visualise if you are growing up in the self-indulgent modern world of chocolate bars, and potato crisps and ice-cream cones, is the all-pervasive grasp of rationing. All those tasty snacks were unavailable or prohibited (*one* Mars Bar was all the sweets, chocolate and cream cakes allowed for one week). It must have been particularly hard on small children. I had been forbidden chocolate and other sweets throughout my years of illness, so the war rationing simply continued the austerity up to my twenty-eighth year (when rationing finally ended).

One result of this was that I still hate leaving food uneaten on the plate. Nor do I feel justified in munching a whole chocolate bar in one sitting. For almost the first half of my life I was accustomed to eating less than my stomach told me it wanted. Through much of this time food was not only scarce, but relatively unpalatable. An omelette made from powdered egg substitute was not the same as one that had been whipped up from a couple of fresh eggs. There was no point in making a fuss; we knew that through much of the war we were in a desperate struggle to beat the German U-boat blockade that was attempting to starve us to defeat. And after the war, in the heroic days of the first Labour government, there were more important issues than a return to gourmandising. (For most of the war and for years after, the maximum cost of a meal in *any* restaurant from Lyons Corner House to the Savoy Grill was five shillings – 25p in modern money). That had its advantages. If you were a poor student, you could still afford to impress your girlfriend by taking her to dinner at the Café Royal or the Apéritif in Edinburgh. Always assuming you could get a table, of course.

All this was just coming upon us in autumn 1940. In the meantime there was a more severe crisis growing in the foreground. Uncle Tom was going bankrupt. That seemed an impossible statement at a time when the government was desperate to cultivate every mouse-hole of ground; when special subsidies were available to farmers with initiative. Tom had a lifetime of experience on the land that had been tilled by his father and grandfather before him. Had any of them made a go of it? No.

It had been his mother's money that had kept the farm going so long. Now that money had run out. What was he going to do about it? He had no idea. He drew his big armchair closer to the fire and buried his nose in the *Yorkshire Post*. There was nothing he could do. Somebody else would have to do summat. They did. Early in 1941 he received an eviction order.

Tom's younger brother Clifford arranged a regular payment from Detroit to his favourite sister, my mother. She found a council house in a terrace in the nearby hamlet of Howden Clough. It was quite a pleasant place, high on rolling moorland. Most of the neighbours kept chickens. The neighbouring fields, much rougher pasture than those at Croft Farm, were successfully turned to arable land that very year.

If Tom had noticed he never let on. That sort of exploitation of his resources would have saved him from bankruptcy. Now he was supposed to be looking for work. Every day he walked to the Labour Exchange at Birstall, a mile or so away. When he came back in mid-afternoon the message was always the same: 'Nowt today.' He never worked again. His wife, my Aunt Laura, got a job cleaning and housekeeping for a widowed cousin.

VI

We must have moved to Howden Clough sometime soon after Christmas 1940. It's a curious fact that I can't remember a single wartime Christmas. 'Peace on Earth and Good Will towards Men' seemed singularly inappropriate in the midst of global destruction and there was little good cheer available when a week's meat ration was one cutlet.

Yet there was one general present given to us this winter: 113,000 Italians. Italy had entered the war on Germany's side at the fall of France, and sent an army to North Africa with the intention of capturing Egypt. General Wavell, commanding a mixed force of British, Australian and Indian troops, had counter-attacked in early December with spectacular success. The collapse of Italy's East African empire was followed by Haile Selassie's triumphant entry into Addis Ababa.

Nothing so bright as this desert victory was to follow. In May, Hitler's Deputy Führer, Rudolf Hess, parachuted into Scotland. The only senior Nazi who actively tried to end the war, he was the only one to be kept in solitary confinement for the rest of his life. Also in May, the German battleship *Bismarck* was sunk. But in April, Rommel and the Afrika Corps reversed the situation in the Western Desert; the British Expeditionary Force in Greece had to be evacuated; after a bitter close combat battle in Crete, the island had to be abandoned leaving thousands of our troops to their fate. All this early summer desperate battles were engaged on land, sea and air. They were like a prelude to the ultimate trial. On 22 June, Hitler launched a massive attack on Russia.

While writing this section, I ran into a northern neighbour, Myles Hildyard, at a Christmas party. Knowing that he had fought in Crete, I told him that for me as an adolescent this summer of 1941 seemed the absolute nadir of our fortunes. He agreed. He had spent months hidden by Cretan peasants in the mountains. Eventually a fishing boat stowed him away and carried him across the Mediterranean to Egypt.

Rommel's reputation in Cairo was such that Myles's commanding officer openly stated that if the British were beaten he intended to go south and set up a colony of English exiles in South Africa. Presumably the Royal Navy would have taken Churchill, the British government and the Royal Family to Canada.

Just to remember those awful times is deeply depressing. The year 1941 seems to be perpetually grey, sunless, dreary and apathetic. The sky over the moors was not even given the interest of clouds, but pallid heat, like looking through a featureless gruel. How well it was described in the journey of the evil spirits to Hell in Milton. Milton, who had lived through that most desolate and chilling of all conflicts – civil war. He understood the range of man's beastliness:

> Thus roving on
> In confused march forlorn, th'adventurous bands,
> With shudd'ring horror pale, and eyes aghast,
> Viewed first their lamentable lot, and found
> No rest. Through many a dark and dreary vale
> They passed, and many a region dolorous,
> O'er many a frozen, many a fiery alp,
> Rocks, caves, lakes, fens, bogs, dens, and shades of death –
> A universe of death, which God by curse
> Created evil, for evil only good;
> Where all life dies, death lives, and nature breeds,
> Perverse, all monstrous, all prodigious things . . .

6

COLD HANDS

I

It was the afternoon post early in January 1942 that brought a long, official brown-paper envelope slithering and twisting like a snake through the letter box. We all looked at it without moving. We all knew what it was.

'Well go on then,' said my mother. 'Aren't you going to open it?'

'I know what it's going to say,' I muttered. 'There's no point in opening it.'

'How can you possibly know?' said my father reasonably.

'I know I did badly. You've got to pass in everything. I know I did badly in geometry.'

'You can never tell. Anyway you'll never know until you've looked.'

'Well if you're so keen to find out *you* look,' I said ungraciously.

So it was my father who announced to me that I had, in fact, passed the Matriculation Examination in all subjects taken and had therefore qualified for a place at London University or at any other equivalent seat of learning.

In the previous October I had taken care of what place that should be. I had attended a selection board at Guy's Hospital, London, another awe-inspiring event, seated in an empty classroom facing five or six grey-suited, friendly, but sharp gentlemen. They nodded approvingly when I explained that my father had always wanted to be a doctor, but had not been allowed to continue his studies, though he had been the head boy at his grammar school. He had passed on his unfulfilled admiration for the profession. Had I thought which branch of medicine I might want to specialise in? 'I don't think I do, sir. General Practice is what I favour.' That produced a general warming of the atmosphere. GPs would always be needed; it was the backbone of the profession.

Was I aware that for the first three years, though Guy's was a great hospital and at the forefront of medical knowledge, I would be engaged in academic studies: anatomy, biology, chemistry and physics? I was aware of that. 'Don't feel too worried about those chemical formulae, eh, Mr Gill?' I thought I could manage them. Sympathetic chuckles and on to the last question. Medicine was one of the few university studies that gave exemption from military service until after the degree was taken. However, some young men preferred to go straight into the forces. A place would be kept for them when the war was over. Would I prefer to start next September or delay medicine until the end of hostilities? 'The latter, sir.'

I had already sorted out my war service, I hoped. In the autumn of 1940, when we were still living on the farm, I had joined the Air Training Corps (ATC) the day it was launched. Three evenings a week I was squeezed into uniform (I was a gangling six foot one inch by now), marched up and down, taught to manipulate the Morse keyboard, studied aircraft recognition and learned to navigate by the stars. I did all this ostensibly because I wanted to join the Air Force when I was eighteen and a half. But I was following my father's good advice that I was more likely to have control of my destiny if I knew clearly what I wanted. I wanted action and adventure, but not in some dusty desert foxhole, or freezing North Sea convoy. The Air Force fitted the bill.

There was one hitch. My eyesight. It wasn't good enough for the exacting air crew medical. But being in the ATC meant that I knew what personnel were in demand. In late 1941 there was a drive to increase the RAF night-fighter strength. The Luftwaffe had shifted to night raids on

Britain and the RAF was desperately seeking more effective ways of night-flying interception. A new aircraft, the Bristol Beaufighter, homed onto the enemy bomber by radar. There was a shortage of trained radar operators. The medical requirements were relaxed. After all, the only physical requirement was to be able to distinguish the blips on a radar screen. In the same autumn of 1941, when I had the interview at Guy's, I saw a senior RAF liaison officer attached to the Air Training Corps. He reassured me on the continuing need for radar observers (he tactfully failed to explain that this was partly due to the Beaufighter's high casualty rate in landing and take-off accidents). All I had to do was to express my preference when I was called up in 1942. My years in the ATC would ensure that I was drafted into the RAF in whatever branch seemed appropriate. It was almost certain radar observers would continue to be needed.

Now, patient reader, you may well ask why are you devoting so much time to something that never happened? You never did become a doctor did you? Or a radar observer in Beaufighters? No, and that is precisely why now I find it interesting to note down the path never taken and to recall the feelings and anticipations I had then. Feelings I tucked away and never looked at for fifty years and more. Would I have been a good doctor? No. I would have suffered too much for my patients. I would have been a dutiful family practitioner, worn out before my time; somewhat disappointed with life and consoling myself by reading philosophy in an escapist manner. And the radar observer? Probably dead at twenty.

I certainly never thought that. Growing up in the war made its risks seem no more than those from riding a bicycle in the blackout. Remember, this autumn of 1941 the war had already been under way for more than two years. And, apart from the Italian debacle in Africa, we had lost all along the line. Yet here we still were. In the concentrated night raids on London and other major cities that lasted from August 1940 to the end of May 1941, more than 43,000 civilians were killed and 51,000 seriously injured. Everyone knew someone who had died. Yet there seemed no failure of morale.

Perhaps it was the scattered nature of the bombing that reduced its effectiveness. The main target, London, was then the biggest city in the world. Hitler would have had to hammer at it night after night for years on end with the sort of weaponry that he had available at the time. (No doubt Teutonic efficiency would have produced something nastier quite quickly.) But, instead, he made his second great mistake. (His first was not to continue bombing the English airfields during the Battle of Britain.) That shrank to insignificance compared with the foolhardiness of attacking Russia on 22 June 1941.

At first it seemed to be a replay on a bigger scale of the Blitzkrieg on France of the previous summer. In one month, the German armies had fought their way over three hundred miles to the very gateway of Moscow. The effect on Britain was immediate. The nightly air attacks ceased. The long snoring notes of the German bombers passing overhead, slow and broken like an asthmatic sleeper, ended as abruptly as a change in position silences the epiglottal tremors. Clearly the searchlights of war had swung to the East.

This was obvious even to my mother (a very unwarlike person). It was decided that we would go back to Canterbury at the beginning of November. My mother and I would return to Wakefield for the ten days that I would be sitting my Matriculation Examination early in December. In the meantime, we would see how we related to being back in 'Front Line UK', as Kent was frequently called. One tempting difference in Canterbury's favour was the fact that it had three cinemas, whereas there were none in Howden Clough. Occasionally we would make the bus journey to Leeds and go to a matinée at the theatre. That way I was able to appreciate the fragile beauty of Vivien Leigh in a revival of *The Doctor's Dilemma*. It was the first stage play she was in after returning from the magic Hollywood years that began with *Gone with the Wind* and ended with *Lady Hamilton* and belated marriage to Laurence Olivier.

But now, back in Canterbury, we were basking in the thought of the silver screen. I remember we were arguing one evening – it was Tuesday 18 November – whether it was worth going to see Robert Taylor as Billy the Kid. I still had a hankering for the Western, but regarded Taylor more as a handsome profile than a plausible gunslinger. How would this Yank at Oxford stand up to the fire and brimstone of the six-shooter? A tremendous explosion temporarily dimmed the lights and reverberated away into the distance. Mother, father, and son – we looked at each other in frozen disbelief. We had heard nothing like it in the war. 'That was a mine,' said my father quietly. But how? 'They must have dug their way into a coal mine,' said my father. There were very deep mines in eastern Kent. But the thought of German commandos digging their way into them did not seem very likely.

My father went away to telephone. His role as an ARP warden gave him useful contacts. When he came back he looked both serious and somewhat relieved. It was a parachute mine apparently. Dropping silently through the evening air it had devastated its target. And its target was? The village of Sturry, some seven or eight miles away on the road to Herne Bay. Its charmingly winding main street was destroyed; some twenty or thirty people killed or seriously injured. Just recently I found a description of the raid: 'One of the first bodies to be found was that of a small girl who had apparently been to the baker's shop: her body was found in the street – and she was still clutching a bag of buns.'

I did not know that detail at the time. In any case, it seems more atrocious now looking down the long perspective of the years that the little girl lost. For what purpose was she robbed of all her expectations? What advantage was it to anybody that she died? I didn't think such things in 1941. I was still alive and later in the week went to see Robert Taylor as Billy the Kid. He was tougher and harder than I expected. That was surely right. It was not called the Wild West for nothing, after all.

II

To someone just eighteen, the war itself, now in its third year, seemed simply part of the unquestionable given of existence. My father was just over eighteen when the First World War began. Perhaps each generation was going to be subject to this fiery initiation. Probably I was so anxious to get into the newfangled machinery of the air war because my father had got into the newfangled machinery of the tank war and behaved, I knew, with modest heroism. So I wanted to find some means by which I could modestly not fall too far behind his example.

He also found something I could usefully and enjoyably do in the six months that I was waiting for my call-up (eighteen and a half was the youngest age for conscription). My father had been told by the local newspaper owner that his staff were very short of reporters as all the young ones had been called up. Remembering my interest in creating bedside magazines, my father put my name forward.

So, early in January 1942 I found myself under the watery, pale blue eyes of Mr Hews, the proprietor of the *Kentish Gazette*. He seemed much more uncertain of himself than I was. His sentences wandered away into a maze of subordinate clauses. He found it excruciatingly difficult to tell me how little he was going to be able to pay me. He led me to think it was only going to be a few pence, and I was pleasurably surprised when he was at last able to murmur 'Seventeen shillings and sixpence.' (Half a pint of beer, I had just learned at my local, was ninepence.) Sensing that I was not displeased, he winced an apologetic smile and gratefully handed me over to the chief reporter, Mr Ovenden, or Gussy as he was universally called.

Now here was someone I could picture shifting his half-smoked cheroot to the corner of his mouth as he growled in the time-honoured way of all newspaper films: 'Hold the front page, you guys; here's hot news.' Just how hot it was going to be I mercifully could not imagine.

Actually, Gussy did not smoke cigars, but he never had a cigarette out of his mouth. A perpetual trail of ash drifted down his greasy collar. His eyes were narrowed to slits and his shoulders shook to almost continuous paroxysms of coughing. It was not only the nicotine, but the poison gas he had inhaled in Mesopotamia in the First World War. 'Sorry laddie, got to cough a bit, get some relief.'

Reeling from side to side with each fresh outburst, he took me along a dark corridor into the oily, fumy, juddering bedlam of the works. Here some half-dozen grizzled veterans banged away at the hot slugs of type. Here the meandering thoughts of Mr Hews in his weekly leader came to a full stop, and Gussy disciplined the pomposities of the city council into a few pages of jerky shorthand. 'Make sure you spell their names right; doesn't matter what they say.'

It was a world that Boz might have recorded. I was to start the next Monday. I thought I might be going to enjoy it. I underestimated. It was actually one of the best times of my life.

III

On the Monday morning I set off from our house at 8.45 a.m.: turned left out of our gate into New Dover Road, and walked for ten minutes or so past the large Victorian houses surrounded by the bare trunks of their trees, over the railway cutting, past the entrance to St Augustine's Road with its modern, semi-detached houses; and then, following the curve of the road to the left, encountered the incongruous square brick shape of the telephone exchange, a terrace of early Victorian houses and the nouveau Regal Cinema. Across the cobbled open space of the cattle market and into St George's Street, well named as the tower of the church elbowed its way masterfully onto what was now about to become the High Street. The big clock face on the church showed it was exactly 9 a.m. as I went into the inconspicuous office entrance to the *Kentish Gazette* on the opposite side of the road.

It was a dingy little place, mostly taken up by filed copies of the *Gazette* and a dark-haired girl who was looking at herself in a compact mirror, busy blackening her eyebrows. She did not seem particularly interested in finding out why I had appeared. I shifted uneasily and eventually produced a mild copy of Gussy's cough.

'Well, boy, what do you want?' she said snappishly. 'Is it BMD or For Sale?'

The questions would have been enough to floor me, but in delivering them she put down the compact and looked at me directly. My stomach, empty after a hurried breakfast, literally turned over. I had never seen such a beautiful person. And she must be working here!

'I'm the new reporter,' I said as grandly as I could.

'Good Law, they must be robbing the kindergarten,' she said turning into the back of the shop. 'Hey Beez, see who's here.'

A plumpish, freckled girl of about the same age came bustling in from behind the ledgers. This was Joan Beasley, who looked after the business side of the paper.

'What about you?' I asked the heaven-sent beauty.

Her name was Christine Wimsett, and it turned out that she registered all the Births, Marriages and Deaths – the BMDs – in the paper.

'You might laugh, but it's the small ads that make the money,' she explained.

I nodded seriously. I was not likely to deny anything she said. Just at that moment, with a tinkle and a crash, a tall curly-haired young man came in off the street lugging a bicycle.

'Keith, here's your new buddy,' said Christine.

'Am I glad you're here,' exclaimed Keith Webb. 'I have to come all the way from Whitstable.'

'Where are the other reporters?' I asked, looking around apprehensively.

There was a general hoot of laughter. Apparently there were no other reporters.

'What about Gussy?' I could hear the distant echo of his cough coming from the works.

'Oh he only does the Circuit Judge cases – the important trials – and the local urban district council. All the rest will be you and me lad.' Keith gave me a welcoming slap on the back.

'Let's see, it's Monday today; that's undertakers isn't it?' said Joan Beasley, generally known as Beez.

'Undertakers?' I asked. 'What have we to do with them?'

'That's how we find out who's dead,' said Keith.

'Who's dead?' I asked.

'By looking in their coffins,' said Christine voluptuously. 'And making sure they're stiff and frozen.'

'Why do I need to do that?'

'So that you can interview them, for their obituary,' exclaimed Christine.

'But if they're *dead* . . .'

'You only need the obit if they *are* dead.' Christine tossed her dark hair and I joined in the laughter.

I could see that it was going to be very different from swotting up Milton.

IV

Storing his bicycle in the corridor that led to the works, Keith took me on a tour of the undertakers. As I remember, there were four or five of them – as different as cremation was from burial.

Mr Herriot employed at least a dozen carpenters. His cavernous shed echoed with hammering, banging and sawing, almost drowning the screech of the green and red parrot that flexed its claws on Mr Herriot's shoulder.

He was immensely proud of the quality of his coffins. Each Monday he insisted on taking me round the works, pointing out the enduring beauty of the latest mahogany masterwork he was producing for some local worthy. 'Nothing', he would murmur, 'will as much become him as his final resting place. Just lift the lid, laddie.'

Unwillingly, I did.

'See that: pure sateen cushions to support his head. I know what you are thinking, my young sir. He may not know where he is himself – though we very much hope he does. But even if the worst happens and he goes to another place – don't let's consider it. But even if it did so happen, his relatives won't know for a long time. And they'll be consoled in the meanwhile with the thought of that beloved head resting on that pure sateen, and the preservative powers of that mahogany come all the way from Burma. Only teak and mahogany can give you that *guaranteed* protection. Believe me, that protection is needed in chalky, porous soil like ours. Indeed it is.'

On reaching such a climax, Mr Herriot would shake his head so violently that the gold rings in his left ear would tinkle and the parrot would rise from his shoulder with a startling screech. I would stumble off into the winding bustling streets, narrowly missing the bicycle boys, the waggoners, the platoons of soldiers, an incantation of rural deans, an imprecation of cattle drovers, basket-laden housewives and the fruit stalls that enterprising farmers had set up on the edge of the great bomb crater with its wild flowers fluttering on the slopes where my favourite bookshop had been.

Visiting the undertakers, my regular Monday morning task, could be agitating when death was all around. But it could have its compensations.

'Hey, come in and sit down. You've been visiting that disturbing Mr Herriot, hasn't he Samuel? In our business it's a great mistake to go metaphysical, isn't it Samuel?'

The brothers Samuel and Jon Jonson rarely disagreed with each other, probably because Jon did all the talking. I don't think they were twins, though they always dressed alike in dark tweeds and bowler hats; an austere appearance which characterised their gloomy profession. They did all the work themselves, but still had time to relax and, when it seemed appropriate, to hand out a thimbleful of brandy.

Halfway in size between the Jonsons and Mr Herriot was the carpenter's shop and funeral arrangers of Meredith and Son. They could provide a horse-drawn hearse with black plumes and music for the procession; Mr Meredith employed an accordion player and a violinist. They often played and sang while hammering away at their latest assignment.

Of course, my purpose in visiting them was neither to discuss metaphysics, nor to drink brandy, nor to listen to a wistful air. I had to get the addresses of their customers; the people who had died in Canterbury during the previous week. Then, on Monday afternoon, I visited those addresses, interviewed the bereaved families and extracted from them the life story of the dead person. Usually it was a son or daughter, brother or sister, who stumbled through the catalogue of their relative's brief life at my prompting.

At first I approached these interviews with dread. An emotional person myself, I could not imagine my appearance, notebook and pencil in hand, as being other than crass and repugnant to the bereaved family. But I quickly came to realise that I provided a symbol of the dead person's importance. It did not matter that the *Kentish Gazette* had a purely local circulation. It was the name in print, included in capitals in the heading, with at least two paragraphs of life and achievements that was important. It visibly rounded off his story and gave it a terminal meaning. In this way I was like Mercury, the messenger of the gods, flying down to convey that all was well. (This was, of course, before the arrival of television and when the radio dealt with the dreadful daily events in a relatively distant and impersonal way.)

I realised how important the visit of priest or welfare worker was. My function, however, was more than just condolence. Like Mercury, I had to connect this simple life with the remorseless flow of world events that was visible in much the same sized type a few inches higher up the newspaper page.

Because death is a relatively rare event in family experience, there would be uncertainty in how to handle it. Quite quickly I learned how to deal with wives who said: 'Would you like to see the body then?' The answer had to be yes, otherwise you were spurning an offer to witness someone whose life had been of crucial importance to the person making the offer.

So I saw a number of the dead, usually stretched out on the bed in the spare room, filling the space in the way the dead do, with a breathless hush that cannot be answered. Some relatives became unnaturally frivolous. 'Feel his hand. Did you ever know anything *so cold*?' One wondered where such conversations might end.

V

So much for Monday. Tuesday and Friday mornings there was the magistrate court. Keith and I would toss for which of us would cover which day. Despite my shaky command of shorthand, I enjoyed this close-up view of the law. It was an interesting way of seeing justice done at a grass-roots level. The principal Justice of the Peace was a squarely plump and decisive tradesman who owned the largest women's dress and drapery store in the town. During the Battle of Britain he had stopped his car to watch a dog fight between two or three Messerschmitts and a lone Spitfire. The Spitfire was shot down. Mr LeFevre saw the pilot bail out and his parachute open successfully. Later in the day he heard that the pilot was his own son.

The war only impinged obliquely on the magistrates. By far the greatest number of war cases in my time related to minor infringements in the blackout restrictions. After a while I noticed there was something familiar in these prosecutions of bicyclists, who were often accused, not of having too much light between their handle bars, but too little. Then I realised all the cases were brought by the same policeman.

When I told Gussy he agreed at once. He explained that an ordinary policeman on the beat would not have much opportunity to distinguish himself. So it was common practice for him to bone up thoroughly on one aspect of his profession, then if he could not bring a charge for overlighting, he could probably accuse the evening pedaller of the opposite. At the end of the year the policeman could point to the number of cases he had successfully brought to trial and hope his zeal be remembered when promotion came around.

Many of the matters that occupied the court seemed unnecessary and trivial. Thus I had to report on my own father being fined seven shillings and sixpence for failing to get a licence to keep a dog. (At the end of the thirties we had acquired a nervous little West Highland terrier called Jane.) This lapse was hardly likely to affect the war effort. On the other hand, matters of great pith and moment often seemed intractable.

The most violent cases involved either coal miners or gypsies. Kent mines were exceptionally deep, dark and dangerous. The miners wanted to be paid commensurately more. The government had outlawed strikes during the war and proposed moving in Welsh miners. The fury of these hard, self-contained men from underground had to be witnessed to be believed.

Equally aggressive in a more feline way were the gypsies. For centuries they had wandered across the southern counties halting to help in the seasonal fruit picking to the irritation and distrust of the local farmers. Now the government had forbidden such movement, as Kent was considered a potential war zone. To the gypsies it was an arbitrary attack on their ancient liberties. But were they so ancient?

On Tuesday afternoon it was my task to go to the public library. There, neatly piled, were copies of every issue of the paper. It had been founded in 1709 and was thus the seventh oldest in the country. I had to choose excerpts from the issues of fifty years before (1892); one hundred years before (1842); two hundred years before (1742) and two hundred and twenty-five years before (1717). The further back I went, the easier it was to find analogies with the present day. In the mid-eighteenth century soldiers had to be marched in to quieten the rebellious miners. Gypsies found guilty of horse stealing were hanged from the gibbet on the Dover Road.

I loved working in the quiet musty-smelling library. As well as choosing items to fit the appropriate dates I also had to pick at random short paragraphs that would fill an unwanted gap on the page. In fact they were called 'fillers'. Here is one I remember from the summer of 1776. German mercenary troops were being shipped off to Boston to put down the rebellious colonists.

'Tis said when the Hessians marched abroad, they was all crying drunk . . .

I particularly like the dots.

A much longer and more detailed account was given of a duel in (I think) 1722. It was fought with swords and one young contestant lost his hand. And lo and behold, there in a case nearby in the museum was the embalmed hand, looking very slight and fragile with the sword which it had once held beside it.

Unless there was some unexpected news story to cover, Wednesday was a quiet day for the reporters. In the morning Gussy put the paper to bed. This was when the fillers came in useful. Mr McNally, the advertising manager, bustled about checking that the adverts were rightly placed. Keith and I retired to the reporters' room on the first floor.

In the afternoon the whole building shuddered and shook with the paroxysms of production. The front office was closed, presumably to stop any of the public wandering into the danger area of the works. The important thing for us was that it released Christine from her desk. She was supposed to type any business letters that Mr Hews required, but this seldom happened. Instead she would drift up to the reporters' room and torment us. Usually Beez would join in. Keith would go out and buy a flagon of cider. From behind a pile of old news sheets we would pull out a battered portable gramophone. On it would go an equally scratched and chipped 78:

> Oh yes, let them begin the beguine
> Make them play . . .

After a couple of glasses of cider we were in the mood to dance and dance we did.

Outside the hustle of the busy High Street went on; below the whole building was convulsed with the grinding clamour of the printing press joined by the sympathetic hawking of Gussy. Did we care? We were dancing cheek to cheek with the most beautiful girl in town. Time stood still.

> When a Broadway baby says goodnight
> It's early in the morning.

VI

I think it was probably my mother who first encouraged my interest in ballroom dancing. Sensibly, she will have seen it as an alternative to the games that I was not allowed to partake in at school. By the time we returned to Canterbury in November 1941 my enthusiasm had been further stimulated by my cousin Douglas's terpsichorean triumphs.

So it was with real determination that I went for a couple of lessons a week to Miss Hanbury. If my timber-toed cousin could get a gold medal, why shouldn't I? I practised the movements of the quickstep, the slow foxtrot, the waltz, the tango and the cha cha cha in front of the long mirror in my parents' bedroom until my Victor Sylvester recordings were wearing out. I preferred the original American versions played by Artie

Shaw or Duke Ellington, but Miss Hanbury insisted on the strict tempo
of the King of the Ballroom.

I obeyed Miss Hanbury in all things. In fact I soon found I was as
preoccupied by Miss Hanbury as I was in counting the numbers of the
chassé and the two-step. Miss Hanbury took her female pupils in groups,
but boys singly. 'Boys are so much more embarrassed at dancing with
each other, and they have to take the lead in so many movements in
ballroom dancing, it's easier for them to learn face to face,' she explained
to my parents. Perhaps this was true but I wonder if she was aware of the
effect she had on at least one of her pupils.

I can recall a host of images from those lessons in the spring of 1942.
She would be waiting, a cigarette in a long holder held between her
slender fingers, smoothing with her other hand her simple silk dress.
I suppose she was in her early thirties and I assume she only thought
of me as a rather gauche and clumsy adolescent. Yet in her lessons
I was principally preoccupied with battling with the unexpected
sensual impressions she produced in me. I was aware of the perfume
that came with the warmth of the body that was so agonisingly close in
the slow foxtrot. My supportive hands told me that beneath the silk
dress was only the ripple of firm skin and the single line of the
brassiere strap. She could judge to perfection how near she could be to
me in the long sweeping movements of the tango without actually
touching. She never talked gossip or small talk, yet below the
disciplined surface of the lesson, I was aware of a preoccupation in
her to which I was not sophisticated enough to respond absolutely.
What should I have done? I did not know, but remembered the lines in
T.S. Eliot:

> When lovely woman stoops to folly and
> Paces about her room again, alone,
> She smoothes her hair with automatic hand,
> And puts a record on the gramophone.

Well she would have been plain daft if she had done any stooping to folly with me, whatever that might mean in practice. Yet there was something. If I did some particularly crass and clumsy movement, she would suppress a deep-felt sigh. When a shimmy or hesitation went quite well, I could sense how her body responded. She would sweep me along into movements I would not have dared imagine. 'Jolly good,' she would murmur under her breath.

What did she do when I had gone? Her house was full of pretty, delicate things: Persian rugs and carved ivory combs and watercolours of some Eastern bazaar; yet it seemed patently too large for one person and there never was a sign of anyone else. One of the tunes we danced to was by Noël Coward. My parents had the record at home. He sang the refrain with his characteristic brittle poignancy:

> Dance, dance, dance little lady,
> Youth is fleeting – to the rhythm beating
> In your mind.
> Dance, dance, dance little lady,
> So obsessed with second best,
> No rest you'll ever find.
> Time and tide and trouble
> Never, never wait
> Dance, dance, dance little lady.

Surely it would not be second best that obsessed her. She wanted some sort of perfection. Certainly it was not anything I could provide or even imagine. Keith and I analysed her in a manly way over a lunchtime half-pint. It was one of the enjoyable perks of having a job. It brought the independence of alcoholic consumption: pub life, darts, snooker, talk about women. Nor were we entirely bereft of experience of the opposite sex. Keith had a sister, and in our office were those two dazzling but tricky examples: Beez and Christine. A book might have been written about their perverse and inexplicable behaviour.

Our knowledge did not stop there. We had got to know a mixed group of people of our own age. We all met every Saturday afternoon at the tea dances held at the Regal Cinema. A tea dance! Does such a thing exist today? The cinema had a properly sprung dance floor, tall, art-nouveau windows and a live group of four or five players: saxophone, alto sax, clarinet, piano and drums. Band, dance floor, pot of tea and cakes, all came to only two shillings and sixpence (approximately 12p). All the *Kentish Gazette* group went along.

It was here that I learned the important fact that women not only laughed at your jokes differently, they responded to instructions on the dance floor in unique ways. No matter how much I tweaked and pulled some (not necessarily the tallest or strongest), they would just go on boring in, pushing you in front of them like a wheelbarrow. Others tried to keep on repeating the same combination of steps. I liked to think out what I wanted to do, putting in surprising new movements now and then. I learned that to be able to do this sort of thing successfully meant having rehearsed it a number of times with your partner. Occasionally you found the ideal: light as a gossamer shawl, intuitive as my dog Patch had been. But even that wasn't the final word. Beez was a more responsive partner than Christine. But Christine was beautiful. And she used her beauty to enrapture you, clinging close to you, leaning her cheek against yours, till you wanted the dance never to end.

There was another good reason why you tried to linger longer on the floor between numbers. The dancers were not only locals. The war, you will remember, began because Germany invaded Poland. Many Poles were captured at the end of the brief month-long war. The unlucky ones were handed over by the Germans to the Russians. In 1940 all the officers, 18,000 young men, were shot. It was done night after night for a month, secretly. Two years later we knew nothing of it. But we did know that many Poles had escaped. A dozen or so regularly attended the Regal Cinema tea dance.

They operated long-range guns that were kept in a disused railway tunnel near Canterbury. They were part of the defences of Kent should Hitler have chosen to invade. But by this time in 1942 invasion did not seem very likely. Instead the guns were wheeled out to retaliate if the Germans started a barrage from their long-range guns which were just across the Channel near Calais.

It was not their enormous weapons that impressed me adversely about the Poles. It was their ability to click the heels of their highly polished boots, to bow over the hand of a girl they were asking to dance. They had the gift totally to ignore everyone except the person who was their selected partner for that afternoon. Not surprisingly this partner was often Christine. She was already engaged to a young British officer stationed somewhere in the Midlands. Much healthier for her to lavish her attentions on solid British types like us, Keith and I reasoned. Unfortunately Christine thought differently.

There was a tragic glamour about these refugees from a faraway land that I could see would impress a susceptible young girl. Christine was just twenty, eighteen months older than me, but she clearly did not understand how flirtatious behaviour might lead these chaps on. They were rumoured to be a hot-blooded lot. I had seen a film in which after responding to a toast they had all thrown their glasses in the fire. They could not have had any rationing in the eighteenth century!

Other, nastier things were whispered about our Poles. The sort of thing you could not really mention to a young girl. Keith and I discussed it of course. They were said to be very sadistic in their love-making. Even going to the extent of biting off a girl's nipple in a moment of frenzy. I found this hard to imagine, especially as I had never seen a real female nipple. But such behaviour did not seem conducive to passion. Eventually we got it across to Christine by Keith telling his sister who told Christine. What did she say? Keith was enjoying being the intermediary. 'Stuff and nonsense, and if anyone tried any funny games, she would jolly well bite off his you-know what.'

So Christine continued to exasperate us by flirting at the tea dances with these courteous sadists. Our only retaliation the next day in the office was to ask if she had had a good bite. At which she was actually seen to blush.

Teasing was one way we could make contact with this superior being, whose very appearance entering the reporters' room stunned us to silence. I went to the extent of analysing all the effects she had on me, from walking into a closed door to falling over my own feet.

The only other group of people who upset my equilibrium to anything like the same extent were war heroes. By this time in the third year of the war a number of my near contemporaries had been in action, either in the Army in the Western Desert or Greece or Crete or in the Navy in battle with the Italian fleet in the Mediterranean or in the Air Force either bombing Germany or patrolling the Atlantic in search of German submarines. One Coastal Command pilot, Johnny McFee, whom I had seen a couple of years before, regularly playing cricket in the local Canterbury side, Keith and I met by chance near the Christ Church Gate of the cathedral. His head was heavily bandaged and he was limping along on a single crutch. We managed to persuade him to tell us his story over a coffee in the nearby Cadena café.

He was flying a Catalina, the American flying boat, on the North Atlantic convoy route often stalked by U-boats. Such Catalina patrols could last for many hours and the pilot often opted for changes of height to maintain alertness and attention. McFee had reached the furthest perimeter of his patrol and his navigator was giving him his homeward-bound course. Something made him look down. Two thousand feet below the water was seething and boiling; could it be a whale coming up for air? Mesmerised, he watched a familiar shape emerge from the foam. It could not be? But it was. A German U-boat was surfacing – out of all the thousands of miles it might have chosen, it was coming up right below him. Any moment it would discover its danger. The depth charge added to the turbulence. Had he hit it vitally? In a moment it would be gone.

Intolerable to lose it in such circumstances. He fired another depth charge and brought the Catalina down in a wide sweep. Something rose like the hand of Neptune from the tortured sea. Flying metal debris from the injured submarine smashed in the front of the plane and split McFee's skull. Slumping forwards he was unaware of his plane following the submarine into the tormented waters. His navigator got him to the surface, inflated a rubber dinghy and sent off the alarm code. The whole episode took three minutes. The dinghy was picked up five hours later on the edge of dusk. It all happened fifteen days before. His navigator got the DSO and McFee, who should not have brought the plane so low when firing depth charges, got the DFC.

Would our war when we got into it have episodes like this? It was difficult to imagine. Hence the chance meeting with McFee was like talking with a figure out of mythology. Our eighteen months in the Air Training Corps with its Sunday morning drill, Morse Code practice, aircraft-spotting slide shows and exercises in astral navigation and dead reckoning brought us the reassurance that uniform and discipline were meant to do. For me they had another great benefit. Here was a group of young men from all walks of life who accepted me as one of them without a second thought. The ATC began the long period of rehabilitation I needed to recover from the self-questioning gloom and despair that the years of schooling left me prone to in any large gathering.

I realised that others had their own problems of shyness and self-depeciation, often cleverly disguised. I found this in my particular group of friends, though one of them was the outstanding figure in our flight of a hundred or so youths. Tony Rickell was a natural leader; he had been selected as our flight sergeant when only seventeen. He radiated humour and a generosity of spirit that would uplift any doubting group. Yet he had a profound tragedy in his life, which he never referred to. I only knew of it through my father. Tony Rickell was illegitimate. His father would not see him or acknowledge him.

Peter Woods was also the offspring of a broken marriage, though at least he was able to continue to see both his parents. He had a more laid-back charm than Tony's. All the girls loved him. He was extremely good-looking with dark curly hair, and a gentle, sweet-natured manner. Indeed for some time, though remaining in the Air Training Corps, he wrestled with the problem as to whether he should fight at all. His religious conscience suggested that he should not. In the First World War this would have led to prison and the delivery of a white feather. In the Second he would probably have been sent down a coal mine. Realising this he opted to go into the Merchant Navy. This was a highly dangerous form of service, but it was only bringing food and needed supplies to beleaguered Britain. As to the white feather: I never heard of any fluttering through the post in the Second World War. Certainly Peter lost none of his wide circle of friends. I was at his farewell party in spring 1942 before he left to join his first ship.

Also present was my third friend, Albert Lewis, though his aspirations were quite different. Albert was a cockney; I do not know what brought him down to the cathedral city. He worked as a shop assistant in the draper's shop opposite the Regal Cinema. When business was slack (and when clothes rationing was as tight as it was in 1942, business was usually slack), Albert would come to the shop entrance and stand, his portly figure rocking slightly on his heels, his auburn hair and freckles gleaming in the late afternoon spring sunshine.

He had a smile for everyone. But he must have realised that his stubby legs and turned-up nose did not easily cast him as a romantic hero. Nor were his mathematics good enough to allow him to become a navigator or a pilot, but he had set his heart on the RAF and when his call-up time came he got in – as assistant cook. Once inside he was able to apply for retraining as an air gunner. He had calculated correctly that there was always a shortage of rear gunners. It was the most vulnerable position in the plane.

As for Tony Rickell, he turned out to be as brilliant a pilot as he was a leader of men. He survived the war to become a test pilot, internationally known.

Alas, I am writing about all these acquaintances in the past tense. They have all been dead so long, it amazes me that I remember them so well. Peter Woods survived torpedoes and shipwreck to die of typhoid fever in Marseilles in 1944. Albert Lewis became a mid-gunner on a Liberator bomber based in India. They were ferrying supplies to the Americans under General 'Vinegar Joe' Stilwell in northern China. Their plane was lost somewhere over the Pamirs early in 1945. Its precise fate was never known.

Tony Rickell's death was watched by millions. He had changed his name to Tony Richards and was taking part in the Farnborough Air Show in September 1952. At this time Britain still had aspirations to contribute new planes and new technology to the air race. Tony was flying with John Derry, a senior test pilot, in the prototype fighter, the DH 110. It crashed shortly after take-off, killing both pilots, in a spectacular inferno of destruction.

VII

The passage of time gives a glamour to events that at the moment seem tragic, exciting or merely suprising. Small happenings can bulk large. Some time around Easter 1942, Christine, Beez, Keith and I went to a spring charity dance. It was held in a lunatic asylum.

At that time I had never been to a loony bin, as we charmingly called it. It was not what I expected. Instead of padded cells there were elegant flower beds; long terraced walks and wooded hillsides beyond; a beautiful eighteenth-century reception hall, which became our dance floor. I expected to be watched by gibbering ghouls, but I think all the inmates must have been locked up.

I had never danced in such grand surroundings. Perhaps their splendour affected Christine also. Quite soon she suggested we should explore and led me away by the hand. The moon was just coming out and nearly full, giving gardens, flowering magnolia, almond and cherry a frosty glimmer. We walked arm in arm along the terrace to where the woods began. And there I kissed her and we sat on a stone seat, watching the moon gathering brilliance as it rose.

I passed the rest of the evening in a daze of happiness. Those moonlit kisses expanded to fill all time and space. Yet I must not omit the climax of the evening. We were boarding the bus that had brought us and was going to take us back to Canterbury. I became aware of a number of people silently watching us through a wire-mesh fence. A tall, imposing-looking man beckoned me over.

I was not in a mood to deny anyone anything. I walked across to the fence and said hello. The figure drew himself upright. 'I am Julius Caesar,' he said in a voice not to be gainsaid. Then in a much more conversational tone he went on: 'I landed near here, you know.'

So people really did imagine they were characters in history. Or was he just having me on? Wasn't that what Christine was doing with me, anyway? The kissing episode was not repeated, but it did mark a change in our relationship. She would ask me if I would like to go shopping with her; or meet her for a coffee on a Saturday morning. I was cast I suppose in the classic role of the *cavalier servente*. I was useful for carrying the parcels. In return Christine lost her snappish, condescending tone and revealed a sharp sense of fun.

Those spring days in the ancient city; sunlight and shadow falling on the crouching oak corbels that must have greeted Chaucer's pilgrims; my mood was in tune with that expressed by earlier travellers: 'The still nooks, where the ivied growth of centuries crept over gabled ends and ruined walls; the ancient houses, the pastoral landscape of field, orchard or garden; everywhere – on everything – I felt the same serener air, the same calm, thoughtful, softening spirit.' What Dickens felt I felt too.

The happiness that came with my affection for Christine was reflected back to me in every aspect of this benign city. Its twisting narrow streets with houses reaching out almost to meet from opposite sides in a plaster and beam embrace; the constant but subtly changing views of the cathedral spires revealed in every twist and turn of the winding lanes, luring one on like the song of the sirens for a yet more expressive and magisterial vision; the calm confidence of tradesman and passer-by in the survival of this passionate yet grand affirmation of the enduring presence of God.

Whatever aspect human frailty took it would be bent to maintain the Divine Will. So it seemed to me on a day in April 1942 when I walked through the cathedral close. I was going to interview the new archbishop. Cosmo Lang, who had held office since 1928 with all the penache of a Renaissance cardinal, was retiring. The new man, William Temple, had made a powerful impact of a very different sort as Archbishop of York. The difference was obvious at once.

When I was shown into his study he stood up rather awkwardly and apologised. His feet were bare and his long ecclesiastical socks were steaming in front of the fire. He explained that he had just been caught in a sudden shower. He had only moved in the day before and had not yet unpacked.

This led him to tell me that the cathedral had been built on a bog and the crypt was still liable to flooding. In Saxon times prayers were regularly made for its survival. It was in fact burnt by the Danes in 1011.

'We must pray that nothing like that happens in our time,' said the Archbishop, looking up at the dominant spires of the Bell Harry Tower.

7

HOT NEWS

I

All the six months that I was so greatly enjoying myself on the *Kentish Gazette* ('Such larks, Pip, such larks,' as Joe Gargery would say), all that time the war was grinding away and our fortunes reached their lowest ebb. U-boats took a greater toll than ever before; in the Western Desert, Rommel proved more than a match for the serious but unfortunate General Auchinleck. The Japanese surprise attack on Pearl Harbor had brought America into the war on our side, but also destroyed the Allied Pacific Fleet. A series of brilliant campaigns captured the Philippines, the Dutch East Indies, Hong Kong, most of Burma and, most devastating of all, Singapore. This was the greatest defeat the British Army ever recorded; more than 80,000 of our men fell into Japanese hands. Some had only just been diverted to the futile defence of an ill-prepared stronghold. Many were to rot away on the building of a Japanese military highway, the Burma Road. The Japanese had nothing but contempt for an enemy that was so easy to defeat, and showed it by acts of the most horrible brutality.

Tucked away in our besieged little island fortress, there seemed nothing for us to do but grit our teeth and bear it; or, as in our little group at the *Kentish Gazette*, to take the pleasures of the moment. There was something else the country was doing: building bombers. We had endured months of destruction in 1940–1. Now, at least, we were in a position to give the enemy a dose of its own medicine.

The RAF carried out its first 1,000-bomber raid on 30 May 1942; 600 acres of Cologne was declared to be completely destroyed. Altogether, 1,500 tons of bombs were dropped in 90 minutes. It was hard to visualise what that would be like. Perhaps we might not have to imagine it for long, Keith said with an uneasy laugh. We knew what he meant. In the last month or so the Luftwaffe had launched a series of reprisal attacks on ancient cities. Exeter, Bath, Norwich, York had all been struck. Might it not be Canterbury's turn soon? Like Cologne we were a historic centre with a magnificent cathedral.

On the night of 1 June I was woken by the ululating call of the air-warning system. It was immediately over-topped by the hooting of our local imminent danger foghorn, and the warning cries of my parents. They wanted me downstairs in the room my father had reinforced with sandbags and a sheet metal ceiling some three years before. It seemed it was going to be useful at last. As I pulled a coat over my pyjamas, my sleepy senses picked out another sound, deeper and more continuous than the warnings. It was the whining of circling aircraft: more of them and much closer overhead than I had heard in the past.

I ran out onto the landing to the accompaniment of a new sound. It was a high-pitched shriek that grew rapidly in volume as I bolted down the stairs. The scream pursued me and dissolved into a tremendous ear-shattering explosion. Still on the stairs I was struck by a sharp blow on the head. The plaster ceiling fell around me. I kept on running. Now I've actually been hit by Hitler I thought.

Two more tremendous blasts punctuated my arrival in the strong room. With it went the crash of glass that we thought (rightly) might be the front windows. Through the next hour-and-a-half we did not talk much. We lay on the carpet pressing as tightly to it as we could. It was as though we might be able to hold down the floor from erupting under the force of those dreadful shrieks. Our fear, unexpressed except by an occasional moan from my mother, was infectious. My small Scottish terrier Janie was trembling and whimpering. She tried to bury herself under my stomach.

It amazed me how quickly we understood what was happing. Like a pack of wolves, the planes circled continuously overhead. From time to time one would peel off and come hurtling downwards, accompanied by the characteristic high-pitched scream generated by the screechers attached to its wings. This note rapidly deepened and grew in volume till it seemed to be vibrating through the very rafters of our house. That was not the end, though it seemed more than the senses could bear. Out of it came a shriller, sharper scream. This was the bomb. Invariably it was not alone, but the first of three. Here was the moment of truth. The explosion was too vast for us to be able to guess how close or far it was. But the second bomb, bursting a few seconds later, would be either closer or further away than the first explosion. If it was the latter, we could take a breath more easily, for it meant that the third bomb, continuing the same trajectory, would be still further away. If the second bomb was louder and closer than the first . . . then there was nothing to do but grit the teeth and dig deeper into the carpet.

There were times when several planes were diving and shrieking at once, when our innocuous anti-aircraft guns were banging away indifferently and the batteries of Bofors guns chattering like a cage of demented monkeys. It seemed the tortured air itself would rip us apart. There was worse to come. The sounds of destruction would rise to an unbearable crescendo and then suddenly pause. It was as though a predatory lion, having achieved the fit of violence which gave it the kill, was drawing breath before rending its victim. So the assaulted atmosphere audibly sucked in silence before spewing it forth in a fountain of falling floors, crashing girders, collapsing walls, pulverised furniture, destroyed lives. This was the most terrible sound I have ever heard. Often it went on for a long time. The bombers' wail, the bombs' shriek, the ear-punching blast of the explosions — these were as nothing to the awful grandeur of the desolation of homes collapsing about us.

Sometimes the collapse began with a mere trickle of falling bricks and sharding windows. Steadily, but mercilessly, the downfall grew in speed and volume, till at its apogee it overwhelmed all other sounds. It was at this climax that we listened most intensely for a human participant. How pitifully small and thin was the occasional distant cry, rarely repeated. Occasionally closer at hand was the exchange of more robust shouts and warnings. Uttered in the chinks and crevices of all the conflicting bedlam, it underlined the casual inhumanity of this mechanistic rape of our cherished home city. Would there be anything left? The cathedral, dominating the approach from all directions, must have been a target. What other motive but destruction of its historic treasures could have brought the bombers to this small market town?

It seemed quite likely that we would not survive to know the answer. Within minutes of the first bombs falling all the lights failed. My thoughtful father had filled a drawer with candles and matches, but so violent were the sounds outside that none of us wanted to get off the floor. Ridiculous though it was, it seemed unnecessarily dangerous to draw attention to ourselves even by lighting a match. We never even discussed it. The only window in our little strong room had been completely blocked up by sandbags; so throughout this cacophony of explosions we remained in absolute darkness. Most of the time I kept my eyes tight shut. I had regressed to the sort of childish fear that a nightmare or ghost story might once have stirred in me. I kept thinking it must be going to end soon. Then a further wave of attackers made itself heard.

A new and menacing sound crumpled still further the overloaded air. It angered me, because it blurred the concentration I needed to pick out the paths of the falling bombs. What good did it do me to know that a particular stick of these was getting closer or further away? None at all, but I hung on to this momentary knowledge as a tiny comfort of rationality in all the rampage of destruction which I could barely imagine. Meanwhile, the crackling sound steadily grew in volume. Fire. You could sniff it in the air. We had heard of the firestorms which incendiary bombs could unleash in crowded streets. Here was a danger we had not considered: to be sucked into a maelstrom of flames.

An absurd idea when you thought of our road lined with massive trees and solid, mostly Edwardian, houses. You could see this was the way panic spread. Get back to analysing the direction of the bomb explosions. That was getting harder to do. Not only was the fire crackle getting louder; there seemed to be fewer bombers circling overhead. My father stood up and lit a couple of candles. We looked at our pale, taut faces. No bombs were falling. Wordless, we hugged each other. My mother cried.

'I can't make us any tea,' said my father. 'The electricity's off.'

'No, don't you remember Gag?' said my mother (she only called him by his initials, G.A.G., in especially unguarded moments). 'Don't you remember? When we bought the emergency food tins you got a Primus stove. It should be in the cardboard box in the corner.'

It was. Though lighting it created nearly as much of a crisis as the Jerry bombers. Eventually, red-faced, my father discovered the knack of pumping it up. By the time we had had a cup it was about half-past three. We reckoned the actual raid had lasted an hour-and-a-half.

As we had thought, the plaster had come down over the stairwell and the front windows had blown out, frames and all. They were four long windows, two on the ground floor and two on the floor above. Thanks to my mother's careful taping-together of the adjoining panes, they had remained unshattered. They lay twisted and tangled across the front lawn like monster serpents. But where had the bomb fallen?

II

We persuaded my mother to take an aspirin and go back to bed. Though relatively lightly damaged, our house had lost all the communicating services: telephone, electricity, gas, radio. Water was running out, and we had not heard or seen anyone since the raid. Our neighbours we knew were away. My father and I decided to go into town to find out how bad the damage was.

First, where was the bomb hole that, judging by the noise at the time, had so nearly contained us? We walked gingerly to the front gate. Our feet crunched over more than gravel. Shining the narrow torch beam that we were allowed to show, dozens of pinheads of light gleamed back at us. Were these jagged fragments bits of our bomb? My father gave them a comprehensive feel and pronounced them friendly ack-ack particles. No wonder they didn't bring many planes down if they burst into such insignificant pieces.

But at our gate we got our first sight of what the enemy could do. In the middle of the gateway opposite was a large crater about twenty feet across by some fifteen feet deep. It was exactly at the spot where every day for so many years our neighbour had turned to wave goodbye. Remembering that, my eyes automatically lifted to the first-floor window where his wife had waved her response. There was something strange in its appearance. A dark cleft ran down the façade of the whole house. It seemed to be leaning inwards about to collapse like a house of cards. And, indeed, it had to be demolished later. The morning farewell ritual had already been interrupted. The war had carried our neighbour into the North African desert and his wife back to her parents in the safer Midlands.

On this night of 1 June 1942, there were other things to occupy us. From our front gate we could normally see straight down the Dover Road to the centre of Canterbury dominated by the cathedral. But now there was nothing but billowing clouds, sooty dark and pink tinged. So the cathedral *had been* destroyed, as we had feared.

We set off at a quick walk in the direction of the town. It was a strange experience; like Dante being shown hell. We did not say much; we met not a soul. After all the deafening cacophony of the raid our ears felt naked not being wrapped in layers of dissonance. At the same time, the clatter of our feet seemed disturbingly loud. Why was there no clangour of ambulance or fire engine? No shouts or cries?

Off to the left, beyond the wayside trees, we could just make out that one of the big Edwardian houses had been reduced to rubble. I tried to remember who lived there. I was almost sure it was an eccentric spinster who kept at least a dozen dogs and many cats. Should we stop and look for her? I shuddered at the thought of what the bomb must have done to all those assorted animals. No, said my father, when we find a fire engine or a policeman we shall report it. We hurried on.

About a quarter mile from our house the road passed over the railway bridge on the main line to Dover. Several bombs had been dropped here uprooting and damaging a number of trees, but, as far as I could see, not hitting the rail-track (more houses were destroyed here and on the neighbouring St Augustine's Road than I could tell in the dark).

Just beyond the bridge the road curved and revealed a spectacular sight. A pair of modern detached houses faced the entrance to Erskine Road, where I had danced the spring evenings away in the clutches of Miss Hanbury. Luckily she was on holiday visiting cousins in Scotland. Her windows had blown out, giving a ghoulish appearance to her house as it glared skull-like across the road. There, the two modern houses seemed to have been sliced in half by some giant trowel. The front wall had been shovelled away, leaving the contents of each room completely visible and hardly disturbed. Baths, lavatory, beds, dressing-table, toys, kitchen plates, armchairs hung suspended in space. All these objects closely resembled the ones in the house next door, as though they might have been models at a House and Garden exhibition. The final weird congruity were two columns of flame that hissed out of the bowels of the houses and shot straight up more than twice their height, illuminating all this part of the road with an unearthly light.

'Gas,' muttered my father, 'they've punctured the gas main. No pipe smoking here.' (Pipe smoking was something I was just trying.)

There were no signs of any victims. Later we were to discover that the occupants had already been dug out. A little further on we saw our first people. Past the ugly new telephone exchange the road widened where the old city wall and the Burgate had been replaced by a car salesroom. Here groups of men were standing silently looking at the sight before us.

Our road narrowed again into a long terrace of Georgian houses. Beyond it was the Regal Cinema where I had so often danced. Perhaps it would be better to say the cinema *had* been there.

We were looking at a huge living mass of flame. It was coming towards us from the heart of the old town. As we watched it leapt from window to window up the Georgian terrace. The speed and gusto with which it fed itself made it seem a monster of pulsating energy, weaving and writhing with dreadful gluttony.

My father recognised that most of the men were from the fire brigade. They could do nothing to fight the flames. Bombs had fractured all the water mains. They were waiting for mobile water carriers. By the time they arrived they agreed there would not be much left of the old city. They believed that the Bell Harry Tower still stood. It was impossible to see through the dense flame clouds. They did not know how many people had died. A senior and popular official, the Town Clerk, had been killed when his home got a direct hit. His house was one of those ruins in St Augustine's Road that we had failed to notice.

The firemen advised us to go home. They did not think the flames would jump this wide open space. We were not the only creatures putting their trust in it. Dozens of assorted dogs and cats were running about distractedly, barking and occasionally chasing each other. The fires cast an unreal, excessively brilliant light on the scene, so that the shadows of the cavorting animals were sometimes longer than the real height of the motionless firemen. This surreal element of fire dogs must have occurred at other blitzed cities, but I have never seen it referred to.

On our way back I told my father that I would take a short cut from New Dover Road to Old Dover Road, where Christine lived, to make sure that she was all right. He did not object. Just beyond the railway bridge a narrow footpath ran parallel to the line, connecting the two roads. I had often used it as a short cut back home after leaving Christine at her house.

Now I ran along it in a mixture of excitement and apprehension. The gas flames from the two nearby houses had stopped. The clouds, rolling low overhead, cast a strange pinkish glow down onto the high brick walls of the cut. My diary tells me it was 5.30 a.m. and just beginning to be light.

Turning a corner I ran full tilt into a mass of bricks some twenty feet high. There was no way round them. They completely blocked the narrow footpath. It was as though a giant had picked up the walls on each side of the cut and thrown them together. And for good luck he had then kicked over the small private hotel which had been on the other side of the wall.

It may seem disproportionate, but nothing that happened that night shocked me so much as this total destruction of a footpath. I had only discovered it in the recent months. I had hurried along it so often, aglow with the pleasure of having just left Christine. Now it was gone, transformed into a barrier between us, just as real life, another aspect of the war, was going to separate us in a few weeks when I would be eighteen and a half and called up. Now I had to find another way to reach her.

I had to run all the way back into New Dover Road; down to where the firemen still stood, and the dogs still barked, and where the Georgian terraces were now one indistinguishable mass of flame. I turned left as though I was going to the railway station. Over another railway bridge and there was the leafy expanse of the Old Dover Road. One of the pleasant small Georgian houses was where Christine lived with her parents. And there outside, on their doorstep as though waiting for me, were the three of them. Here the fires seemed further away. The first rays of the summer sun tinted Christine's dark hair. A new day was coming.

III

Later on that day I wrote in my diary: 'Went round for Christine again at 9.30. Found Keith and Joan B. there. Tried to go down town with them' (in an attempt to reach our office). 'Place a terrible mess, fires still burning, our office, like all Upper High Street, gone. Lost Keith.' (He could not push his bike over the piles of still smoking rubble.) 'Made way by devious route back to C's house. J.B. left us there and I stayed with C. all morning as her people out. Glorious weather for first time this summer so picked her up at 2.30 and went for long country walk round Bishopsbourne and Bridge arriving back 5.30 pretty tired. Strange such a beautiful afternoon should follow such a night of grotesque horror. C. never looked lovelier.'

There followed a strange hiatus; a sort of regrouping of psychic forces. Often such moments are referred to in memoirs of wars. About this time I clipped the following quotation from Siegfried Sassoon's memoirs of the First World War: 'What I felt was a sort of personal manifesto of being intensely alive – a sense of physical adventure and improvident jubilation, and also . . . a feeling that I was in the middle of some interesting historical tale . . .'.

With the town centre, including the office of the *Kentish Gazette*, crumbled to ashes there was nothing to do but read, walk and talk. This we did. Even in this benign midsummer the war maintained its surreal presence. In one field we came across a peacefully grazing herd of cows. At least they appeared to be grazing until we saw that one was lying on its back with its legs sticking straight up in the air like a child's wooden toy. Another had leaked yards of snakelike intestines across the field before falling on its head. The field, we now noticed, was pockmarked with bomb holes. The most curious and repulsive detail was the behaviour of the uninjured cows. They were munching their cud in a characteristically bovine way, apparently unmoved by the fate of their companions.

The damage to the old part of the town stupefied the senses. Teams of workers came down from London, digging, sawing and carting away the beams and rubble that had been the preciously preserved homes of many generations. Now, rising above the clouds of dust and smoking debris in all its untouched majesty, the cathedral had never seemed so triumphant. Only the Victorian library sheltering besides the cloisters was destroyed by a direct hit.

This providential delivery was not only the work of God. Hundreds of fire bombs rained on the parapets, but the devoted civilian guardians scrambled all over the roofs throwing the venomous hissing sticks of flame down onto the surrounding grass and gravel. No damage came to the cathedral. Its saviours were not firemen by training, but mostly middle-aged townsfolk who had chosen to volunteer for the Auxiliary Fire Service, or, like my father, to be an ARP warden. Yet for the superstitious there was another fact to ponder. Throughout the war, fifteen bombs fell in the cathedral precincts. Not one scored a hit.

As the shattered ruins of ancient streets, pulverised pilgrim inns and the wreckage of the Georgian mansions of minor clergy were cleared away, long-masked views of the cathedral were revealed. Never had it looked so dominant. Even the smoke and ruin of those sunlit days of June 1942 had an echo in the distant past. Marauding Vikings had burnt the city and martyred the clergy in the eleventh century. Then the citizens settled down to rebuild: plaster and wattle dwellings that had now been finally destroyed. So what? There was comfort in the thought of that earlier rebuilding. Canterbury would rise again, and in the meantime we could rejoice at the revelation of so many new visions of the cathedral.

Nor did it take long for the battered city to get on her feet. The morning after the raid a bucket of drinking water was delivered to every house, an essential aid in avoiding the spread of typhoid. Hand delivery continued morning and evening for three weeks, until the main water supply was restored. A communal restaurant was set up for the many hundreds who had lost their kitchens. Situated in a big marquee on a school playing field near the West Gate and run by the Women's Voluntary Services, with a choice of freshly cooked food, it became a popular social gathering place. The Archbishop, Mayor and other visiting worthies such as the Royal Family and Mrs Roosevelt patronised it. There was no problem either about having a hot cup of tea at home. In those days virtually every house still had an open fire or two. It would be very different today. Loss of electrical power would probably lead to a panic, darkness and looting. Nothing less gloomy than lunch in the communal kitchen could be imagined. The lovely sunny weather probably had something to do with it; so had the feeling – pretty generally shared – that an unprecedented challenge had been faced and mastered.

A symptom of this was the huge congregation that turned out for the funeral of Mr Marks, the Town Clerk, who was the most distinguished of our victims. I know it was a large gathering, because I had the almost impossible job of stopping every mourner and ascertaining his or her name, initials, address and function. Many people regarded this as an impertinent impingement on their private grief. Others were only too anxious to make sure that their presence was noted. Perspiring under my heavy dark suit and unaccustomed black tie, I counted it the most unpleasant job I had had to do for the *Kentish Gazette*.

It was to my considerable surprise that I was still working on the local paper. On the morning of 2 June I had managed to get into the area that had been our office only with the greatest difficulty: the offices had vanished and in the works puddles of coagulating molten metal showed where the printing machines had been. But in the crisis Mr Hews had been less indecisive than I would have youthfully expected. He had persuaded our rival paper, the *Kent Messenger*, to allow us to use its printing machinery (the two papers went to print on different days).

Altogether forty-three people were killed in the raid and forty seriously injured. Many, including our family, stayed out of the town for a few days, sleeping with friends in the local farms or villages. There were a number of small follow-up raids, but their impact compared to the attack on 1 June was similar to a *Volkslied* following a full performance of *The Ring*. Now that the damage had been done the

British authorities increased the defences, including a layer of silver balloons. Their presence, turning pink in the summer twilight, was definitely comforting, though I never heard how many planes they actually brought down with their trailing cables.

A few days later we were visited by another placebo, the Duke of Kent. Why a tour of the sites by minor royalty should be considered an encouragement to the bereaved masses is hard to define. But its practice must go back to the appearance of the king before his troops on the morning of battle. It would be hard to see the languid Duke in that role. I've been trying to think of any memorable remark he made in the whole of that day when I was at his elbow with pencil at the ready hoping for a *bon mot* to start off my article: nothing. The most startling thing about him was the thick yellowish-orange make-up that plastered his weakly pleasant face.

Another childhood illusion gone. His marriage to the beautiful and elegant Greek princess, Marina, had been one of the fairy-tale romances of the 1930s. Now its magic was as rapidly dispersed as the medieval streets of our city. I was beginning to learn that proximity did not necessarily increase respect.

8

STAMPING ON THE HINGE OF FATE

I

The train was packed. I squeezed myself into the last possible seat, pushing my small suitcase uncomfortably behind my knees. This being England, a series of protesting grunts and sharp exhalations of breath were the sole acknowledgement of my rickety progress over the trampled feet of my neighbours. Once I had snaggled and wriggled and eased myself into the notional free seat – a few square inches on the middle of one side of the compartment – all my fellow travellers let out a collective sigh of sympathy for the suffering my late arrival had inflicted on my immediate neighbours and proceeded to examine me from behind their papers with an icy and suspicious reserve. An attitude no doubt reinforced by the posters prominently displayed on such public places as railway stations warning us that careless talk cost lives. With it often went a grudging dislike of all the young people in uniform, who might for some illogical reason be thought to be enjoying the war. The sort of attitude that expressed itself about our American allies (who were just beginning to appear in considerable numbers on the streets) as over-paid, over-sexed, and over here. Yet where would we be without the potential self-sacrifice of the young of all the allied nations?

As I thought this, it came over me with a powerful shock wave that I was one of the possible young victims. All my life I had been protected, nursed and pampered by my doting mother. I had just left her (on Paddington Station) for the very first time. I was journeying into an unknown future without her. Whatever happened to me at the RAF Reception Centre at Cardington, I sensed with bitter fright that I would never be able to shelter behind her again. When I thought of all those thousand acts of gentle kindness that she had given me, my eyes swam . . . Hastily I pulled out the *New Statesman and Nation*, which she had thoughtfully provided for my last journey as a civilian. But for once V.S. Pritchett was not an adequate escape. I could guess enough about the future to know that. No sharp-brained Squadron Leader was going to discuss with me Pritchett's left-wing politics, nor warm-hearted NCO tuck me up with a hot-water bottle when I had a feverish cold. (Curiously, both these incidents were to happen to me in the next few months, but I had not got the benefit of fore-knowledge.)

Nor could I know that on this very day when I was joining the Air Force a very much more exalted person was leaving it. The Duke of Kent would be making no more demands on liquid make-up. His plane crashed through Scotch mists into a mountain top killing all on board.

To me, on that grey Tuesday 25 August 1942, the future was clouded with fateful uncertainty. I would have to face it alone without my mother. My desperate knowledge of my loss, my recognition of the end of my boyhood, was too much to bear. Oblivious of the portly middle-aged civilians bulging on either side of me, I cried and cried. It was not only the loss of my mother, but of all the happy days at Highfields, Jack Packham's blood-curdling stories, my friendship with Patch, Grandma Taylor's memories of Victorian England, playing on the beach with my father; a world that the bombing of Canterbury had visibly shown to be over.

Once the tears had begun there seemed no stopping them. I tried disguising sniffs with coughs and splutters; it only drew attention to my emotional collapse. Nothing was said, but I was uneasily aware of being examined by eighteen pairs of critical eyes. It was too much. I got up and plunged across the assault course of legs and feet. The grunts this time rose to verbal protests: 'I say look out there'; 'Cor watch it mate'; ''Ave an 'eart.' Forgetting my bag, I scrambled into the corridor. It was blessedly empty save for a few lonely figures contemplating the passing scenery through the wraiths of their cigarette smoke. I pressed my forehead against the sooty window-pane and abandoned myself to my misery.

Nothing that happened on that beastly day made me feel that I had gone too far in expressing my despair. Quite soon we reached Cardington. I got out and was looking for the RAF squad which was supposed to be meeting new recruits, when there was a shout and a heavy blow on the back of my neck. The train was leaving and one of my fellow travellers, noticing that I had left my overnight bag in the compartment, had kindly and accurately thrown it at me.

Immediately afterwards an RAF Sergeant materialised in the station entrance.

'Aircraftman Second Class Gill? Come on, hurry up. You're the last. Get on board the transport and quick about it.'

Every single communication from higher authority issued in the next six weeks included an admonishment to move faster. But what transport? I looked wildly around for some sort of bus.

'Up on the three-tonner now. Stop being so dozy, Aircraftman, unless you want to run all the way.'

A large open lorry was backing out of the station entrance. Sitting or squatting among the old tyres, spades and other implements were some dozen pimply morose-looking men of assorted ages. No doubt these were my fellow conscripts.

Have you ever tried to get on board a large lorry when its movement precludes you climbing up the wheels? Eventually three of my fellows seized me under the arms and threw me down among the tyres, further bruising elbows and knees. For the second time in ten minutes my overnight bag was hurled after me. Despite the skinned shins, my main preoccupation was how dirty the tyres were getting my sports jacket. But then I remembered I would not be wearing my own clothes any more . . . for how long I wondered? (Four-and-a-half years as it happened.)

Here, in the midpoint of the war, Cardington was the bottleneck which equipped all those entering the Air Force. It had never been built with such a massive intake in mind. Yet I suppose one has to say it did not do too badly, if you accept queues of Gracie Fields-type dimensions. The Air Force gave you everything from the mug to drink your tea, to the billycan to boil your water, from the tin hat to protect you from enemy shrapnel, to the knee-length woollen underpants (three pairs) meant to save you from lice. It was said that many of the poorer intake had never worn underwear till the Air Force gave it to them.

But it could not protect you from everything. At the end of an exhausting first day we were herded into a barnlike wooden building, crowded with metal beds each with an issue of four woollen blankets. So far I had hardly spoken to a soul. Now my next-door neighbour started a probing conversation. Dark and shifty; instinctively I distrusted him. My mother had given me £5 in ten-shilling notes. How should I hide it with this sharp-eyed neighbour watching my every move? Eventually I took advantage of a drunken fight that caught his attention to slip my wallet under my pillow.

That first night in the Air Force was a breath of hell; literally, as many of the new arrivals expressed their nervousness through upset bowels and the toilet facilities were totally inadequate. The transition from being relatively free agents to obeying instantly sets of rules that we neither knew nor understood affected us all. The authorities recognised that we were undergoing a severe self-adjustment. For some, drink was a help. There were several bars (run by the NAAFI) on the camp. All through the night recruits were tottering into the dormitory, falling over the beds, vomiting on the unfortunate occupants, fighting each other, cursing and shouting their discomfort. To all this the RAF police turned a relatively blind eye.

Lying awake in the darkness (lights were put out at 10.30 p.m.) my thoughts returned to my family. This time not so desolately as on the train. I recognised that I was in a sort of limbo. If nothing got much worse than this I reckoned I would survive. But it seemed likely that it

139

was going to be a lonely sort of life. I had not seen anyone among all those frightened faces who might be a chum. With this gloomy thought I fell asleep.

When I woke up it was light and people were stirring. I looked across at my neighbour's bed. It was empty. I pushed my hand under my pillow. My wallet had gone.

II

I never saw my bed neighbour again. Nor did I report the theft. What could the authorities have done about it, except to tell me to be more careful next time? There was nothing I could have spent the money on anyway. The whole day we were occupied marching from one depot to another. There was something irresistibly comic in our gradual transformation from a polyglot group of civilians, shuffling and stumbling under the rising pile of assorted kit, from plastic gas capes to black leather boots, to the sort of parody of a military squad that we evolved into. Divided into groups of thirty, we were constantly passing and repassing the other groups. The donning of a crucial item, like the blue serge tunic, brought a rousing cheer from other squads that had not progressed so far.

This irrepressible good humour seemed a characteristic of the British serviceman. It could cushion the severest shocks: one of which was about to hit us. A man of considerable authority (I expect that meant he was a leading aircraftman: I had not yet learned to read all badges of rank), this wielder of our fate, called us to attention. Having repeated this command three times and each time told us to be quicker about it, he got to the point. As the weather was so good, the kindly station commander had decided we would all enjoy a spot of camping. Tents were being put up at that moment in an adjacent field.

He failed to tell us that the input of recruits had surpassed the numbers that could properly be dealt with. The neat rows of bell tents looked very handsome from a distance. Each tent might have contained four sleeping figures at a pinch. *Ten men* were allocated to each. And every one of us now had a bulging kit bag of equipment to look after.

There was only one possible solution. Each of us must lie on our side facing in the same direction, with our legs bent up under our chins. I suppose now this would be called the foetal position. It did not allow for any individual movement, like stretching the legs or turning over. Nor, of course, did it account for calls of nature.

Such superhuman immobility was beyond our control. When a pair of hairy legs descended on top of ours it was impossible for us not to wriggle our legs out from under and put them on top of the heap, shortly to be pushed aside by another pair of interlopers from the other side of the tent. It was very like that game where you pull your hand out from the bottom of the heap and slap it on the top. Naturally we got very little sleep that or the next night. It did, however, perforce get us to know our neighbours. The man on my right was a barber from Putney, one of the gentlest, kindest men you could ever meet. He was thirty-nine years old with spectacles and a bristly moustache. I knew all about the bristles as several times I woke up with my face jammed against his.

It was remarkable how calmly we all took these total invasions on conventional privacy. To get out of the tent once we had all jammed into it was a major exercise. How to urinate in the middle of the night was therefore a serious problem. It was most easily solved by easing the penis out of its covering, pointing it upwards and in the general direction of the open tent flap, and letting rip. A waving motion created a sprinkling effect, not unlike a rain shower on which you could loudly blame the sudden downfall. Several people who had thought themselves lucky by getting head space near the entrance decided to try sleeping out the next night. Being England, there was a genuine rainfall in the early hours and a sudden descent on us of four or five soaking and unwelcome tent mates.

Those nights in the tent seemed to me the limit of conceivable discomfort. But I was soon to be proved wrong. By Thursday morning we were completely kitted out, dressed in blue and learning how to salute correctly. Once more we were formed into long lines, this time waiting for the interview that was to decide our fate in the Air Force. In my case it took less than five minutes. The blond and clearly bored personnel officer confirmed that there were no vacancies for radar observers. 'Now,' he said, 'I would suggest clerk SD; that's what most of you failed air crew go in for.'

I didn't particularly like the idea of being a clerk.

'It's not a desk job,' said the officer, glancing at his watch. 'You'd be a plotter. You'd have to pass a trade test first.'

'When would I take that?'

'I'll give it to you now.' He looked down at a typed sheet on his desk. 'How many times will six go into twenty-four? How do you spell accidental? What's the capital of New South Wales? Here's a page of geometrical figures; point out an isosceles triangle. Good, good, good. You've passed. After six weeks on the general training course at Skegness you'll go to the plotters' school at Leighton Buzzard. Send in the next man as you go out.'

That afternoon we said goodbye to our own clothes. Crudely wrapped up in the brown paper and string we had been instructed to bring with us, and left at the subsidiary post office in the camp central block. Our facetious leading aircraftman told us that there was nothing more he could load onto us and that the rest of the day was our own, except that there were one or two odd jobs that some of us would have to volunteer for. He then called us out in turn and told us what those jobs were. They were mostly cleaning out the kitchens, weeding the entrance drive, polishing the silverware in the Officers' Mess. Eventually everyone had been allocated a task except for me and one other. The leading aircraftman sauntered over to us.

'You might think that I've saved the best for the last and in some ways I have. It seems to me just listening to the way you talk that you're a fastidious couple. I'm sure your mothers always insisted you left the bathroom just as you found it.'

What was he talking about? At this point I and the other man had not exchanged a dozen words. Nor were we physically alike. I was six feet one inch and he five feet four inches. He had dark, aquiline features and straight dark hair. My hair was lighter and tended to wave. Yet it was true that we had noticed each other during the morning. His voice was surprisingly much deeper than mine, but we both spoke with what might be described as a public school accent. The leading aircraftman was right in putting us together; our powers of cooperation were about to be severely tested.

Beyond the orderly rows of the bell tents was a single long tent. This was the WC: a long pole perched above a series of large metal buckets about three feet deep and three feet across. They had not been emptied since the tents had been put into service the day before. Like everything else at Cardington, they were exuding signs of over-wear. Our task was to dig a pit in the next field, carry the buckets across from the other field, empty the contents into the pit and eventually cover it over with the original earth.

The task was not made easier by the return of the sunshine and an August heat wave. It took three hours for us to dig a pit in this high-summer-baked ground. In fact, our progress was so slow that three more amateur labourers were put to work with us. While we toiled and sweated, blistering hands and aching shoulders, the object of our attention two fields away became more and more apparent. At a distance the stench was appalling. Close to it made you feel sick and suffocated.

Full to the top and slopping over, the buckets were not easy to carry. I had not realised how much of human excrement is liquid. Our persecutor had gone to the trouble of getting us working overalls; a very necessary protection for our brand-new uniforms. The path across the fields between the WC and the pit we had dug was quickly dubbed Shit Street.

People came out to watch us at work, but they did not stay long. The smell defeated all expectations of participating in a gloat.

Resting frequently on our slobbery journey along Shit Street gave us plenty of time to get to know each other. It was not advisable to go into a long conversation. Movement at least gave the illusion that you were creating a breeze. Nor could you afford to take deep breaths. So talk was a sort of rapid mutter between the teeth. Like:

HE. Which do you read; *Spectors* or *Staggers and Natters*?
ME. Oh, *S. and N.*
HE. Me too and how.

This meant that of the two weekly journals, the *Spectator* and the *New Statesman and Nation*, we both favoured the left-wing *New Statesman*.

He had been to a well-known school in the City. His name was Wyndham Davidson.

HE. Come from Canterbury, eh? Had a grandfather who was Archbishop there [Randall Davidson].

By the time we had filled in the pit, and covered it over and struggled out of our sticky stained overalls, we had agreed to try and stay together at our next posting in Skegness.

III

The following morning we were up at 5 a.m. This was no hardship after another shin-breaking night in the tent. Others probably had it worse than me. The unfortunate barber told me mine was the pongiest hair he had ever slept next to. However, the journey to our next billet was a reminder that I was not really as fit as my height and youth suggested.

The distance from Cardington to Skegness was probably only some sixty to seventy miles, but it was across England from west to east, a journey never as easy as travelling north to south. As I remember, we had to make a couple of changes which involved lengthy waits in rural stations. So that, while we left tainted Cardington without regrets at six in the morning, it was some twelve hours later that we were installed by the North Sea in Skegness.

For all that time we had been literally strapped into our gear. Let me see if I can make clear what this entailed. From the skin outwards: woollen underwear, heavy woollen socks, blue linen shirt, separate collar and tie, blue serge uniform with brass buttons, fore and aft cap, heavy black boots; webbing belt and complete harness, to which was attached: small pack containing personal gear, metal billycan, knife, fork and spoon, iron rations, water bottle; large pack containing all spare clothing, blankets, etc., heavy overcoat neatly folded and strapped onto the top of the large pack, anti-gas cape also neatly folded and strapped onto the bottom of the large pack. The kit bag, which was as heavy as a large suitcase, was meant to contain all private possessions as well as such additional blankets and towels as might from time to time be issued.

It was the kit bag which was really my undoing. Other trains were converging on Skegness, bringing recruits from Scotland and the north of England. They had to be infiltrated into the long columns unloading like ourselves from the Midlands and the south. Each stop meant lifting down the heavy kit bag from its precarious position balanced across one shoulder and standing it upright between you and your immediate neighbour. Each start meant lifting it up again onto your aching collarbone. Often we moved only two or three steps before having to repeat the whole action.

Lifting the kit bag up began to take a tremendous effort of the will. My breathing came in short gasps. My marching lost its rhythm and I wavered from side to side. Just forcing myself on occupied my every blurred attention. I could see nothing, experience nothing, except the need to totter on. I began to collide with the marchers on either side of me. Much, I am sure, to their alarm.

'Hey, laddie, give me that kit bag for a bit,' said a kindly voice. Without its weight I was able to concentrate on getting command of my breathing. I saw the man carrying my kit bag was a corporal (in fact, by great good luck he was the NCO in direct charge of our contingent).

Skegness, like some other seaside holiday towns of pre-war days, had been largely taken over by the RAF. The narrow side streets that ran straight down onto the sand dunes and had once been awash with crowing and caterwauling children now echoed to the equally infantile bellowed commands of drill sergeants and the obedient responses of their victims: 'One pause Two' or the even more complex 'One pause Two pause Three pause Four'.

These side streets were housed with a variety of modest-sized, but stylistically ambitious residences. They appealed to holiday-makers who might really have preferred to go to a Swiss chalet or a turreted French *palais* or even a Tudor manor. Their owners would hardly have recognised them now. Entirely stripped of all furniture, carpets and every item that gave character, each room had two to four uniform metal beds of the sort with which I was to grow very familiar over the next few years.

When we eventually arrived at the house which was to be our home for the next six weeks, Corporal Barker quickly allocated us our beds. When Wyndham and I asked to be put together he said sharply that there could be no preferential treatment for individuals. However, it so happened that we were the last to be allocated, and so came together in the top floor, where there were only two beds and a splendid view of the sea through dormer windows.

How quickly the corner where you slept became home. Most young men reinforced the territorial claim by pinning up a photograph of their dream companion, Betty Grable or Phyllis Dixey the fan dancer or – if they wanted to show how classy their taste was – Vivien Leigh. A few would put up a picture of a favourite dog or even – very daring – a family photograph with Mum and Dad and younger Sis. That was daring, because in these first days of communal living, few had the self-confidence to reveal so much about themselves to those strangers around them.

Wyndham and I quickly decided to be different. We came across an old Christmas edition of the *Illustrated London News* that a previous occupier had left behind as rubbish. It included a number of colour reproductions of great works of art from the National Gallery that were now hidden for safety in a Welsh slate mine. So, instead of Gable's emphatic legs, our waking vision slid along the sinuous curves of the *Rokeby Venus*; not a real mum and baby brother, but Giotto's *Madonna and Child* watched over our uneasy dreams.

While we were hammering in the last tack on a wintry Dutch scene of skating on the Zuider Zee, Corporal Barker came in, no doubt attracted by the knocking. 'I say lads no nails allowed,' he began, then let his eyes wander up the backside of Venus. 'So this is what you call art,' he said in puzzled tones. He peered at a crowded Dutch fair where a middle-aged man was urinating against the town hall. 'Mind you, I can't say I wouldn't prefer to watch a good game with Arsenal myself. But I suppose this is what we're fighting for.'

IV

When I recall those six weeks at Skegness it seems one long parade, the crash of boots stamping up and down again, the shouted commands and our bellowed responses. One pause Two . . . By the front . . . qui-i-c-k march . . . At the double, now . . . Ab-o-o-o-u-t turn . . . About turn, about turn, about turn. Oh my blistered feet. Every movement had to be stamped into the concrete with an energy and precision that seemed likely to crack open a passage to Australia.

Each morning began with three hours' foot drill and if we weren't coming up to scratch another couple of hours were thrown in in the afternoon. There was something mesmerically satisfying in spending so much time achieving such a pointless perfection. The Air Force would say it was not pointless, but gave us a solid core of discipline which would be needed when we came under fire. But would it? We were not going to march across Europe to arrest Hitler in Berlin.

Some of the other things we did seemed equally daft. We learned how to take apart a Bren gun, how to clean it and put it together again. But we weren't issued with Bren guns. We were also ordered to run through a hut in which a tear-gas bomb had just been thrown. It was not lethal, but equally the Germans were not likely to use it against us.

There were thirty-two of us in 28 Squad under Corporal Barker. We were a mixed crowd. There were two or three lads from the slums of Liverpool and Manchester whose dialect was so thick I never fully understood them when they talked together. They had the rapid understanding and cocky confidence that came from maturing in gangland. At the other extreme was Deaken, a Norfolk farm-labourer's son, who had never been more than a dozen miles from his home village, addressed everyone as 'thee', and knelt by his bed to say his prayers every night before lights out. Gidney, at twenty-nine, was the oldest member of our squad and much the cleverest. He was an electrician from Staffordshire. He had taken the trouble to read up RAF law, and was always quoting King's Regulations to the authorities in order to protect our interests.

Tall and gangling with protruding eyes, a sharp nose and diminutive chin, there was something rather comical about Gidney's earnestness, though we all benefited from it. Our indebtedness was recognised in his nickname, 'the colonel'. It was a tribute both to his authority and his undershot jaw and bulging eye. Only a few of us achieved the doubtful distinction of a general epithet. Our single coloured recruit, a tailor from the East End named Da Silva, answered cheerfully to 'Blackout'. A very pretty young man, who had been a shop assistant in Eastbourne, was 'Blondie'. Most of these epithets were first expressed by a cockney, Maconachie, who was too individual a character himself to pin down in a

Mary Gill, my mother.

My father, George Arnold Gill, served in the First World War as an officer in the Tank Corps.

This is me at fourteen months being held by my nurse.

My father relaxing in our garden.

My mother and her younger brother Clifford.

My mother's parents, William and Emily Taylor.

The wedding of Sarah Jane Taylor, my great-aunt, at Croft House, Upper Batley, 1893. My mother is sitting just in front of the bride, with her brothers Tom and Clifford on either side of her.

Fred and Will Taylor, my great-uncles (seated on the right) on their ranch in Colorado, 1884.

Here is my great-grandmother Taylor, in formal pose for a Victorian studio photographer in Scarborough.

William Taylor, my grandfather.

My grandmother, Emily Thomas Taylor.

My grandmother Taylor (on the right) with a friend.

Henry Talbot, my grandmother's admirer (whom I called Tor), with me in the garden at Winchester.

At Winchester with my grandmother.

My grandfather, George Gill, and me.

Out and about with my mother at Herne Bay.

This is me at eight.

Here I am in my spinal chair with my father, grandfather and dog Patch.

My cousin, Carolyn Taylor.

Stephen Coltham, my tutor, who was an important influence on me as a boy.

No. 28 Squadron RAF, Skegness, 1942. I'm in the back row at the extreme left; Wyndham Davidson, second row from the front, extreme right, looking very serious; John O'Connor, our wild Irishman, in the second row from the front, second left.

HEADQUARTERS (UNIT)
ROYAL AIR FORCE IN NORTHERN IRELAND

Christmas Day, 1943

MENU

◆

BREAKFAST
Cornflakes   Fresh Milk
Fried Egg and Bacon
Tea   Coffee   Breakfast Rolls   Butter   Marmalade

DINNER
Cream of Celery Soup
Roast Turkey   Roast Pork
Sage and Leek Stuffing   Apple Sauce
Brussels Sprouts
Roast Potatoes   Creamed Potatoes
Savoury Gravy   Dinner Rolls
Christmas Pudding   Rum Sauce   Dessert Apples
Beer   Minerals   Cigarettes

TEA
Cold Ham
Winter Salad   Rich Fruit Cake
Assorted Biscuits   Sweet Mince Pies
Tea   Coffee   Bread and Butter   Jam

Christmas Day menu, 1943.

Jimmy Blair and me in Dublin, September 1943.

Pilot Officer Michael Gill.

The ops board at Hartford Bridge on D+1, 7 June 1944, listing aircraft and crews of the three resident bomber squadrons.

An RAF Mitchell bomber takes off to attack a target in Northern France shortly after D-Day, 1944. (*Imperial War Museum*)

No. 137 Wing, Hartford Bridge, 1944. I am in the back row, seventh from the right.

The special fog dispersal aid 'Fido' in operation at an RAF bomber station, with a Lancaster taxying in the background. We had 'Fido' at Hartford Bridge. *(Imperial War Museum)*

The King and Queen leaving the Officers Mess at Hartford Bridge with the station commander, Group Captain Macdonald, September 1944.

Medal presentation parade at Hartford Bridge, September 1944.

Enjoying a drink at a café on the Champs Elysees with Hillerby, our Met Officer.

In the ops room at Vitry-en-Artois, near Douai, in Northern France, 1945. I'm the one with the pipe.

Germany, 1945. I'm on the right.
We both had revolvers.

A knocked-out German Tiger tank on the Vimy–Lens road. Sergeant Metcalfe, Les Rates, me, Leading Aircraftmen Boulter and Nichols, April 1945.

Ruined Cologne, but the cathedral survived.

In Germany, 1946.

couple of words. I enjoyed his company and that of a southern Irish volunteer, John O'Connor. He intended to be a film star. Another, and thoroughly detestable, cockney was 'Chummy'. That derived from his habit of continually attempting to borrow everything from boot blacking to money — forays that invariably began with him sidling up to his victim and saying in wheedling tones: 'Oh, chummy, I wonder if I could have a loan of . . .'. Unabashed by the nickname, he continued to importune us in the same terms all the six weeks we were together.

I rapidly became 'the Professor' or 'Prof', though I think I was, by a month, the youngest in the squad. My years of enforced idleness had led me to read a great deal, and I had information available on most subjects. Knowledge I was only too ready to impart. Wyndham was better read, but a great deal more sophisticated in revealing it. Like all these epithets, mine was double-edged. It suggested learning, but also pedantry, and an inability to cope with the practical side: a reputation well deserved.

I was not, as I had gloomily expected, the most inept and unhealthy member of the squad. This unhappy distinction fell on a young man called Robbins. Incapable of walking in step or of swinging his arms synchronously, with thick pebble glasses and a vacant, heavy face, he could only just have reached the requisite intelligence level for call-up. Continually preoccupied with his own opaque thoughts, never apparently knowing what was going on, or joining in the jokes and badinage that flowed between us, or acknowledging any of us as individuals, he was brilliantly christened 'the Lodger'.

'Can't you see 'im if we got a direct hit from a Jerry raider. He'd walk into the flaming billet and say, "What's frying up?"'

Even Robbins was tolerated, turned in the right direction, helped into the appropriate clothes and shouted into line. He got sworn at more than anyone else; he was also helped more. There were never any fights in our billet. We were too tired to quarrel.

It came as a surprise that, after my years of illness, I was able to cope not much worse than the average. Yet, however hard we tried, Wyndham and I seemed prone to disaster. Perhaps it was being tucked away so snugly in that little room at the top of the house that made senior NCOs on tours of inspection sniff for blood. There was nothing in regulations that said you should not have flowers in your billet. Wyndham had bought a cheap vase in Woolworth's and placed it, regularly filled with sweet peas or violets, on an up-ended orange box between our beds. We had made a shelf in the box on which we put our library: two or three volumes of poetry, Lawrence short stories, *Point Counter Point*, and the latest editions of the *Listener* and *New Statesman*. I can see now it was not a tactful mixture.

In my fourth letter home I wrote: 'Our Flight Sergeant is a beast. He used to be a schoolmaster in private life and he has a very acid temper. On the other hand, our Squad Corporal, Barker, could not be nicer. He is a Yorkshireman, rough on the surface, but kind-hearted underneath.'

The truth was that, despite blistered feet and other aches, I was enjoying myself. Sharing a room with someone my own age was an exotic thrill. In many ways our tastes were complementary, but different. Wyndham introduced me to D.H. Lawrence. *The Woman Who Rode Away* swept me into a disturbing new dimension of experience.

I was reading it one evening when Wyndham came in looking rather pleased.

'I've just seen Auerbach. He's asked us out for a meal tomorrow night.'

'Auerbach has?'

'Yes, it's to celebrate. He's got his commission.'

'Gosh, what a compliment.'

Tall and portly, with curly grey hair, Auerbach seemed nearly as old as my father and twice as imposing. I suppose he was at the beginning of his forties. Like my father, he was in banking, but as the editor of a trade journal. Not in our billet, he often chatted to us during breaks in drill. He had a rumbling laugh, a witty tongue and an air of gracious condescension.

'Will you be going into Intelligence?' I asked him, once we were settled at the small café table.

'Catering, actually.'

'Well placed to look after No. 1,' nodded our fourth companion, another ageing recruit who had been introduced as Bill Varley.

'I suppose so. Apparently there are no immediate vacancies in anything else.'

'Mind you, it won't be a doddle. Not everyone knows about writing, but we all have an opinion about what goes into our stomachs.'

The easy way he talked to the formidable Auerbach surprised me. He was not very impressive in appearance. Though perfectly clean with Brylcreemed dark hair, his lined face looked as though iron filings had been stitched into the seams. I wondered what he had done before joining the Air Force.

'That'd take some telling. I was a cook once in Calgary. Last couple of years I've been driving a crane.'

'Where do you do that?'

'All over. Wherever it's needed.'

'Our young friend is from Canterbury, Bill.' Auerbach bent forward.

'Yeah? I was down there a couple of months ago, clearing the wreckage. Bloody shame about those old houses round the cathedral.'

'Yes.' I began to like him better. 'Is that what you'll do in the Air Force?'

'No. I've had enough of shovelling rubble. Bomb disposal is what I'm aiming for.'

'You mean, you'll be defusing bombs?'

'Yeah. I've seen so many that don't go off. Bloody menace they are.'

'That's a hot job.'

'Not really, if you know what you're doing.'

'Won't your family mind?'

'Bill's on his own,' said Auerbach.

'I am now. The old woman bought it in the Blitz.'

'Oh, I'm sorry.'

'Well, we weren't married. We'd have parted sometime.'

'Don't you believe in marriage?'

'It's for the birds, isn't it? Look, sonny, nothing is for keeps in this life.'

He got up and strolled out, leaving me confused. I believed in romantic love and a marriage that would last a lifetime.

'Those are often conflicting aims,' Auerbach lowered his voice confidentially. 'Though I have reason to believe Bill was with his old lady thirteen years.'

Varley was coming back with four glasses and a jug of water from the kitchen. Auerbach produced a flask of whisky. The café was an unpretentious place and the fried Spam, peas and chips not much above the resources of our cook house, but it was a pleasure to eat off a table cloth, even if there were a number of coffee stains underlining the check.

'Mike's just started on D.H. Lawrence,' Wyndham explained.

'Lawrence? He's a mixture of sense and bilge.' Varley had a way of dismissing a topic with flat finality.

'Surely he was right to put such an emphasis on sex?' I was full of the convictions of one who had never even touched the flesh of a naked breast.

'He was right about getting rid of sentimental Victorian nonsense. Then he put up a lot more of his own.' Auerbach was waving a lighted cigarette in his chubby hand, though we had not yet had the apple pie and custard. To smoke in the middle of a meal; that seemed the height of decadence.

'There's a passage in Flaubert in which he says he's never able to see women standing under lamp-posts at night, or walking up and down wet streets, without excitement. It's the accessibility, the possibility of a relationship of the most intimate kind when there is no relationship at all: intimacy without sentiment.'

'I've always found the idea of prostitution disgusting,' said Wyndham with diffidence. 'I think prostitutes when you see them in Soho often look repulsive. Great wide mouths, like sharks or lizards.'

'My dear boy, there are as many varieties as in any profession. Don't malign whores; you can ask them to do things no respectable person would.'

What did he mean, I wondered. I hardly understood what went on in normal sex.

'I saw a woman done by a donkey once,' said Varley.

'Was that in Cairo?' said Auerbach, perhaps annoyed to have lost the floor.

'No, Marseilles; the dock area. It was a show, of course; but I reckon it was for real.'

'How could it be?' I asked.

'What happened?' said Wyndham.

'Well it was just a little place, full of sailors like myself. We'd been told what to expect and all paid up. This woman comes on. She wasn't young or particularly good looking, but I don't suppose the donkey cared. In fact, she looked as if she'd been fucked to hell, thin as a wraith. First of all she danced about, took her clothes off, cracked a whip. She had a couple of younger assistants. They brought on the donkey. Quite a little beast, but when she played with it, it came out a yard. Then she lay back on a low table and pulled it in her, first by the ears and then by its cock.'

'And you reckon it really entered?' Auerbach was attentive now.

'I'm sure of it. I was sitting off to one side and had a good view. Not all the way, of course. But enough. After a bit the donkey let out a terrible bray. Scared the living daylights out of us. We'd all been sitting as silent as the grave, and there it was rearing up and pawing with its hoofs. The attendants rushed back and pulled it off. It came out dripping.'

'Good Lord,' said Auerbach.

'Surely that's not possible. She'd have been injured,' said Wyndham.

'Told you I had a good position. I saw a glint of metal up her. I reckon she had a series of stainless steel rings up there getting smaller and smaller to stop it over-reaching itself.'

When we got to the Camp coffee, Auerbach went out and came back with a port for himself and three more whiskys for us.

'There's nothing like frigging,' said Varley dreamily. 'I envy you boys, you have so much of it to come.'

'Mind you, a lot of it's in the head,' said Auerbach. 'Anticipation; it's often the best part.'

'I think about it all the time,' said Varley. 'Maybe it's being in the company of all you blokes. I'm beginning to wonder what it was like.'

'That's just the trouble,' I said. 'I can't imagine what it's like.'

'Don't worry, boy,' said Varley. 'It comes naturally. Just get an older woman at first. Use your imagination.'

'Imagination: the frenzy of creation.' Auerbach was much more pompous than I'd realised.

'There's a game I've often thought of playing,' said Varley. 'You get her to lie on her stomach, and you paint a picture on her back. With your cock of course. She has to guess what it is. You dip your old man in this tingly substance, so when you put it on her back it leaves a sensation behind.'

'What's the tingly substance?' asked Wyndham.

'That's the trouble; I've never been able to find it. But it's a great idea, isn't it? Sensuous, but thoughtful: fizz and a quiz.'

'I would paint God creating the Universe from the Sistine Chapel ceiling,' said Auerbach. 'Such broad, sweeping strokes.'

'There's a drawing by that Frenchman, is his name Doré?' said Varley. 'It's the devils descending into Hell. Dozens of them with flapping wings. A long fall all the way down into that hot, seething pit. That's the one for me.'

As we hurried back through the blackout, there was not another airman on the streets. 'We'd better run, it's nearly lights out,' I muttered.

Corporal Barker was already on his rounds of the ground floor as we crept hastily up the stairs. We were still making our beds when his head came round the door.

'Been on the booze, eh lads?'

'Oh no, Corporal,' we chorused.

'Get down to it quietly now. I'll give you a couple of minutes before I turn the lights out.'

Tucking in his blankets Wyndham chuckled. 'Amazing chap, that Varley.'

'Yes. I didn't like Auerbach so much as I expected.'

'He's a bit of a poseur, I'm afraid. He's very generous anyway; the evening must have cost him twenty-five bob.'

'More than that. I reckon with the drink it was six-and-six a head. I hated all that stuff about prostitutes.'

'I agree with you,' said Wyndham, wriggling into his bed.

'I *do* think girls are magical and mysterious:

> She walks in beauty like the night
> Of something something and starry skies
> And all that's best of dark and bright
> Meets in her aspect and her eyes.

'That's what I think of them.'

'They're certainly hard to understand.' Wyndham sounded sleepy.

'There was something nasty in the way Auerbach talked – gloating almost.'

Wyndham opened a cynical eye.

'Do you think he was talking about ladies? Why do you think he likes our company?'

I did not really understand what he meant, and before I could ask him Corporal Barker banged on the wall for quiet.

Sleep took me the instant my head touched the pillow, but in the night I had a complex dream. I was kneeling in front of a fireplace, oval and splendidly decorated, putting together lengths of a broom. I stuffed it up the chimney, further and further, adding more and more lengths, and pushing it vigorously. But it got more difficult and eventually I was thrusting against some obstacle. I pushed and shoved so hard back and forth that the whole wall began to sway and buckle. Just as it fell forwards over me, it turned into my mother, enveloping me in her youthful arms. I woke as the last twitches of sticky liquid fell on my thighs. That, I suspected, was what sex was going to be like: a bit of a fiasco.

V

There seemed to be something about us that provoked surprising responses. Mealtimes were made more unappetising by the reaction of the cook-house staff. Big sweaty men in dirty overalls, spooning greasy stew, cabbage and watery mash on the line of passing plates, the appearance of Wyndham and myself galvanised them to mysterious action. They would chant in unison: 'Here come the queenies, the queenies, the queenies, here come the queenies, the faery queens.'

What did they mean? I could not understand it, but I knew it was insulting and it made me flustered. It seemed a continuation of all the teasing I had suffered at school. Primly, I accepted it as my lot: horrid, but inevitable. Wyndham ignored it also, or I might have learned what it meant. I felt it clearly had to do with our being nice, refined people. Probably an adverse comment on the way we talked.

I was confirmed in this belief when we were out for a stroll one Sunday afternoon, the only time we had the opportunity to walk about. We were stopped in the street by the Quartermaster in charge of the dining-halls, such a high-ranking figure that we had seen him only once or twice, looking authoritative above the seething meal benches.

'Where are you boys off to?' He was perspiring and seemed oddly ill at ease behind his jutting moustache.

'Just taking a walk, sir,' said Wyndham somewhat unnecessarily.

'Like a cup of coffee? My rooms are near here.'

This was so surprising that we said nothing, but a greater shock was to come.

'I hear you like art.'

How could he possibly have heard that? Or know anything at all about us?

'I've got a nice collection myself. I'd like to show it to you.'

Why was he asking us? Why did he not just order us to go with him? There must be something wrong. Senior NCOs did not mix with the likes of us. In the uneasy pause we looked at each other.

'It's very kind of you,' said Wyndham, 'but I think we ought to get some fresh air.'

'Yes, we should be getting on, thanks very much though.'

He did not try to detain us, but walked rapidly away.

'Poor chap, he must be lonely I suppose,' said Wyndham after we had gone some distance in silence.

'How could he know about us?'

'Goodness knows.'

A few days later I was queuing at the entrance to the dining-halls for tea when I suddenly felt an urgent tug at my sleeve. Looking round I saw only an ornamental pillar, a vestige of the time when this had been a smart holiday restaurant, and behind it an archway covered in a dirty white linen curtain. I was moving on, under the impetus of those behind me, when the curtain parted. The red face and dark moustache of the Quartermaster appeared fleetingly. His lips parted, showing a flash of white teeth. He said 'hist', like a character in Shakespeare. At the same time, in one frantic gesture, he put his fingers to his lips and gestured me to him. Then the curtain fell.

I continued with the queue. He was obviously as mad as a hatter. Then I heard his voice, low but peremptory.

'Boy, come here.'

That was an order. I turned round reluctantly. He was holding the curtain aside, but standing back from it so that only someone in my

157

position could see him. Behind him, white-clad figures were moving about. I walked through the curtain into a sort of scullery. There were shelves and cupboards of food and utensils and, beyond a further arch, the kitchen, frantic with noise and activity.

'Here boy, have a mince pie.'

He held one out, crispy brown and dusted with sugar. He himself was gleaming in white, belted overalls. He watched me eating with watery intensity.

'Take some more. Take some for your friend.' There were rows of them on a table beside a card with 'Officers' Mess' written on it.

'Sorry we can't give them to you all, but for you . . . how is your friend?'

'Wyndham? He's all right, thanks.'

'I missed seeing him today.' He was bundling about a dozen pies into an old newspaper.

'Don't forget. You must be tired sometimes. If you and your friend want to put your feet up, have a little quiet, my rooms are at your disposal.'

He spoke urgently and quietly. As he handed me the wrapped-up pies, he seized my hand in both of his.

'Dear boy . . .'

Thanking him, I was turning away when he stopped me with one of his hissing exclamations.

'Wait: the address.' He pulled out a showy fountain pen and wrote it in a large flowing hand.

'Do come, any time.'

Needless to say we never went, though the pies were delicious. They were more than a luxury. Every letter I wrote referred to food. We were constantly hungry. I did not bother to mention that several people in a neighbouring street had been killed in a tip-and-run air raid. What was important was that the bombs had broken the power lines and ensured that we had only cold food the next couple of days, thus diluting our already meagre rations. Officially we were not allowed to receive food parcels, but everyone did. As well as fruit, my parents sent cheese, small packets of butter (bought in the country on the black market), biscuits and sweets. It was not enough. I wrote: 'I should love a really nice cake. I have had some scrummy home-made cake provided by other chaps in the billet.' Night dreams were as often occupied by mountains of grub as by equally inaccessible girls.

September was one of the worst months in the war for shipping losses. The Germans had stepped up the production of U-boats to such an extent that, despite increased casualties, twice as many were operating as at the beginning of the year. If they could squeeze that iron ring of torpedoes a little tighter we would be forced to capitulate without an invasion. Hunger was the incalculable joker in the war game, and the one that worried the Allies most in this critical time.

Churchill had recently made one order that directly affected us. He visited the Eighth Army in the desert in August. The front line was only fifty miles from Cairo. All the Headquarters Staff there were armed with rifles and ordered to defend the city should Rommel make a breakthrough. He attempted to do so, during our first week in Skegness, but was held at bay. The dour drawn battle of Alam Halfa lasted six days and ended with both armies back where they had begun. The last-ditch defenders were not needed.

A similar situation applied at Imphal, on the borders of India, where the survivors of our forces in Burma were mustering. RAF ground crew were armed to defend the airfields. With the enemy advancing on all sides, there was no place for the non-combatant. So our six weeks' course was reorganised to contain more battle training.

There was something incongruous in our gingerly practised unarmed combat. It seemed more important not to break Robbins's arm than to get him down smartly on the sunlit sands. We had to take it on trust that a blow with the side of our hand to Gidney's prominent Adam's apple would kill him if applied with sufficient force. Charging at a stuffed sack and poking it with a bayonet to the accompaniment of shrill yells made me feel silly, not aggressive. I could not imagine any circumstance where I could bring myself to do such a thing. Even stamping on a spider, a creature I viewed with loathing, was quite beyond me. When it came to rifle fire, I could muster only 16 per cent, though a number of others, including Wyndham, did not hit the target at all.

I might have made some progress at foot and rifle drill, but as a military machine I was far from effective. The most elaborate part of our field training was a night exercise in which we were to attack the neighbouring Butlins camp, now occupied by the Navy. Our job was to reach and mark with chalk the Headquarters huts, thus signifying we had blown them up. The main assault was across the dunes from the sea. I was part of a diversionary attack from the land. We had to crawl up a shallow hill, cut the barbed wire defences and run through the camp to the enemy HQ, hopefully unobserved. Speed and silence were essential. We rubbed mud into our faces, pushed branches of laurel and clumps of grass through the netting on our helmets till our necks bent under the weight, loaded our rifles with blanks and set off at about 10 p.m.

Our NCOs were just as excited as we were. There was a long sustained rivalry with their opposite numbers in the naval camp. We were exhorted to do our best in passionate terms. The duds, like me, were begged at least to keep quiet and not to shoot a blank up the next man's behind while crawling. This was quite easy to do, as we had to cradle the still relatively unfamiliar rifle across our elbows while wriggling forwards in what we hoped was a snakelike manner. The rifle was continually sliding back and bumping our noses, or bouncing off our extended arms altogether and landing noisily in the grass.

I was put in the middle of a group of nine, led by Corporal Barker. We set off on our stomachs in single file. In my anxiety to shine I was continually overtaking the man in front. It was the moronic Robbins. Alone among us, he moved with his cheek rubbing the grass and his bottom jutting high in the air. When my rifle got entangled with his boots he let out a strangled yelp. Corporal Barker came crawling back.

'For Christ's sake keep quiet Robbins. And Gill, you keep your distance. Don't crowd him or he'll think he's being raped.'

I did my best, though it was a dark night and easy to lose touch. As we neared the top Corporal Barker paused more and more frequently. We could just make out the dull gleam of the wire and hear the crunch of a patrolling sentry. We made a supreme effort to move silently now. It was fortunate I had the porcine hulk of Robbins's bottom for a fix. Just below the perimeter the halt stretched interminably. Heavy drizzle came on, darkening the scene even more. A distant star shell, the rattle of small arms fire, and confused shouts told that the frontal attack had gone in. We remained in frozen immobility, joints aching, the sodden state of our uniforms slowly spreading down to our skins.

Gidney, who was right behind me, shook my boot. I looked round at the interrogative pallor of his raised face. Silently I pointed forward at the looming bulk of Robbins's behind. More time passed. I went into a dreamlike reverie, pleasantly released from the soaking discomfort of the body. I was called back to the wet earth by giving vent to a dozen staccato sneezes. They came on without warning and I had no time to smother them. Lord, that would be enough to rouse the whole garrison. Worse was to follow. Gidney crawled fast past me. Suddenly he was standing up and kicking Robbins. The bulging bottom disintegrated. It was a large pile of earth. Gidney turned and grabbed my shoulders.

'You fucking stupid gint,' he yelled into my face. 'Now we've lost 'em.'

'Ssh, ssh, hadn't you better keep quiet!' I whispered soothingly. 'Corporal Barker wouldn't want us to make a noise.'

At that moment there were three heavy explosions: firecrackers going off. Yells and shouts and then a number of sharp blasts on a whistle. The noise maddened Gidney further.

'It's all over and we've missed it,' he screeched. 'We've missed all the fun. We've been lying here, perishing to the bone, all because of you, you blind bugger.'

I tried to explain, pointing out the deceptive similarity of contour and volume between mole-hill and posterior.

'You wouldn't know your own arse from your elbow. You wait till the Corp gets hold of you. He'll have your guts for garters.'

Actually, Corporal Barker was looking uncommonly pleased with himself when we finally met up at the rendezvous point. His eyes, surrounded now with streaks of gun-powder among the mud, fairly twinkled over the top of a mug of Navy tea.

'Well, well, I did say keep your distance,' he murmured. 'You just shouldn't have taken me so literally.'

With Robbins and two others he had found a way through the wire. Unnoticed by the defendants, they had reached their objective and put on their chalk marks. As a final triumphant flourish, Corporal Barker had scaled one of the huts and, leaping from roof to roof, had dropped a lighted firecracker down each chimney, to the consternation of the occupants. Stirred out of his usual catatonic indifference by the explosions, Robbins had jumped at an emerging senior naval officer and fired his rifle in his face. Though it was only a blank, the unfortunate man suffered shock and a broken nose from the blast. Robbins had to be refrained from clubbing him to death with his rifle butt.

'Perhaps it's as well that you weren't with us, Gilly,' said Corporal Barker. 'We do still need the Navy, I suppose.'

He had been personally congratulated by the RAF Commanding Officer for the excess of zeal and ardour he had instilled in his squad.

My nemesis came three days later. The climax of our field training was a newfangled assault course. Under lowering clouds and flurries of rain we struggled through barrels, climbed ropes, scrambled along poles and swung across a specially constructed pit of mud. I managed all this fairly well, only putting one foot knee-deep in the mud, and not falling backwards into it as some did on letting go of the rope. Then we were told to double back to our billets and parade again in full kit – tin hat on head, full back-pack, side-pack and water bottle, respirator slung at the ready on chest, rifle and fixed bayonet in hand. We were paired off with someone approximately our own weight and ordered to carry him over a two-hundred-yard course in three minutes. I was unlucky enough to draw Da Silva, the amiable East End tailor. He was at least a stone heavier.

Picking him up was difficult enough. It was like two hornets embracing, cluttered as we were with bulging equipment front and back, and with the additional hazard of the sharp pointed bayonets always threatening to go up our noses. Eventually I got him on my back in some sort of fireman's lift and set off. I discovered it was better to pitch yourself forwards and run as fast as you could, utilising the pull of gravity from the weight on your shoulders to increase your impetus. The trouble was, however hard your legs went, gravity kept gaining on you, and your body sagged lower and lower. Eventually one of the rifles got between my legs and brought us down. Our helmets banged together with an ear-ringing crash. There was no time to get him on my back again. I embraced him, and lifting him bodily, trotted through a red haze. His heels were dragging on the ground. My knees were melting. The pain in my chest made me believe one of the bayonets was sticking in it. The course seemed interminable. We fell several times. I had no idea how long it took to reach the finishing line. No one commented.

I realised yet again how very unfit I was. Four years on my back in a spinal chair, the total prohibition on playing any sports that followed, had left me with no reserves of energy and muscles that had never been used. I was still trembling with fatigue when we were assembled for the last test of the day. Still in full kit, we had to charge at one of the sea-front shelters, scale the ten-foot-high brick side wall, run along the flat concrete top and, jumping down the other side, run past a table where the dreaded Flight Sergeant Jones was sitting with a stopwatch. The time allowed was fifty seconds.

We gathered in a watching group and ran forward in turn as our names were called out. The first few made it look quite easy: a running jump, fingers clutching the top, a scrabble of boots against the brick, and they were up and away. Then Gidney, missing the hand-hold, fell on his back with a sickening crash. When it came to be my turn, my grasping hands failed to reach the roof. My jump had not lifted me high enough. And I was over six feet tall. Smaller men were going over with apparent ease. After some humiliating fluttering against the wall I was ordered back to the starting line. The jumping went on. Some fifteen or twenty out of the two hundred failed. We were told to try again. This time all but four made it. My fingers reached the flat concrete, but my arms were incapable of levering my body, weighted with all its equipment, upwards. I fell back with a jarring thud.

The voice of the Flight Sergeant rang out cold and clear from where he sat at the distant table.

'Those four men will go again.'

Two more got over, leaving only Robbins, the clumsiest and stupidest man in the Flight, and me. Surely I would not be bested by such an idiot. Yet there was a crablike power in that misshapen body. On his fifth attempt he got one elbow over the top and hung sideways, grunting and jerking like an impaled pig. A frantic cart-wheeling of legs and other arm and he was on the roof. Wheezing and gasping, he pulled himself to his feet, clattered away without a backward glance, and dropped heavily down the other side.

I ought to have been pleased for him, but I felt only consternation at being left on my own. This time I must make it. I succeeded only in grazing my chin. None of my friends looked at me as I limped back to the ranks.

'Stand forth that man.' The Flight Sergeant's diction was so precise that he hardly needed to raise his voice, though he was seated fifty yards away. I marched out alone, still gasping for breath. In the space midway between the watching Flight and the table, I was halted.

'Aircraftman Gill, you have so far failed to carry out a trial at which all your comrades have succeeded. Some are nearly twice your age; others are at least as unfit and ill-prepared as you are. Never mind. You will stay here until you have completed this test successfully. For the rest of the Flight, the day's duties are over. You may go to tea. Flight – dismiss.'

I stood rigidly to attention, my cheeks burning. Behind me the lucky ones turned on their heels and bustled off. Through the receding footfalls a single low farewell reached me.

'Good luck, Mike.' That was Wyndham.

It seemed so unfair. Some of them might be a lot older, but I doubted if any had passed a quarter of their life in bed, and had had to be taught to walk all over again at the age of eleven. And how was I going to be able to make it, when each attempt further sapped my feeble strength?

I flung myself against that dreadful wall with increasing despair. Each run required a nerving of energies, a steeling of bruised and aching flesh for the impact. I recognised the greater the force with which I threw myself upwards on that last step, the more chance I had of getting my reaching fingers onto the top. There was no alternative: no cracks or misplaced plastering allowed a toe hold on that rough, but unseamed surface. Each failure jarred every bone, produced a new bruise or graze or added to an earlier one.

It was like being punched by a brick fist, ten feet high and eight feet across. I could not imagine how I would ever master it. My breath was coming in fiery gulps; I was close to tears. Fatigue lifted me out of the body, to which I remained attached by sharp threads of pain. Remotely I heard the clatter of iron-tipped boots on the concrete increase their momentum, till the collision shocked me back into the knotted contusion that I was becoming. What was I doing? The situation seemed more and more unreal as I ran, jumped and fell into the gathering dusk of the early October evening. The solution could only be a horrid calamity.

After one frenzied effort I crashed heavily and lay gasping for breath. Light footsteps approached.

'Get up Airman. Being sorry for yourself will not help.'

Shakily I pulled myself to my feet. How could the Flight Sergeant be so unfeeling? Against my will I found myself appealing for sympathy.

'I was ill when I was young.'

'Possibly. Your medical record shows you as A4B now. That is a higher rating than many of those who got through this test this afternoon. You also are going to do it, however long it may take. I am prepared to stay here till breakfast if need be. Rest for ten minutes before we proceed.'

His merciless, judging voice drove me to anguish. What had I done to deserve it? The other NCOs had all vanished. This morning had begun like any other, with the expectation of a million similar days to follow. Now it had changed, like one of those trick picture postcards: looked at from one side, it showed a sunny seaside; looked at from the other, the lines of the picture blurred over into a storm at sea and a shipwreck. I was in the eye of the storm and, absurd though it was, this trial was reality; my skinned hands, grazed legs and bruised body, the pain in my chest, the ache in my limbs, all confirmed it. Yet it was also a nightmare, the wall growing higher and higher as I shrank with hurt and tiredness. And lowering at the side, flogging me on with his acid, contemptuous tongue, the monstrous Flight Sergeant, pale, inflexible, vindictive.

'Right, Airman, you've had your rest. Let's see if it's given you any more guts. Proceed with your next attempt. It will be your sixteenth.'

I hated him. It was not a feeling with which I was familiar. My life had had its pain and fear, but I had been carried through the trials of illness by the devotion of my parents. Their loving care had made grim times happy. Only in the two years at school as an adolescent had I experienced malice. Spite came my way because I was singled out, not able to play games, allowed home at the weekends, treated solicitously by the headmaster. I remembered the flaying inquisitions that probed every weakness, the mean surreptitious bullying, the uncomprehending nastiness of my classmates. I had hated them as I now hated this evil Flight Sergeant.

Usually I suffered the endless silly witticisms in silence, but there had been the time, when I was about fourteen, when I was driven over the breaking point by a boy smaller than myself. He was one of my chief persecutors. Over and over he repeated a fatuous torturing rhyme, putting his face close to mine while I was reading and trying to take no notice. At each repetition the sniggering crowd of followers grew behind him. Suddenly, without warning, I lashed out. I was completely inexperienced at boys' tussles, but I hit him so violently that the blood spurted from his nose. He said nothing, put his handkerchief to his face, and went away. He never teased me again.

Thinking of this, and of all those other yapping monsters at school, my hatred grew and wrapped around the silent tormentor who was watching me now as I ran forwards in the twilight. He had humiliated me in front of the whole Flight. He was going to keep me here all night was he? I would show him. I found myself further up the bricks than before, my hand over the top. It slipped on the damp concrete and I fell full length on the asphalt.

Jarred and breathless, I was up and trotting back to the starting mark before I had fully pulled my wits together. If it was only him I was throwing myself at, I would kick him until his teeth rattled, just as I was kicking at the bricks now. I would get my arm around his stiff neck and break it, as I had it over the wall. My elbow would be pumping between his ribs, in the way it was levering me over the edge. Flinging my tired body on top of the concrete shelter, so would I flatten him and squeeze the breath from his hateful frame.

He had not finished with me yet. As I dropped shakily down the far side and lumbered to the table where he sat, his face gleamed pallidly upwards.

'You have nothing to congratulate yourself on, Gill. You have taken seventeen attempts and two hours and twenty minutes to carry out a simple trial that on average took the members of your Flight forty seconds. Not good enough, Gill. This fiasco will go in your records. More will be expected of you in the future. You may dismiss.'

What a bastard. Going on right to the end. I had done it, after all. Stumbling painfully back to Trafalgar Avenue, I never thought that without the spur of the hatred he induced I would not have made it.

No one in the billet asked how I had got on, or made any reference to my earlier failures. Bruises made sleep difficult, and the next morning I felt very odd: hot as a furnace and aching intolerably. It did not take much persuading from Wyndham for me to report sick. This time it was as well that I had brought my satchel with overnight kit. I had a temperature of 104 and was sent straight by ambulance to the nearest military sick-bay at Boston.

VI

I remember little of the next twenty-four hours. My condition was diagnosed as influenza with a high fever. My body was taking a revenge that for years was customary: following a period of intense effort with a relapse into the ill-health that had accompanied so much of my childhood.

I was in the sick-bay only three days, being discharged as soon as my temperature returned to normal. During this time I missed our final passing-out parade and the celebratory football and hockey matches that followed. I could not have cared less. Once my fever began to abate, I thoroughly enjoyed myself. Illness was a familiar condition. I knew how to get the best out of it. There was the additional comfort of a real mattress instead of the hard biscuits of the billet, and sheets, coarse but clean. Even the sharp, alcoholic tang of drugs and antiseptics were old friends.

I sipped my Bovril and Ovaltine contentedly and luxuriated in the frequent bed baths, meant to bring my temperature down. The male nursing orderlies were an easygoing crowd, and the other patients a cross-section from all the services. Talking to them had an odd effect on me, considering the incompetence I had recently displayed. I wrote to my mother: 'There were chaps in our ward who had escaped from Greece, one from Dunkirk, one who had come from New Zealand to fly a Wellington bomber, a stoker in a submarine and another who was in an armed trawler, not to mention several men of over fifty who had served throughout the last war and volunteered again for this one. I wouldn't like to think that my war effort was confined to living in absolute safety and moderate comfort.'

How best to serve? It was a recurring problem, triggered not so much by patriotism as by social conventions. Most of my peers in Canterbury had been, like myself, in the Air Training Corps, and were now training as pilots or navigators, as I would have done had I not failed the last medical. Others were in the commandos or Merchant Navy. Not to be at risk, when so many others were, seemed morally unacceptable.

I discussed the problem with Wyndham the evening I got back.

'It's silly to think we would be much good in a scrap,' he said calmly.

'That's not the point. We ought to be in danger.'

'Seems to me we're all in danger. Like you in Canterbury. It's more dangerous to be a civilian living in the docks in Plymouth or Liverpool than to be in an army unit stationed in Iceland.'

'I know all that. It's true of course. Total war and so on, it comes to everyone. But that's *passive* suffering.' Wyndham looked up quizzically.

'You think we ought to volunteer for something nasty?'

'I don't know. If you'd seen these people in hospital . . . Then there's that friend of Auerbach's, the one who's in the other Flight. Remember? He'd been a gunner in Wellingtons, crashed, and got so badly smashed up he was totally discharged, yet here he is, signing on as an airman – he had been an officer before – anything to get back into action.'

'I know what you mean,' said Wyndham, diving into our bookshelf. 'While you were away I was reading your Stephen Spender. Do you remember this poem?'

He read it slowly, in his surprisingly deep, thoughtful voice.

I think continually of those who were truly great

. . . . .

Near the snow, near the sun, in the highest fields,
See how these names are fêted by the waving grass
And by the streamers of white cloud
And whispers of wind in the listening sky.
The names of those who in their lives fought for life,
Who wore at their hearts the fire's centre.
Born of the sun, they travelled a short while towards the sun
And left the vivid air signed with their honour.

The grave splendour of the words brought tears to my eyes. For a moment I saw myself plunging ashore on some rocky moonlit coast, a knife between my teeth, an image that changed instantly to me dragging an injured pilot from the burning wreckage of his plane. It was pure sentimentality of course; I would have cut my mouth on the knife and burnt my toes. I was a liability, best kept out of trouble.

Reading my thoughts, Wyndham said gently: 'I don't think action is the most important thing. I think we need to keep clear in our minds what we want to preserve. So much is falling . . . We need to hang on to what we believe to be good, so it doesn't go down with everything else.'

Part of my mind agreed with him, but I found the idea of this giant melodrama moving inexorably past on the stage, while I was still in the wings, intolerable. I must be in it somehow, but how? The thought of actual fighting, of killing Germans, was impossible and disgusting. It was most unlikely I would ever be trusted with a rifle again, now this course was virtually over. The chances were I would end up in some quiet backwater. That was what my parents would prefer and my general weediness made appropriate.

The paradox was still teasing me the following night. At the very beginning of our six weeks, everyone in the squad had contributed sixpence to a sweepstake that was to be drawn at the end. This had been done while I was in the sick-bay. I won and, richer by twelve shillings and sixpence, took Wyndham, John the Irish film extra, and Maconachie the cockney out for supper in the little café across Drummond Road. It was both a celebration and a farewell. Any day our posting would come through and we would be scattered.

Maconachie was particularly caustic about my dreams of glory.

'That's all a wank, mate. The thing to do is find a cushy billet and keep out of trouble.'

'You don't really mean that, after everything that's happened to your part of London.'

'I do, and how. I've had the war up to here. My war was being scared shitless in my granny's cellar, night after night, in Brixton. Now I'm in it I'm going to have a soft time.'

'I don't see how it's in our power to choose, any more than we know where we are going in the next few days,' said Wyndham.

'I don't agree with that,' said John. 'After all, we're only just in. There's always ways and means of getting what you want. In my experience, the best is to walk straight towards it.'

'You can do that if you like, mate. But if anybody asks me to volunteer for anything, my answer will be the same as the feller who, when he'd made his girl pregnant, was asked what steps he intended to take. "Bloody big ones," he replied, and was never seen again.'

Maconachie, with his crumpled anxious face, could always deflate us into laughter. But he meant what he said.

'I don't think it's so easy to find a quiet corner,' said John. 'There's danger everywhere. Even here. We've had a couple of raids, some chaps killed.'

'Don't worry about me, I'll find a place,' said Maconachie with conviction.

'It would be easier if you were an officer,' murmured Wyndham. 'We're just pawns in the game.'

'I don't know about that,' contested John. 'Did being a brother of the King stop the Duke of Kent crashing?'

'I saw him just a few weeks before he died,' I said. 'He came to Canterbury a couple of days after the Blitz. I was one of the reporters who went round with him.'

'What was he like?'

'A bit of a ponce. He wore lipstick and yellow make-up.'

'Effete bugger,' said Maconachie.

'No, they all do,' explained John. 'All the Royal Family. They think it makes them look better in photographs.'

'Well,' I said, 'I think it's a shock for ordinary people when they meet them. Blue round his eyes and a black outline – might have been an Ancient Egyptian.'

'Could as well be an Ancient Egyptian now, couldn't he?' said Maconachie. 'Dead as Pharaoh, isn't he?'

'That's what I mean,' said John. 'Death levels us all. Look at that general who was going to take over in the Desert. He was shot down on his way to Cairo.'

'General Gott that was,' said Wyndham.

'He was doing what you said earlier, John,' said Maconachie. 'Stepping forward to take command. Fat lot of good it did him. He'd been better getting his men growing cabbages in Lancashire.'

'He was said to be a jolly good tank general,' I said.

'Pull the other one, mate. We haven't got a general that's won a battle, except against the Eyeties. When we did have one that looked promising, that Wavell, we shipped him double-quick out of the way to India.'

'The one who went out to replace Gott my father says is very good,' I said.

'How does he know?'

'Well, this Montgomery was head of Southern Command. He was stationed near Canterbury. He made all the big-wigs under him go running every morning. Said they ought to be as fit as their men. Some of the other generals hated him.'

'Sounds as if he'd got the right idea,' said John.

'Probably a nutter,' said Maconachie. 'There's something about getting to be Top Brass. Turns your head to metal, too.'

'Oh, I don't know,' I said, 'you can't say that about Rommel.'

'Ah, but he's a genius, isn't he? There aren't many of them around.'

'Perhaps he'll find his match in this Montgomery,' said Wyndham.

'Garn,' said Maconachie. 'You mark my words. The days when a British general could mean anything are over. Only two things count in this war now: Russian manpower and American machinery. We'll lose if the stuff isn't made quicker than the men are killed off.'

His conviction put a temporary chill on us.

'I think you're wrong,' said John quietly. 'Individuals still count. Leadership counts. Look at Churchill.'

Maconachie could change his opinion as fast as his tongue could wag.

'You may be right, mate. Fact is, I hate generals 'cause not many of them come from Brixton.'

Thin slices of ham with chips had been followed by small portions of synthetic almond tart and cups of tea, the consistency and colour of liquid mud. These could be our last moments together.

'We must all meet after the war,' said John. 'Where shall it be?'

'How about Veeraswamy in Regent Street?' suggested Wyndham. 'The food's delicious and it's fun. All the waiters wear turbans.'

'That's Indian, isn't it?' I said. 'I've never had Indian food.'

'You may have too much in the next few months,' said Maconachie. 'How we going to know how to meet anyway?'

'Just leave your name with the doorman. He'll pass it on. I know him well,' said Wyndham.

'I wonder what adventures we'll all have before then,' said John, raising his tea cup. 'Here's to that meeting anyway.'

'It's probably years away,' said Maconachie.

'We may not recognise each other,' said Wyndham.

'Or want to know,' said Maconachie.

'What are you going to do, after it's over?'

'Me? Back to the barrow, I suppose. If this bloody rationing ever ends.'

'Won't it be marvellous,' said Wyndham dreamily. 'I can't even imagine the lights. Do you remember Piccadilly, all those colours flashing and moving?'

'One year my parents took me up specially to see them,' I said. 'I was about twelve years old.'

'My mum and dad took me every Christmas to Regent Street. They used to have lit-up angels and things strung across,' said Maconachie. 'As a treat I'd look round Hamleys. That was a great toyshop, but too expensive for us. They'd buy me some little thing that had caught my attention without me knowing. Then it would turn up in my stocking.'

'My parents used to take me, too,' said Wyndham.

'I've been there. It had the most amazing model trains,' I said.

'I suppose your childhood was spent in a bog, John,' said Maconachie.

'Not at all, there are some fine shops in Dublin.'

'And theatres too, I've heard. But you wouldn't go back?'

'No, there's no film industry to mean anything.'

'How about you, Windy? What will you do?'

'Not much choice, I'm afraid. Nose back to the balance sheets.'

'You don't like it in the City?'

'The City's all right. I'm not sure I'm cut out to be an accountant. It'll get better as time goes on, I suppose.'

'What about you, Prof?'

'Well, I'll be up in London, too. I'm going to Guy's to be a doctor.'

'You, a doctor! Gawd help your patients!'

'What do you mean,' I said huffily.

'No offence meant, mate, but let's face it, you are likely to sew up the operation leaving the scissors inside.'

'Rubbish,' I said briskly. 'Anyway, I probably won't be a surgeon. My father wanted to be a family doctor.'

'What's what your father wanted got to do with it?'

'Well, he wasn't able to be a doctor, because they had no money, so his father put him in a bank. It was a white collar job, and safe. So my being one will fulfil his ambition, you might say.'

'Seems a rum reason. My dad always wanted to be a millionaire, but that won't help me to be one.'

'My father's a surgeon, in Cork, as it happens,' said John. 'It's a dramatic life, but I can't be sure you'd be cut out for it, Mike.'

'There is one thing.' Maconachie's spectacles glinted evilly. 'You have to deliver babies, don't you? They say there'll be a baby boom after the war. Perhaps you'll help to bring it down.'

'You watch it, Mac,' I protested. 'Or some day I'll prescribe gripe water for you when you've got an appendicitis.'

Their ribbing flustered me. Medical studies seemed far away, and I had none of the confidence about mastering them that John seemed to have about his acting future.

'I'll be out of your clutches, anyway,' he smiled. 'I'll be in Hollywood.'

'You so sure you'll get there?'

'Of course. It's the place for stars, and I'm going to be a star. Bigger than Errol Flynn.'

He grinned with all his glittering even teeth.

'I wouldn't mind going overseas,' muttered Maconachie. 'Australia perhaps.'

'You mean, emigrate?' asked Wyndham.

'Why not? England's all right for you lot, but it's not so hot for my sort. Old Gidney goes on a bit, but he's right. Things ought to change. Not that I suppose they ever will.'

I could not imagine how things could change and be better. The England I knew, the orchards and farms and coastal towns of Kent, seemed perfect; and after the war, like Canterbury itself, must be restored and renewed and revitalised to continue, just as before. That was why we were fighting the war, wasn't it?

On my return from sick-bay, I had celebrated by stopping off at Skegness's only bookshop. There I had bought a book by Lord David Cecil, *The English Poets*. It was one of a new series, *Britain in Pictures*, and with eight colour plates seemed good value at *2s 6d*. Cecil, whom I had heard of as an Oxford don, began by saying:

> Every great nation has expressed its spirit in art: generally in some particular form of art . . . German music and Italian painting flourished, at most, for two hundred years. England has gone on producing great poets from the fourteenth century to today: there is nothing like it in the history of the arts.
>
> Nature placed England in the Gothic North, the region of magic and shadows, of elves and ghosts, and romantic legend. But from an early period she has been in touch with classic civilisation, with its culture, its sense of reality, its command of form.

Yes, and the variety of language was matched by the infinite subtlety of the English climate; those endless gradations of light and shade, those sudden reverses, melodramatic shafts of sunshine, Ibsenian gloom of torrential rain, Celtic twilight of mists and mellow fruitfulness, soft dews of springtime, grandeur of autumnal woods and purple hillsides, feathery clouds of summer and towering Babylonian stormscapes of winter. And above all and around all, the sea; the sea that dashed against her shores on all sides and every mood, changeable as the spirit of man, more vast, more powerful. A constant corrective to arrogance and pride, a consolation to all merely human misery, a parable for every emotion, the highway to all the lands of the earth. Thrice lucky Englishmen, to be given this climate, this island, this glittering ocean home. I had never been abroad, but lying on a Kentish field in summer I knew I was in the best place on earth.

Not for us the fierce contrasts of continental heats and iron frosts, the endless winters of the north, the barren deserts of the tropics. Our equable damps and cools had produced an equally temperate race, balanced but argumentative, judicious yet capable of passion: the stolid Saxon given a heady dash of Welsh rhetoric, Scots iron, Irish magic. A nation of shopkeepers, nature-loving country parsons, contentious dons, poetic cricketers, cheeky City chappies, women novelists, long-striding fair-skinned beauties, great actors, noble talkers, eccentric squires, philanthropists, iron-masters, robber barons, Puritan soldiers, breeding geniuses such as Darwin and Newton, James Watt and Faraday, Thomas More and David Hume, Boyle and Rutherford, Charlie Chaplin and Frank Woolley, Livingstone, Captain Cook, Nelson and Alfred the Great.

Englishmen produced not only the Romantic Movement, but the Industrial Revolution; not only the bowmen who stood firm at Agincourt, but the sailors who charted the Seven Seas; the explorers and legislators of the greatest empire the world had ever known. The sun never set on the dazzling kaleidoscope of her peoples, enriched at home by embattled minorities seeking freedom from oppression, Huguenot refugees in the sixteenth century, Flemish Protestants in the seventeenth, Lithuanian and Russian Jews in the nineteenth, right down to the Poles and Czechs and Norwegian and Dutch and Free French of the present day. We might have had our dark Satanic mills, but we were also the outstanding bastion of freedom, the forerunner in the fight against slavery, in the defence of free speech, the development of justice and democracy. Unconquered for nearly a thousand years, we would come yet again to the rescue of captive Europe and liberate her from the tyranny of the new dictatorships as we had in the past from Napoleon and Louis XIV, and Catholic Spain.

> The meteor flag of England
> Shall yet terrific burn,
> Till danger's troubled night depart
> And the star of peace return.

The tricky thing was to get a hand to the flagpole without being frizzled by the sparks. Unthinkable to moulder these halcyon days in some cushy Home Counties billet; equally unpalatable to be thrust, a hapless pawn, into an outpost airstrip in Burma, easy road-building fodder for the encroaching Japanese. To create a bang not a whimper; that was all important. But how you do that at eighteen, when a ten-foot wall was nearly an insurmountable obstacle? It was obvious, I needed influence and a clear view of what to aim for: I had neither.

An example of the general haplessness was upon us with the end of our course. Days of indecision followed while we waited for our posting. We had no idea where we would be going. Most of us were put to work on neighbouring farms. I had two days' potato picking, back-breaking work in the enormous fields of Lincolnshire, where the end of the furrow curved away over the horizon. Then, returning with chapped hands and broken nails in the mid-October twilight on an open lorry, I heard we were to be off the following morning.

There was a typed movement order pinned on the entrance to the billet. I was to go to the Plotters' School, Leighton Buzzard, whatever that might be. Wyndham was posted to the Clerical Reception Centre, Chipping Walden. There was no time for considered farewells. It was already 8 o'clock and we were to depart at 3.30 in the morning. A desperate scurry of packing, polishing and final cleaning followed. The billet had to be made as shiny as we had found it. We left the pictures from the *Illustrated London News* on the walls, by special permission from Corporal Barker. He said they looked cheerful and appropriate, as the next intake would be running up to Christmas.

'Besides, it'll remind me of you daft couple, my terrible twins,' he winked, giving Wyndham a cuff on the chest.

We were going to miss Corporal Barker. We were going to miss our little room with its dormer window looking on the phosphorous lines of the sea. For six weeks it had been our home, an intimate haven above the vast impersonal pistons of the war machine. We wondered how long the new occupants would find Piero della Francesca to their taste. We were even going to miss the comical peaked turret of our billet and the stubby curve of Trafalgar Avenue, with its abrupt termination in the gorse-covered dunes. For the last time, we formed up in the grey pre-dawn and marched away from the murmur of the shore line.

This time, loaded though I was with all my equipment, I was able to carry my kit bag without assistance. It took three hours of short marches and long halts to reach the station. Every airman in the place seemed to be leaving, and in their wisdom the authorities had planned we should all reach the station at the same time. There was another very long halt on the road outside. We were given hot tea and a packet of sandwiches.

Eventually, at about 8 a.m., names began to be called. Mine came up quite soon. I shook hands with Wyndham; we promised yet again to write. A wave to the others standing in their ranks and I shouldered the kit bag: a lumpy burden. Why had I not learned to pack it neatly?

'Hurry up, you there,' shouted the NCOs down the long lines of the squads. 'At the double, now; we haven't got all day.'

I broke into a rickety trot, stumbling under the weight. I was far back in the ranks and I could hear the hiss of the waiting train. I was sweating in my greatcoat, an unaccustomed covering, made more constricting by the webbing buckled over the top of it. Water bottle banged against one thigh, side-pack against the other, main pack sawed against backbone, bending under the kit bag. Some protuberance in it, jouncing against my ear, tilted my cap over my eyes and threatened to skitter it at my feet. Ramming it on my head, my free hand caught my glasses, slipping them down my nose. My exit from Skegness threatened to be as ignominious as my arrival.

There was a muffled cheer as I reached the station entrance. Was it a farewell from my friends, or an ironic acknowledgement of my dishevelled appearance? No time to look back: far down between the slender metal pillars I saw Auerbach among those getting into the train. He was on his way to the officers' training centre at Cosford. There was no one else I knew. I bundled into a crowded compartment of strangers, just as the train began its premonitory jerks and whistles. I leant back with a long huff of relief, nearly dislocating my neck on the sharp edge of the back-pack as the train surged away.

What could I have put in it that was so rigid? The tin helmet was strapped on the outside of the pack as regulations demanded. Clumsily, I undid the shoulder braces and shrugged it off. Might as well be as comfortable as possible, on what I expected was going to be a long and tedious journey. How awful that after all that hanging about there had been no real chance to say goodbye to Wyndham. Now he had gone out of my life, perhaps forever, leaving not a trace behind. I should at least have asked for one of his paintings or drawings. I knew that in some ways he was the first adult friend I had, and I would have dearly loved a keepsake.

Heaving the back-pack up onto the clothes rack, I paused. How had I ever managed to make it so square and neat? My packing was always a disaster; somehow it must have subsided into tidiness during the hours of marching and waiting. Hastily pulling out the flap and digging in an exploratory hand I pulled out a drawing of myself. 'M. in the billet at Skegness' it was captioned. You could see the Piero della Francesca on the wall. I was reading and looked rather too plump. Behind the drawing there was a wooden frame with a whole lot of watercolours pinned to it. It was Wyndham's collapsible easel. I had the mementoes now, rather too many. I also had all his underwear, his shirts and his spare uniform and spare boots. By the same token he would have those that belonged to me. I had his back-pack and he had mine. We had obviously picked up the wrong ones in the flurry of leaving the billet. On the outside they were, of course, interchangeable. But in the contents . . .

He would have my *English Poets* and *Point Counter Point* and Joad's *Guide to Modern Thought*. More importantly, his spare uniform would now be intended for someone six feet one inch, mine for someone five feet four inches. I looked at his shirts, neatly folded in front of the easel. Collar size fourteen; and he had acquired mine with collar size fifteen-and-a-half. His boots, which I now owned, were size seven; I needed size eight. I tried on the tin helmet: even that was tiny, resting on my head like an inverted ashtray. What a disaster. I groaned aloud. How could I go to a new posting carrying such a weight of demonstrable incompetence?

The other airmen watched my investigations with beady interest. Imagining the sort of charge I would be put on, the fines I would be subjected to, the time it would take to retrieve the lost items, enlivened the tedium of the journey. At the least, I would be put under open arrest for wilfully jeopardising RAF property. I glared out of the window in despair, trying to ignore their sniggering innuendoes. It was like my first train journey to join the RAF. I was a hopeless case, cut off and alienated from my fellow men. The comradeship I had managed to establish at Skegness was only a temporary illusion.

I could not help but blame Wyndham. I should have been sorry for him, swamped in shirts that would come over his ears and down below his knees: instead I felt anger that he had not prevented the disaster. He was older than me, more level-headed and sagacious, and he had not foreseen it. Once you thought about it, it was obviously an easy mistake to occur. A last-minute check of the contents of our equipment would have revealed it instantly. My mother would have done just that. Cautious, caring woman, she always checked and counter-checked everything. Of course, she would have done my packing for me in the first place. I would not expect Wyndham to replace her exactly, but he might have looked after me better.

I looked out at flat wide skies that seemed to have the reflection of the sea in them. Seagulls, like tiny flecks of white paint, were landing on the fresh brown of a ploughed field. Strutting about, they were each an animated question mark to my competence. Why had I not noticed that the shape was different? I could never have created those neatly packed rectangles. Why had I not sensed the difference on my back? And how had little Wyndham borne that misshapen hump that would have been my pack between his shoulders for so long without question? No doubt we were two of a kind. Our mutual insufficiencies had drawn us together. Briefly, we had been able to shove up a fragile bastion against fate. This catastrophe appropriately terminated that blissful interregnum. Now, alone once more, we would suffer the unchecked buffets of malignant fortune.

The train chauntered slowly on, past level-crossings and little houses and gardens spired with dead sunflowers. Wainfleet, Thorpe Calvert, Little Seeping, Sibsey: the porters had the faces of wise old cobnuts. At last my compartment had lost interest in my fate. It was discussing the German campaign in Russia. A terrible battle had been raging at distant Stalingrad. For four weeks the Germans had thrown in attack after attack, but the defendants fought on among the ruins. The opposing strategies were analysed as the train proceeded cautiously along a canal. It was an October day of transient sunlight and high cloud. Old men sat fishing in their overcoats. Near Hubberts Bridge suddenly there was a heron, red beak and grey feathers frozen on one leg above the green slime.

My compartment dwelt with wincing relish on the privations suffered by both sides. In hushed voices it luxuriated in the horror: the disgusting things that the Russians did to captured Germans, the sickening atrocities meted out by the Germans to entire villages. It was well known that the Germans, especially the SS, were fiends incarnate. As for the Russians, they were barely human. Meanwhile, we were making rather better time, each little red brick halt reeling past in its pocket handkerchief of ploughed fields: Swineshead, Heckington, Sleaford. The names proclaimed a long-matured care for the land, a pride that gave each cottage its unique dignity. Unimaginable that the mayhem of total war should ever harrow here. Or that disaster should befall oneself. Yet the final terror lay in this: the whole world was now drawn as tight as a single membrane; distant pain caused a twinge to one's own skin. The same contagion that had desolated the cottages of the Ukraine might spring up in the back gardens of England; had in modified form already done so, as I had witnessed a few weeks before, looking along the main street of Canterbury, ablaze from end to end. Would the disease be mortal for all mankind? Only time would tell. I was a pessimist by nature, and my brief experience had not made me more sanguine. The sharp rectangles of Wyndham's back-pack demonstrated that it was only a matter of luck.

We lurched to a halt. NCOs ran along the platform ordering us to de-train. It was Grantham, a largish station, crowded now with troops, standing singly or in bemused groups in the surrounding clutter of their equipment, like so many defrocked Christmas trees. I looked for someone in authority, to whom I could report my loss. No one seemed remotely interested. I supposed it would have to wait until I could report it at my new station. What a way to appear on a course, which I had been selected for on supposed grounds of high intelligence.

I paused on the edge of the platform indecisively. At that moment another train came through. It did not stop but, with airmen leaning from every window, passed with a steady clank and warning shouts from the guards. As if in slow motion, Wyndham passed before my nose. He had not seen me; he was looking off into the middle distance, an absent smile on his lips, obviously entranced by the animated scene. I rushed after him, screaming his name. Startled, he looked round, and broke into a smile of delighted recognition. Trying to keep up, impeded by the crowds and the mass of equipment that covered the platform I waved the back-pack at him. He waved his free hand cheerfully back. Obviously no inkling of the disaster had yet struck him.

'I've got your pack and you've got mine!' I shrieked. 'Throw it out!'

We were surrounded by laughing, cursing, bawling troops; by warning guards; by other cries of recognition as other acquaintances were renewed and last messages passed; by shouted imprecations as I kicked through piles of gear; by the increasing clatter of the train as it began to pick up speed, the end of the platform coming in sight. Wyndham could not understand what I meant. I shouted again and again, getting hoarser and more desperate. Eventually I threw the pack hard at his chest. He reeled back with the shock but instinctively clutched it.

'That's your pack,' I screamed. 'Now throw out mine.'

The train was beginning to outpace me, but I caught the look of understanding dawning on his face. He had recognised his own pack, but instead of throwing back mine, he plunged back into the interior of the coach, to be instantly replaced by several other airmen.

'Get out of the way, let him get back,' I shrieked and gesticulated, but they only grinned and waved. I knew what had happened. He had been standing in the corridor and was now forcing himself back into the compartment, struggling to retrieve my pack from under the piles of others in the racks, falling over people's feet, being obstructed by uncomprehending and belligerent multitudes. Meanwhile the train was getting into its stride. I had to run full pelt to keep up with it. Fortunately this was easier because the waiting troops thinned out towards the end of the platform.

In a moment it was going to be too late: the airmen at the window were pulling up the sash. To be cheated at the very moment when all might have been retrieved. Just as I reached the end of the platform where it sloped down into the gravel, Wyndham precipitously reappeared and shoved the window down again.

'Michael!' he shouted.

'Wyndham!' I shouted back.

For a moment we looked at each other eye to eye. Then the train shot away in a triumphant burst of speed, and the drumming on the tracks beside me rose to a crescendo, drowning the cat-calls and whoops from the platform. From far down the rapidly receding coaches, a hand and arm appeared and tossed in the air a squarish grey canvas object. Heavy, it described a lazy parabola and fell on the gravel between the tracks. Disregarding the warning notices, I leapt over the barrier and sprinted the intervening fifty yards or so. Suddenly I felt light as a feather.

Perhaps fate was not going to be unremittingly unkind. Perhaps my war was going to be that mixture of solace and boredom that was the dominant tone of life. Perhaps the RAF would turn out to be a sort of extended family, protective, authoritarian, but kindly. Perhaps the terrors that were unleashed and stalking the world would only be allowed to pace nearby at night, in the dreams and perceptions of sleep.

I bent over the fallen pack. Lumpish and now mottled with wheel grease from the tracks, it was undoubtedly mine. I seized it in triumph. As I straightened, a heavy grip fell on my shoulder. I turned to face a couple of Military Policemen.

'Can't you read, Airman?' said one sternly. 'You're not allowed on the tracks. And what are you doing, exchanging property? Seems to me you've got a lot of explaining to do.'

I had.

9

HUT 50

I

My memory of Leighton Buzzard is scanty. I thought that I was there for a couple of days; letters home show that it was nearly two weeks. Time flies when you are occupied in learning a mass of new and interesting things. Even the detail of that slips away. What remains is a sense of the atmosphere; a not very large private house with lecture halls and demonstration rooms and a comfortable library in which to sit and study the new world of radio direction finding. What we would later call, under American influence: radar.

All that was fascinating and miles away from the spit and polish of Skegness. Most of our instructors seemed to be middle-aged men who smoked pipes and strolled about in their shirt sleeves. If they weren't turning *Finnegans Wake* into a crossword puzzle there was likely to be a volume of Euclidean geometry under their arms. I was more concerned in reconstituting the Gill parcel service. Apples travelled up from Kent and in return I posted home my dirty underwear. This system continued pretty well until the end of the war. As for the war itself, the decisive stage had been reached this very week: the battle of El Alamein in the Western Desert and the far more ferocious siege of Stalingrad away in central Asia. As Churchill said (afterwards): 'Before Alamein we never had a victory. After Alamein we never had a defeat.'

Not that there weren't some nasty moments still to come. One was just round the corner. Once the course was over we expected to be posted to a regional centre. Each of those centres had a control room where the aerial defence of the region was planned. But four or five of us were simply given a route order. We were to report to King's Cross at midday to take a train to an unspecified destination.

'Ah ha,' said Peter Williams, a bright lad from Sheffield, 'you know what that means don't you? We're going somewhere by sea.'

'Why should it mean that?' I asked.

'Ships taking troops overseas never get announced,' said Peter wisely. 'They don't want to tell the U-boats they're coming.' That was an unpleasant thought.

'But we haven't had any embarkation leave,' protested Barry Shepherd, a twenty-one-year-old Irishman who had come over from neutral Eire hoping to fly a Spitfire. His will was strong, but his heart proved to be weak; so, like Peter and me, he was regraded to special duties, whatever they were.

'Embarkation leave is not a right, but a privilege,' said Peter. (He was going to be a lawyer one day.) 'Besides, we might not be travelling so far away. Iceland perhaps, or Gibraltar; perhaps even Northern Ireland.'

'Well of that lot I'd prefer Gibraltar,' said Barry, 'at least the sun shines there. But all those glaciers in Iceland: it's such a long way from anywhere.'

'And King's Cross is a northern line station,' I said. 'Perhaps we'll go to the Outer Hebrides.'

For a long time we appeared not to be going anywhere. We were sent to the forces canteen on the platform to have powdered egg and sausage. At last, whistles blew and loud-speaker announcements herded us aboard a very long, very dirty train that still stank of its last occupants.

It was 3 p.m. by the time we chuntered slowly out of London. We talked, some played cards. The train was pretty full, entirely of soldiers, airmen, sailors and tough-looking characters who might have been builders or miners. Through the evening, we stopped occasionally at darkened stations; a few, loaded with kit bags and rifles, got off. Similar shrouded groups got on board. It was impossible to read by the dim blue light that blackout allowed us. We were a subdued lot; nobody sang or played the mouth organ as they did in films of troops on the move. As the night progressed, boredom drew us into a disharmony of snores, groans, gasps, coughs, farts and the mumbled expression of uneasy dreams.

Some other sound startled me to wakefulness. The rhythm of the train had changed. The clanking had taken on a deeper, slower note and above it was a shrill squalling. It took a few minutes to recognise the calling of seagulls.

Peter Williams gave me a triumphal wink. It was 4.30 a.m. Shadowy giants slowly passed the carriage windows. With a final grumbling of brakes our train stopped among them. The pallid sky lightened minute by minute revealing the monstrous shapes as the cranes and derricks of a quayside. Among much shouting and clattering of arms we were assembled on the dock and marched in any sort of order up the gangway onto a large grey-painted ship. Lines were cast off and very quickly we were heading out to sea.

It seemed as though our chain of command was anxious to get us out of reach of observers on the land. Yet there were few who could have seen us from the shore. As we passed the last arm of the harbour the landscape fell back and widened. Mountains, snowy-peaked range upon range, rose above the horizon. It was my first view of the Highlands; touched, as I watched, by the earliest gleams of sunlight. This was grandeur beyond anything I had seen.

Leaning on the rail I half-remembered lines by Wordsworth, the first extract from one of his long autobiographical poems, describing a similar vision of mountains appearing when he rowed away from them.

> And, as I rose upon the stroke, my boat
> Went heaving through the water, like a swan;

When from behind that craggy steep, till then
The bound of the horizon, a huge cliff,
As if with voluntary power instinct,
Upreared its head. I struck, and struck again,
And growing still in stature, the huge cliff
Rose up between me and the stars, and still,
With measured motion, like a living thing,
Strode after me . . .

. . . . .

Magnificent
The morning rose, in memorable pomp,
Glorious as e'er I had beheld . . .

'That's Stranraer in Galloway where we embarked.' Barry had come up besides me. 'We'll be landing at Larne. It's just north of Belfast. We'll soon see Ireland. This is a very short crossing. Just as well perhaps.'

As if to underline his words, a staccato burst of gunfire made me nearly jump out of my skin. It was the Bofors gun in the stern, testing its readiness to respond if any Jerry submarines put in an appearance. Luckily none did.

By 8 a.m. we had landed. Another train journey took us by midday to the grey, rainy city of Belfast. So it was to be Ireland where my wartime adventures were really to begin. I did not take much to the first view of this dreary city seen through the windows of a camouflaged bus. Office blocks gave way to residential suburbs. The bus carried us into a hillside park, topped by an imposing neo-classical building. This was Stormont Park – the Parliament building now taken over as the headquarters of the RAF in Northern Ireland.

On the far side of the park, Nissen huts were scattered among the trees. We were told to find Hut 64. Close up, it was no more inviting. Pools of rainwater lay on the concrete floor between the metal-framed beds. Now we saw the value of the rubber boots we had cursed having to carry all the way from Cardington. We soon grew used to putting them on before we put a foot out of bed.

That first day it was impossible not to think nostalgically of the cosy little room under the eaves at Skegness that I had shared with Wyndham. No chance of putting up an intellectual pin-up through the rusting corrugated iron walls of Hut 64. We had plenty of time to contemplate the shortcomings of our new abode. In acknowledgement of the stressed strain of our journey, all the new arrivals were stood down until the following morning. It was the middle of the afternoon. We had been given a meal that seemed a mixture of breakfast, dinner (it was never called lunch) and tea. We were confined to camp. In Ireland we always had to sign out and back at the guard house.

There seemed nothing to do except go to bed. I was just working out how to get my trousers off without getting them soaked when the door was thrown open. A strange humped figure hopped in. I recognised him as Crawford, the least attractive of the group from Leighton Buzzard. Much older than most recruits, he was always making himself unpopular by his sour, spiteful remarks. Now he seemed to be bubbling over with unexpected glee. Positively dancing with delight he shouted: 'Someone here is from Canterbury. Who is it?'

I said nothing, but several of the others pointed me out. He came huddling across, snorting and grunting like a tetchy pig.

'Yes, I thought so,' he leered. 'Do you know what's happened to your town, eh? Do you know?' I had never seen such an embodiment of real evil.

'I don't know what you mean,' I said as haughtily as I could.

'No you don't do you? I'm the one to tell you.'

'Come on, get on with it,' someone shouted from the other side of the hut.

'Yes, you all want to know, don't you? Well, I'll tell you. Canterbury has been wiped out, destroyed, blitzed to bits.'

I felt a wave of relief. 'The bombing was last June. The damage was terrible, but people carried on. Ceilings came down in our house, but my parents were able to go on living there.'

'Were living there. All gone now. There was a new raid yesterday in daylight, made the one in June seem like a tea party. It was a market day. All the local people in from all round. Huge casualties.'

I felt that I had been struck with a knife. Yesterday *was* the market day. What if something had happened to my parents? They would not know how to reach me. They had no address since Leighton Buzzard. Nor did I know how I could get in touch with them. We had already been told that all mail to and from England would be subject to censorship. We had to pass unsealed to the duty officer of the day any letters home. This rigorous scouting of anything crossing the Irish Sea was because southern Ireland was the independent state of Eire. It was supposed to be neutral; but it was widely believed to be passing on information to the Germans and even sheltering U-boats in the many coves and inlets on the rocky south coast.

And what about my parents? They would wonder why I had not made contact with them. Perhaps they were hurt and needing me. Not being able to reach them was intolerable. Barry, coming from southern Ireland, understood better the peculiar relations engendered by his part of the island being neutral. He suggested we went to the guard room in the camp to see if the Military Police could help. It was from one of the police that Crawford had heard about the bombing.

So Barry and I set out. A true new friend, he did not ask me if I wanted his company, he just came along. I don't know whether I could have coped alone. Remember that we had reached the camp only that afternoon. We did not know its layout. It was now evening; a damp mist dripped from the trees and joined the tenuous wisps of fog that hung around the narrow pathways. What lights there were were dim and heavily masked. All the buildings were the ubiquitous Nissen huts, whether they served as canteen, NAAFI, Orderly Room, ablutions,

Medical Office or toilets. At this time of the evening there were few
people about. Later I was to realise that several hundred airmen were
living there at the time, and that our living quarters occupied by far the
greatest number of the huts.

Eventually we found the guard house. It was better lit than most of
the camp. Two police sergeants were sitting chatting by a window that
must have looked towards the main entrance to the park. Their assessing
gaze had that chilly regard which tends to go with authority. Barry did
most of the talking. He began by questioning whether there had been an
air raid on Canterbury the day before. There had; why did we want to
know? I explained that my home was there. Was it a big raid? As far as
they knew, yes. It had been in daylight and at low level. They didn't have
statistics of how many people had died. The police seemed inclined to
end the conversation at this point. I asked if there was any way I could
telephone my parents? The police looked sceptical. There was a public
telephone box at the side of the main square. It took the coin of the
realm, but it was often very difficult to get through to England.
However I could try.

I did try; on and off for three hours without avail. I would get an Irish
operator. He would explain how much it would cost and where I should
put the money. Then nothing would happen except a sound like the
rollers of a mighty sea. Sometimes I would get my money back,
sometimes not.

I came to learn every smudge and scratch on the glass panels of the
telephone kiosk. The main square was bordered by what seemed to be a
wood. From it gleamed a number of small lights. As I watched, several
of them moved and others appeared. They were not lights at all; what
could they be? Were they . . . eyes? Ugh, too big for mice. The flash
of a long tail gave the answer. They were rats. The camp was infested
by rats. They did not seem to mind the rain, which was now coming
down steadily. As I trudged back to Hut 64, their scuttling gaze
accompanied me.

Inside, the hut was no less wet than outside. The separate pools of water had become one continuous cataract which ran from one end of the hut to the other, following the natural incline of the hillside. Everyone was busy learning how to make the three separate sections of bedding into a mattress, without getting the blankets soaked by trailing them on the floor. Everyone, that is, except Crawford. His sneer followed me round the hut.

'Did you find out about your parents then?' he said with mock concern. When I shook my head he could not resist a malicious cackle.

'All the telephone lines will be down, of course.'

Never had I felt such isolation. Even being confronted with that awful wall on the Skegness battle course had been a challenge that was up to me. Now I felt, as people so often did in the clutches of a war as vast as this one, a helpless pawn in a ruthless game. If I could have prayed, it might have helped, but I had not kept up the momentary involvement in the church that followed my confirmation.

As I tried to compose myself for sleep on the hard greasy pillow which stank of the miseries of previous owners, I tried to think what I might have done to reach my parents. It was no use. I kept returning to my own separateness: this awful hut; the rat-infested camp; the viciousness of Crawford; the indifference of the Military Police; the hundreds of miles of sea and mountain which lay between me and my loved ones, and beyond them all the innocent millions who were facing destruction not from any fault of their own.

The next morning we were dismissed quite early having been allocated into various groups called watches. I went into the shopping district nearest to the park, found a post office and sent the following telegram to my parents: I UNDERSTAND THAT CANTERBURY WAS BLITZED LAST NIGHT STOP PLEASE WIRE 1638828 AC2 GILL HUT 64 HEADQUARTERS RAF NI HOME FORCES AND LET ME KNOW YOU ARE ALRIGHT STOP HOPING ALL IS WELL LOVE MICHAEL GILL.

As I wrote to them a day later:

I became more and more anxious as Monday progressed and brought no reply from you and in the evening I again tried in vain to get you on the telephone for 3½ hours. It is almost hopeless to attempt to ring up people from here – there is often a six-hour delay.

I should certainly not have got through to you yet but for the fact that I was discussing what to do about it with the other members of C Watch in the canteen at our place of work this morning when our squadron leader happened to overhear us. He asked me a lot of questions without saying anything, then said in his abrupt way, 'You can try and get through on Fighter Command Priority Line upstairs if you like.'

So I went on to the gallery among all the big-wigs, liaison officers, etc., and on that priority line got through in ten minutes! That was the reason I could not say much. I should have paid for it, because the call had to be booked as a personal one to an officer. One of the WAAF officers offered to have it in her name and would not let me pay her for it. That is typical of the officers here, though, they are a very decent lot; as are the other ranks.

It is very difficult to tell from the newspapers how bad the damage at Canterbury was or how heavy was the raid. Was it worse than the June blitz? Were you in at the time?

In fact, my mother had been gardening. The immediate danger warning sounded at the same time as the German planes flew directly overhead at treetop height. Looking up, my mother saw the black crosses on the wings. One pilot waved to her. Other onlookers were less lucky; thirty-two people were killed, including six children, and fifty-five seriously injured. Ninety Germany fighter bombers took part; far more than I was ever to see on the plotting table at Stormont.

II

Every third morning at 12.30 the airmen in C Watch assembled in front of the guard house. If it was raining (as it often was), there would be a small camouflaged bus waiting to take us to the Filter Room. If it was fine, Corporal Esmond got us into line and marched us off. It was only a twenty-minute walk out of the lower gateway to Stormont Park, along a pleasant country road, turning right up a small hill to the village where the RAF had taken over the local school and converted it into the brain centre of the air defence of Ulster and the western approaches to Britain.

Considering that most of us had just recently been on the introductory square-bashing course and loathed it, it was odd that we took the march to work as a pleasure. There was no steely flight sergeant to nag at our heels. Corporal Esmond was, like most of us, an air-crew reject and hence a friend. But it was also enjoyable to swing along in unison. Being over six feet tall, I was usually in the front rank with my new pals Barry Shepherd and Jim Blair, a bank clerk from Liverpool. When the sun shone, and the birds were a-twitter in the hedgerows, we often sang. It helped to keep us in step and expressed our general feelings:

> There once was a troopship
> Just leaving Bombay
> Bound for some blighty shore
> Heavily laden with time-expired men
> Bound for the land they adore.
> Bless 'em all. Bless 'em all,
> The long and the short and the tall,
> Bless all the sergeants and W O ones,
> Bless all the corporals and their blinking sons;
> For we're saying goodbye to them all
> As back to their billets they crawl.

You'll get no promotion
This side of the ocean
So cheer up my lads: bless 'em all.

This lively ditty was said to express the feelings of the ordinary service
man in the inter-war period, when the greatest danger was picking up
malaria or VD in some far corner of the Empire. But it enshrined one
uncomfortable legend that was still believed to be profoundly true: no
promotion on the *far* side of the ocean, east of Suez. If you were hustled
overseas before you had the time to establish your value, you would have
little opportunity for field decorations in the Burmese jungle or on one
of the Pacific Islands engulfed by the Japanese. More likely, an
uncomfortable and lingering death in a prison camp. We didn't know
how bad conditions were for Japanese prisoners. But some inkling had
trickled through. Enough to make us look anxiously at the notice board
in the Orderly Room every few days. Sure enough, after we had been in
Stormont about three weeks, a brief typewritten list gave seven or eight
names as the nucleus for a forthcoming draft overseas. My name was one
of them.

Well, wherever it was going to take me, it could hardly be wetter or
more uncomfortable than Stormont. Yet oddly enough I felt quite sorry
at the prospect of leaving so quickly. Why was this? Follow me past the
wooden sentry box that was the only outward sign of any change in the
school playground. The entrance hall was still lined with pegs about two
feet off the ground for the children to hang their coats on.

Beyond that, the entire school had been turned into one big room,
two storeys high. It was dominated by a huge table about twenty-five
feet square. On it was painted a map of the whole of Northern Ireland
and the Atlantic approaches. It was squared off like an Ordnance Survey.
Round it crowded some fifty men and women – airmen and WAAFs. At
first sight they appeared to be playing an abstruse form of tiddlywinks.
Some, wearing headsets, were leaning across the table putting down a

path of small counters; they were either red, white or black. Every thirty seconds the colour changed in accordance with the two large synchronised clocks that hung on opposite walls.

Those headsets were connected directly to one or other of the RDF stations which were scattered around the coast of north-west Ireland and the Irish Channel. There, on some lonely headland, the engineer on duty looking into his radar screen would spot the blip which might be a flight of seagulls or an approaching aircraft. He would speak into the microphone which connected him to one of the airmen clustered round the Filter Room table. His message would be terse; something like this: 'North West. Irish J for Jig, 54 32, one unknown at 8.' The direction told you which way the blip appeared to be going; the letters and figures synchronised the radar sweep with the grid on the Filter Room table; the description told you this unknown blip seemed to be on its own and at 8,000 feet. How quickly it was travelling would soon become apparent from the plots put down on the table at the command of the engineer watching his radar screen. Their change of colour every thirty seconds made it possible to get an accurate assessment of the unknown's speed. This would eliminate the flight of birds; and upstairs on the balcony the squadron leader who was the duty officer of the watch would look through his flight plans and decide that the relatively slow speed meant that this was a Catalina from Coastal Command that had been blown off course by the high early winter winds. (On the other hand, it might be a Flying Fortress or Liberator of the USA Air Force. Streams of these four-engined American bombers were flying to England at this time, signifying the decisive change in the balance of power which was coming with America's entry into the war.)

Everything that was flying at any time would be picked up by the radar stations and represented on the Filter Room table. As soon as the squadron leader in command had decided that in this case it was not a lonely German bomber looking for a suitable target, he would call out:

Unknown Friendly. That would be put in a little metal dish that went on the table beside the leading edge of the plots.

A continuous flow of information was broadcast to the two Operation Rooms, which actually had command of the fighter wings whose job it was to defend Ireland and the northern approaches. This was exactly the sort of job I would have volunteered for had I known it existed. There was an element of theatre about it and really tense drama when some *Unknown Friendly* turned into *Hostile One at 10* and a fighter flight scrambled to attempt an intercept.

It suited my temperament to have an overview on one not inconsiderable area of the war, and to feel I was looking down, like some minor god on Olympus, at the tangled fortunes of the actual contestants. I knew, too, that the speed of my response could have a brief impact on these far-flung waters. It was also a very sexy job. Moments of excitement were interspersed with periods of quiet. There were more WAAFs than airmen round the table jostling to get down the latest counter. The leading arrow of each identified plane was put down by a filter officer. They were all attractive, clever and emancipated young women. Often they would be humming the latest Gene Kelly number as they brushed past you. 'Swing your foot way 'round and bring it back, now that's what I call Ballin' the Jack,' or, 'I've got spurs that jingle jangle jingle,' murmured almost in your ear, accompanied by a whiff of perfume and a reminder that you had to call her Ma'am . . . No wonder that on our days off we would make for the nearest dance hall, where there were girls you could touch and who would be happy to follow your steps in the latest foxtrot.

The year 1943 was my great year for dancing. It was aided by the watch system which gave us twenty-four hours off every third day. It went like this: the first shift was 1–6 p.m., followed by five hours off, then back on duty at 11 p.m. A night's work might give you a couple of hours' snooze in the rest room, but might not. If you were sensible, when you came off duty at 8 a.m. you would have a late breakfast in the canteen, then go to bed for four or five hours so as to be sprightly and ready for the evening shift which was 6–11 p.m. Another short night's sleep and then you would be marching through the early morning mist to relieve the watch that had been up all night. You took over from them at 8 a.m. and were on till 1 p.m. Then began your twenty-four hours off duty.

The trouble was that every two or three weeks you had to spend a night guarding the entry gates to Stormont Park. Again, there were four of you and you got some time to relax on a camp bed between the two three-hour shifts marching up and down and stamping your feet in the mud to keep some feeling in them. There was little to keep you alert except the odd drunken airman whom you had to keep out of the sight of the Military Police Sergeant. Once, there was a rifle shot from the woods quite near by. It sounded like a whip crack against the fungoid dripping of the everlasting moisture from the trees. Perhaps it was the IRA. They were not very active in those days.

I was much more alarmed when nodding off in the sentry box another time I nearly dropped my rifle and hastily pulling myself together saw the whole road oozing and crawling towards me. For a moment I thought it must be an earthquake or the magma from a Celtic volcano (I had just been reading *The Story of San Michele*). Luckily, I now saw that the flood was crossing the road and was not going to engulf me. And the next moment I realised it was an immense army of rats. They were several deep and moving in an entirely purposeful way. There must have been thousands of them; I have never seen so many.

Usually one or other of the guard would find the opportunity to bayonet too bold a rodent; I never wanted to kill them and they rarely came near me. During the summer, guard duty could be quite a pleasant change with its smells of the damp earth and the rustle and twitter of the woodland.

We also had to guard the Filter Room itself. There in the village we only had an ancient .45 revolver to protect our plotters. Quite often, one of the off-duty WAAFs would come out with a cup of tea, and chat for a while.

Someone it did not suit at all was Crawford. Like me, he was down for the overseas draft. As time went on he became more and more edgy, shut off in a world of his own. This was literally true for guard duty. One evening, I went out to take over from him. It was a moonless night. As I neared the back of the sentry box I had the sense to call out. In response there was the metallic click of the revolver being cocked.

'Hey Crawfy, it's me: Gill from Canterbury,' I shouted as loudly as I could. I had a torch and shone it on my own face.

In its reflected light I saw two things. The twisted, fearful and fearsome face of Crawford peeping round the sentry box and just below it the gleam of the revolver, wavering, but pointing in my general direction.

'Hey, you don't want that any more.' I rushed forwards and grabbed the barrel; it didn't seem a time to delay. In fact, he merely dropped the gun and squeezed into the back of the sentry box. He stayed like that all night. In the morning two burly Military Policemen took him away. We never saw him again, though we heard he had gone into an asylum.

Less dramatic, but much more tiring, was another regular night chore that came our way every three weeks. This was to 'guard' Stormont. 'Guard' was a misnomer. Built as a parliamentary building, it housed some forty offices, each with a parquet floor that had to be polished and buffed. Each office was covered wall-to-wall in maps with flags and multi-coloured pins that had to be carefully dusted. I expect it must have been from here that one of the most vital strategies of the war, the Battle of the North Atlantic, was planned. Taking a breather from the hard labour on the floor, you could regale yourself on the secret statistics of U-boat losses and the thousands of tons of merchant ships sunk. Later, my curiosity was to have an unexpected reward.

III

A number of what seemed at the time to be quite minor events had long reverberations in my future life. My letters home showed how little anticipation I had of this. I suppose it was in part because all our mail had to be censored – and by the very officers we worked elbow to elbow with around the Filter Room table. Censorship was pretty strict. In an early letter home I referred to Dublin and Belfast: they were surely large enough cities for any snooping German to know that he was stealing a look at them from my account of going to a main street with an excellent bookshop and several cinemas on it. However, all names of towns were carefully cut out. As I wrote on both sides of the paper, my account on the reverse side of a game of golf, which I played with a South American volunteer, consisted of more holes than bunkers. (We quickly learned to write on only one side of the page.)

Our letters were made lengthier at this time than at any other period of the war because my parents were worried about my state of health. In 1943 I had three spells in the military hospital with bronchial fever. They were made memorable for me because as soon as my temperature began to go down I would be put on what were optimistically called 'light duties' in the cook house. This invariably included scraping out the half-dozen enormous pans that had contained the breakfast porridge for some fifty or sixty hospital inmates. Now if I see any other guest in a hotel slurping up that glutinous, adhesive, vomitous-looking substance, I can barely repress a shudder. If the Highlander can be considered somewhat phlegmatic at the start of the day, some of the blame must stick to this joyless cereal.

The Medical Officer was also a Scotsman, so I could hardly complain to him about this essential part of the hospital diet. Especially because he also put me on ultra-violet ray treatment. Sitting in underpants and dark glasses for five or six minutes at a time, three times a week, seemed a funny way to help win the war, but it was quite enjoyable. It was also bi-sexual and most of the patients were officers. I did not expand on this aspect to my father, but simply pointed out how well I was being looked after. After all I would need to be accustomed to tropic sunlight when I was posted overseas.

That particular fate seemed to have temporarily receded. A week or so before Christmas the draft notice which I was on was abruptly cancelled – not postponed, but cancelled. At the time, there was no obvious cause. Now I think it must have been the Allied victories in North Africa, which led later in the year to the invasion of Italy and the setting-up of a whole new theatre of war. There was no further overseas posting for us till July and then it was to Sicily.

In the meantime, various things had happened to me. In February we all sat a trade test – an examination on the various aspects of radar. I got 95 per cent; not only the top mark but, I was told, the highest figure ever awarded in Northern Ireland. The result was that I did not have to wrestle with my conscience about the ethics of applying for a commission (as my father wanted me to do; whereas I pompously thought it would be more self-sacrificing and heroic to serve in the ranks). Now I was simply informed by the Education Officer that he had put me up for a commission. This led to an interview with the station commanding officer. He was an old regular airman who had risen through the ranks to be a Group Captain. He was keen on discipline and hadn't much to say to a young squirt like me. But he supported my application once we discovered that we both played golf.

I also had to have a medical check-up. As I got on well with the Scots Medical Officer I thought this would be a mere formality. To my surprise, he delayed my application by three months. When I asked him why, he explained that he wanted the ultra-violet treatment to have time to take effect. I considered that as soon as I was no longer living in an Irish bog my bronchial tubes would clear themselves. Now I can see that the ultra-violet set up was a new toy for the Medical Officer to play with and I was one of his star pupils. Most of his patients were officers and it looked better on paper that they should come from all ranks.

The very day after my interview with the CO I was put under open arrest. It happened like this. Most of our hut was on the same watch and on this particular morning we were off duty after an all-night shift. Most of us were putting our beds together, getting into our pyjamas (if we had any of our own, it was not an item of clothing that the RAF admitted existed), debating whether it was worth going across to the canteen to scrounge an extra cup of tea or having one of the apples with which my parents constantly kept me supplied. My bed was the nearest to the door and I was just about to get into it when the door was flung open. In came a couple of Military Police corporals with a great stamping of boots and bawling in unison: 'By Your Beds: At Attention Now: Orderly Officer.' And in between them came a little figure with a bristling moustache and a high-pitched grating voice. No doubt he didn't like the look of us either. And the first person to cross his sights was me – half-in and half-out of my brightly checked Chilprufe pyjamas.

'Airman! Stand to attention now. What's all this filth you're wearing?'

I thought it best to be as truthful as possible. 'They're a present from my mother, sir.'

'And what are you doing wearing them at 10 o'clock in the morning? You know I could have you on a charge for this?'

At this point I made a crucial mistake: never tell a person senior to yourself in the forces that you know his business better than he does.

'We've been on night duty, sir. We're entitled to sleep during the day. We work on shifts and we're off duty now.'

'Entitled to sleep, are you? Off duty are you? Don't you know there's a war on! Shift duty, eh. I'll have you shifting, Airman. Sergeant, put this filthy fellow under open arrest. Insubordination, laziness and keeping a filthy billet.'

'I say, sir . . .'

'No you won't say anything, Airman. Another word and I'll have you in the glass-house. Sergeant, see that he tidies up when he appears before the CO tomorrow.'

'Yes, Quartermaster. Airman Gill, report to the Orderly Room in ten minutes. Full parade kit. Subsequently report to the Orderly Sergeant every two hours for the full twenty-four. Until you've appeared before the CO.'

Being under open arrest was no joke. Every two hours throughout the twenty-four you had to dress in full parade gear – all buttons polished, webbing scrubbed, boots shiny – march up to the guard room, shout your name and that you had the honour to appear before the Orderly Sergeant under open arrest and on what charges. If he was an officious type he could look you over, tell you your brass buttons were not shiny enough, and to report again once they were polished enough for him to see his reflection in them.

The next morning was a double exposure: first before the Military Police, then the Quartermaster in charge of camp discipline (the Orderly Officer of the previous day). Finally, I was marched into the Orderly Room where the CO was dispensing justice. A military policeman on either side and a sergeant right behind me giving the time: Leading Aircraftman Gill: Quick march, *left* right, *left* right, *left* right, Aircraftman Gill, *halt*. On the last word, the Sergeant came to attention behind me and knocked my hat off. (This was officially to ensure that you did not throw it at the CO. It also made you feel curiously impotent, which it was undoubtedly meant to do.)

The Quartermaster gave his account of my 'crime' in surprisingly clumsy sentences. The Commanding Officer did not wait for him to finish, but, turning to me, asked if I had not been on night duty immediately before. When I said yes his brow puckered. 'Case dismissed,' he snapped. 'Quartermaster, I would advise you to check your facts more carefully in the future.'

That was the nearest thing to a reprimand that a senior officer could deliver to a senior NCO within the hierarchy-bound confines of RAF discipline. I had the common sense to maintain a totally inscrutable expression. We had no more trouble from the Quartermaster.

A minor irritation followed from my twenty-four hours of house arrest. I became known to the Military Police as a potential trouble-maker – a totally fictional position. No more careful follower of the King's Regulations existed, so I gave the police no opportunity to lock me up. They responded in various niggling ways. For instance, on a windy late March day with bright patches of sunshine, you might not want to go down to the big city in your heavy blue overcoat. But you would wish to wear your warm woollen gloves. Ah, but strictly speaking you were not allowed to wear gloves except *with* your overcoat. Don't ask me why. It was such a ridiculous rule that many police turned a blind eye to it. Everyone leaving the camp had to be inspected by the guard room for shiny buttons, neatly brushed hair, etc. Gloves and no overcoat would be passed a dozen times. I would be going out through the main gate when I was called back.

'Airman, don't you know the rule — no gloves except with overcoat.'

I would have to decide whether to have cold hands or over-heated arms and chest. In any event I would have to go back to Hut 50 to make the change.

IV

An observant reader of the last sentence will have noticed that I was no longer living in Hut 64. This could have been due to my well-timed bronchitis, or to the fact that whenever an orderly officer called, causing all the inmates to leap to their feet, the said officer would get a splash of water right up his leg from our stamping dutifully to attention. In any event the rain got no less in springtime, though it could be expected that the in-house torrents would not be quite so chilling as they were in mid-winter. But who can read the administrative mind? One morning in March we were abruptly told that Hut 64 had been categorised as unfit for human occupation. The very next day we were to move down the valley to Hut 50. Same basic construction, but newly painted, only seventy-five yards through the wood to the ablutions, still only cold water, but no Niagara on the back doorstep; best of all, a weekly allocation of coal so that we could actually light our stove. We imagined sitting round it, smoking our pipes, competing to see whose spit would sizzle longest on the hob.

We fancied ourselves as devilish sharp: there was Frisco, the Latin-American volunteer from Rio; and Jack Torgelsen, the Norwegian tailor from Hull; and Barry Shepherd from neutral Dublin; and Corporal Esmond, just down from Balliol; and Too Too, who had been a name at Lloyds and had the longest dong any of us had ever seen; and Dick Homewood, who was also in the City and frightfully debonair and called everyone Darling and was going out with our Flight Sergeant Marjorie, whose father was the General in charge of Britain's barrage balloon defences; and Bruce, who permed his ash-blond hair and had a thing for Too Too, so we put their beds at the opposite ends of the hut. And then there were the three babies: Peter Williams from Sheffield, Jimmy Blair from Liverpool, and me from Canterbury.

We knew we were the tops, but a close second were our next-door neighbours in Hut 51. They were another of the Filter Room watches. We played golf and cricket tournaments against each other and just occasionally perpetrated elaborate japes that called forth immediate punitive reaction. Mostly this consisted of sending in a commando party of four of the youngest and most active: two at each end of the rival hut. Their aim was to flip over as many of the metal frame beds, depositing their sleeping occupants on the floor, as they could before bedlam broke out. The raiding party then had to escape, hopefully leaving the assaulted hut in a state of confusion. If captured, punishment was immediate. It usually consisted of white-washing an appropriate part of the anatomy.

Often a longer retaliation would follow in a few days. These responses rapidly escalated into such spectacular and dangerous raids that armistice terms had to be drawn up and signed by all concerned before elbows and collar bones got broken. Months of calm ensued. Then, inexplicably, two or three bouts of action would occur. The unadmitted cause was that tossing some innocent sleeping person out of bed is an immensely enjoyable exercise. Skilfully done, the victim feels no pain. The sharp upward jerk of the bed frame lifts him above the corners of the bed legs and should deposit him on his own mattress.

We were living in a backwater of war. Later, passing in the street, we would exchange glances, half acknowledge each other. 'You know him?' my partner would ask. 'Yes, I think so. We were in the RAF together . . . a long time ago, during the war . . . perhaps it was only a momentary likeness.' We were going to meet every year . . . a Hut 50 reunion. We never did, of course.

We had a number of guests we would not have asked back. When, in the evening, we went out to pee, they were sitting just beyond the range of direct light. Their eyes followed us through the wood. When the lights were out they grew bolder. We were kept awake by their gnawing at the concrete floor, pattering along the shelf that ran just above our heads.

The climax came when Peter Williams was sent a home-made cake for his birthday. He locked it up in a leather-bound suitcase and put it on the shelf above him. The rats sent in a platoon. They tore the suitcase to shreds and ate the entire contents in a single night. Peter's bed looked as if it had been in a snowstorm, the tiny particles being all that was left of a man-sized suitcase. He had heard them at it, but was afraid they would have turned on him if he had interfered.

Corporal Esmond called in the station rat-catcher. He put the fragments of the suitcase in quite a large cage. It had a guillotine door poised to fall behind the rat as it followed its nose to the back of the cage.

Early the next morning we were all awakened by a furious squealing and rattling. Torch-light revealed a large and very angry rat trying to chew through the metal bars of the cage.

No one had told us what to do once the guillotine fell. Corporal Esmond produced the only rifle we had, an old-fashioned 303. We agreed we were far more likely to blow one of us away than damage this pocket of whirlwind energy. Then the Oxford-trained mind of the corporal came up with an ingenious solution. Close by the back entrance was a bucket of sand and a bucket of water in case the IRA came in the night and set us alight. But water could also kill. If we dunked the cage in the bucket and held it under the rat would be done for.

But how were we to get the cage *into* the bucket? The rat looked quite capable of chewing us up if we got near it.

'That's easy,' said John Esmond briskly. He hooked the barrel of the 303 through the cage and swung it round and down towards the bucket. The rat went into a frenzy of screaming and leaping. Did it open the cage door or did John bang it against the edge of the bucket and inadvertently release the catch? Nobody could remember, for as the cage swung open, the rat leaped out and we jumped in all directions. Who jumped furthest and fastest was another subject of scholarly debate.

The rat never came back; and we never caught another.

V

The summer of 1943, which saw me heading towards a commission interview, also saw Too Too and me on a junior NCOs course. Another two weeks of square-bashing. Not quite as bad as Skegness, but on the same lines. We both got passes and remained Leading Aircraftmen. I had not the vocal cords for bellowing at a platoon, and Too Too was preoccupied with his personal equipment.

Much more engaging was the week's attachment to the Radio Direction Finding Station at Kilkeel. Only twenty-five people tended the two giant radar masts that dominated the remote inlet of Carlingford Lough in the extreme south of County Down. As I wrote at the time: 'Life in such a small camp has a charm of its own. The only officer, commonly referred to as the Old Man, could usually be found pottering around the kitchen, doing odd jobs to help the cook. Although so small and fairly isolated, the camp food was excellent, and the wooden huts had lino on the floor and a shaded electric light over each bed . . .'.

The June weather brought a glitter to 'the rolling green countryside, dotted with little white cottages and small fishing villages'. Here was the very place where the purple mountains of Mourne swept down to the sea. I went on several long hill walks with Kay Cassidy, the Irish WAAF who shared the attachment with me. We were on a different watch at the Filter Room, so I had not met her before. She was attractive in a characteristically Irish way: tall and well-built with curly dark hair and freckles and a twinkle in the eye. She was a cheery companion; but even in this remote beauty spot the war dominated.

The most modern radar equipment, the Chain Home Low (CHL), had just been installed at Kilkeel. It allowed the operator to pick up a low-flying enemy at a range of sixty to eighty miles. This was a great advance on the Static Chain Home, which could operate against high-flying enemy at ranges up to 180 miles but was unable to give a warning of anything at seagull height.

This was not the only message that Kay was involved in seeking. Her father was dead and her mother's only son was captured in Singapore early in 1942 in what was said to be the worst disaster the British Army had ever suffered. For a long time there was no news of him. His bereaved mother started to consult psychical researchers in the hope of establishing contact. After several abortive attempts, she believed she had found a medium in Belfast who purported to have received messages from her son. They were not reassuring. The young man was grieving to return to his family. He was not well and in a dark place.

To hear such strange and terrible news walking on the magical mountains of Mourne made it seem more disturbing. I wondered whether Kay believed the messages. No, she had not at first. The medium said they were to come next time with a personal object, which they must not let the medium see. If the voice recognised what it was, that would be a confirmation of his authenticity.

They took a large gold pocket watch, which had belonged to the boy's father. You have to understand, said Kay, that the voice which gave the messages was nothing like the voice of her brother. It sounded, she said, as though it had been distorted and relayed through aeons of space. Her mother was told to hold the watch in her right hand and think about it. After several false starts the voice said it might be something to do with time, but it was covered up. (It was indeed a half-hunter, which meant that unless you pressed the button only the centre portion of the watch face was visible.)

Her mother had been back several times, but the medium continued to give chilling news. The brother was weaker; he wanted to see them, but could not. In the meantime, an official card had come from the Red Cross saying that the brother was a prisoner of war. 'That, at least, was a fact,' said Kay. 'I'm not sure what I think about the rest.' Neither did I, but I volunteered to go with her to the next session.

It must have been about two months later that I went with Kay to an implacably respectable address in Belfast. It was rather like a Conservative Party meeting; mostly middle-aged well-dressed women with a scattering of scrawny old men with beards and blood-shot eyes. The host was plump and self-confident. He arranged us around three tables. They were smaller than I had expected. We had to press our knees together to get a touch on the table top. We were not allowed to take notes; that would be upsetting. The atmosphere was all important. Repeating this several times, our host put those who were actually hoping for news at the tables. I squeezed in next to Kay. The majority formed an audience at the back of the room, sitting in upright chairs.

The lights dimmed. Our host spoke now rapidly in a language I could not understand, but it would be reasonable to think it was Gaelic. After a short time movement began – swaying from side to side, gently at first. I can't say how the table started to move, but it did. Something was on it sliding across the shiny surface. Perhaps it was a censer. Certainly there was some smoke in the air. And other voices, mumbling. Some of the women at our table were panting or groaning: responded to from across the room. I did not know whether to giggle or feel I was intruding. Supplicating, that was what the tear-filled voices were doing. I felt discomforted and out of place.

As I felt that, the lights went on with a shocking brilliance. Our host was sweating in the middle of the room. What was he saying? That would be the end for tonight. The atmosphere was not congenial. Was he looking in my direction? Whether he was or not, I did not go back.

Kay kept me in touch with developments. The psychic messages changed direction. Her brother was happier now. He expressed his love for his family. It was no surprise for Kay when her mother received, just before the end of 1943, another formal communication from the Red Cross. Her son had died in the prison camp.

VI

There was a special privilege to being stationed in Northern Ireland. If you wanted, you could take part of your leave in Eire. This gave you forty-eight hours not only in a neutral country, but in one that had not suffered the deprivations and devastation that had affected most of the British Isles.

Jimmy Blair and I had decided that we had better get on with it, when new rumours of overseas postings came up in autumn 1943. Wearing a rag-bag of civvie clothes borrowed from other inmates of Hut 50, we set off with our newly stamped leave passes in our pockets. The weather was fine; the three-hour train journey cost 21*s* 5*d* return. The first surprise was on the platform when we arrived. Through the throngs of people were a surprising number of grabbing hands: beggars. Something I had never seen on an English station. Even more startling were the almost naked small children playing in the mud outside. I quickly learned that it was Irish wits who had invented the paradox.

We had a four-course meal at an underground café recommended by Barry; he had also fixed a decent clean hotel nearby and given us the telephone number of his elder brother. The brother insisted on taking us out to dinner that evening. In the meantime, we looked at the shops. As I wrote at the time: 'It was like a visit to wonderland. To our eyes all the shops seemed absolutely packed with goods of every description – fruit, clothes, jewellery, chocolates, stockings, fountain pens and luxury goods of every description, boxes of eggs outside the grocers, whole hams hung up.' That somewhat breathless list gives an idea of what were luxuries in Britain in 1943 – fresh fruit and fresh eggs as much as jewellery.

When Barry's brother, Howard Shepherd, took us out to dinner, we had the impossibly difficult task of choosing between four cuts of steak: fillet, point, rump or porterhouse. It was to be nine years, yes, another nine years, before meat rationing came to an end in Britain. But food was not the principal memory this trip evoked. It was refreshing to hear a subtly different interpretation of the war news, and reassuring to sense how deeply the people of Ireland were on our side. More volunteers from neutral southern Ireland were serving in the British forces than from the north, which was officially at war (another Irish paradox).

Howard Shepherd rang up and cancelled his evening engagements. 'We then went on to the Theatre Royal: this is a huge affair with a moving stage and three bars (each of which we explored after the show). The latter was a very lavish revue with a chorus of eighty and lots of spectacular scenes and pretty music.

'I think the highlight of the whole outing was coming out afterwards into a world aglow with lights, and wandering along the Liffey admiring the reflections in the water.'

I can still summon to my mind's eye a brilliant image of a double-decker bus crossing the river on the next bridge to ours. Moving all aglow at such a stately pace, it might have been Titania's chariot on her nightly rounds.

This trip to Dublin was in mid-September. The three-month postponement ordered by the doctor was over. Sure enough the Orderly Room delivered a terse notice the next week. It empowered me to travel third-class to London to attend a board for the post of filter officer in His Majesty's Royal Air Force. Said board would be held at Penn Corner, off the Strand, on the next Thursday, and I should present myself at

10.45 a.m. And so it came to pass. I found myself elbow to elbow with four or five youngish men, all looking heavier and more responsible than me. I was only too aware of my wavy hair and horn-rimmed glasses and squeaky voice. My rivals (as I assumed I must think of these others) seemed to be going off to be interviewed at a much quicker rate than I would have expected. Actually there were two or three boards going on simultaneously. When I was called, my interview seemed to be over in a flash, though the other candidates assured me that I was 'in' for more than half-an-hour. After this there was an excruciating wait while your fate was decided. You were informed of the result by the playing of one of two recordings. One said: 'Would the candidate just seen return to his unit forthwith.' That was failure. The other message said: 'Would the candidate just seen report to the medical section on the second floor.' That was success, or at least left it to Fate, Providence or the Will of Allah.

I floated down to the medicos in a haze that seemed to remove me entirely from the common parlance of mankind. How had it happened? They had all laughed two or three times: what had I said? Now there were just these routine nooks and crannies to offer up; put your tongue out, bend over, read the bottom line . . . then there will be the suit to order, Simpson's I think . . . 'I'm sorry to have to tell you this.' What was he saying? They had all gathered round, looking serious. 'I don't understand,' blinking as they switched on the main lights again. The senior one bent over confidentially. 'It's this job you are in for, you have to have an A1 vision, yours is A4.' 'But I do it already . . . have done for a year, nearly.' 'Ah, but as an officer you'll need to have especially perfect eyesight. You carry the responsibility . . .' 'It's just the same, we're just looking down at a lot of tiddlywinks on a great big table.' 'Ah, but it's this electronic equipment isn't it? It's what they were developing before the war, television they call it. Well to look at that distorted flickering imagery all the time you'd have to have perfect eyesight. I'd say you're as well not dabbling in that.' The second doctor came back with a large book. 'It's quite clear, A1 vision required.'

One of the board members came bustling in: 'Bad luck old chap. Go back to your unit and we'll be in touch. You did a good board.' Much good it had done me.

I had arranged by telephone to meet my parents after the board at the entrance to Penn House. They had come up from Canterbury for the day. I could not bear the thought of descending the stairs into the foyer where successful candidates would be embracing admiring loved ones. I needed to creep unseen into some dark corner and clear my mind of foolish dreams of glory. After all I had *expected* to fail. Yes, but not in such a tormenting way.

I got the surprised Sergeant-in-Charge to direct me to the back door. Beyond the Strand were the fast-flowing grey waters of the Thames. I walked down to them. There in the Embankment Gardens were statues to great men. I would never fall into that category; destined to be an also-ran; a disappointment to my devoted parents. I must not keep them waiting any longer. I must have been an awful responsibility, being so ill so often.

They were waiting at the entrance to Penn House. A neatly dressed couple passing into the dumpiness of middle age. We had a caring lunch together and said a lot of cheering things. And that I thought was that, as I settled into the sixteen-hour rail and sea journey back to Stormont. Next time I travelled I would be going overseas.

But, as with my matriculation results, I had underestimated life's endless ability to surprise. When I reported back to the Orderly Room, the CO came out of his office. 'I heard the result; damn silly. I'll recommend you for an admin job if you like.'

The next day a twenty-page typed list of all the commissioned posts available to RAF ground personnel was sent down to me. They covered everything, from armaments storage in the Hebrides to building protective zariba hedges in East Africa. At first I thought that I should take up the CO's kind offer and apply for a job as an administration officer. At least I would get a good send-off from him. Then I thought:

did I really want to spend the rest of my time in the RAF signing movement orders, sentencing drunken airmen to a week's confinement to camp, arranging proper toilets for visiting WAAFs at a station dance, and ending up adjutant in some moribund camp, which I would have the tricky and boring job of running down with the ending of the war? No, I did not.

So, I turned back to the list and looked at it entirely from the selfish point of view of what I would enjoy most. The answer came immediately. Intelligence: that covered a multiple of things; all in the spearhead of action. The principal drawback was my age: I was still only nineteen; secondly, I had no foreign language except French, and that only to schoolboy level; and thirdly, I had not been to university and was down to take a medical degree at Guy's. But what the hell, that was in the far distance after the bleeding war was over. Might as well be hung for a sheep . . .

Surprisingly quickly, in the middle of November 1943 I was ordered to report to the Group Captain i/c Intelligence in the main Stormont building. He was middle-aged with a quiet, gentle manner. As I remembered from all the times in the last year that I had spent polishing the parquet floors, there were two interconnected offices. He gestured to the larger one. 'Have a look in there, then come back here and tell me what you've found out.' 'Can I take notes?' I could. After twenty minutes he called out to ask how I was getting on. I gave him an analysis of the various war fronts and the latest figures of German submarine losses, Royal Naval casualties and merchant shipping sunk in recent months and in what oceans.

'Stop, stop. You can't have taken all that in just now.'

'No, I knew what to look for.'

'How could you know that?'

'I've often studied these walls before.'

'How could that be? This placed is kept locked all the time we're not in it.'

'Not entirely locked, sir. It's open to the hoovering and dusting and polishing squads that come round every night. When they are officially guarding the building, they are also keeping it ship-shape and tidy.'

'And do you fall in that category?'

I explained that the various clerks on shift duty also did night guards around the camp. This office was much the most interesting to keep clean, because it gave a picture of how the war was going.

'Hmm. So from your privileged position, Aircraftman Gill, how do you think the war *is* going?'

'Not so badly as last year, sir.'

'That's a cautious answer considering we lost more ships in early 1942 than at any time in our history.'

He launched into a brilliant analysis of war strategy. Altogether it was going to be a close run thing. The Germans still had some nasty surprises for us, but we had our own secret weapons. But he believed it would not be possible to beat an enemy like Germany (or Japan) without invasions. 'You'll probably be in one of those assaults, Gill.'

He took me to the door, wished me well and shook my hand. The interview had taken more than two hours.

Two weeks later I was summoned back to Penn Corner. This time there were only three on the board – a much younger panel and much more rowdy. They constantly disagreed with each other. If the Stormont interview had been like a chat with a very clever uncle, this was a corner of an Oxford college. One of them summed up:

'You see Gill, you're not coming to us with a special talent; you don't speak Cantonese for instance . . .'

'God, wouldn't that be great if he did . . .'

'We could send him to the Nursery; basic Sino-Japanese languages in thirteen months.'

'No, no, no. The war would be over by the time we'd got the task force ready. I keep telling you to think *strategically* Crispin . . .'

'Well, whatever you say, if Jerry gives us the Christmas present we think he might . . .'

'It'll all be over, one way or another. Where are you off to now Gill?'

I explained I was returning to my unit. And somewhat frostily pointed out that I had come a thousand miles for a ten-minute interview.

'A thousand miles,' muttered one of them. 'God, one doesn't think of the Empire still being so big.'

'Getting some time with the old folk while you're over?' asked the small one named Crispin.

Even more frostily I pointed out that the movement order that got me to Penn Corner made no reference to a forty-eight-hour leave pass.

'Boobed again, have we?' beamed the chairman with false bonhomie. 'We'll have to make it up later.'

I left, feeling more depressed and confused than at any time since the early days in RAFNI.

There were consolations. I had a new and delightful girlfriend called Bunny, a Filter Room WAAF, who was on the same watch as me. (This meant we could spend our days off together.) She was light as a feather and loved dancing. At a Hut 50 party held in a private room in a restaurant in town, she performed the dangerous-looking feat of dancing on the table top, covered in used glasses and small plates. This was for my birthday, 10 December 1943. But it had another more solemn reason. Just as a year before, a really large overseas draft had been posted up at the beginning of December. It included everyone in Hut 50 except Too Too (he must have had some inhibiting condition like diabetes) and me.

This time there was no last-minute cancellation. Everybody left on 11 December. What a curiously devastating effect their going had on this familiar scene. What had housed argument, laughter, occasional tears, the odd fight, sing-songs, and dirty jokes, relapsed into concrete and metal. Like a stage set, which you hardly notice when the actors are in the foreground; once they have left, its very inertia, its seediness, gives it a finality, which increases the mournful sorrow of the one surviving actor.

At that time I thought that the relationship of the ten of us was unique, that it would be something we would all look back on as a powerful experience. In part, I think that was true. What was unique was what was left when we had all gone. Hut 50 itself created the social relationship, the close living, the bareness of our situation. I have lived, later in the Air Force, and for years afterwards in a student hostel, with other males, but nothing was quite as socially basic as this stretch in Stormont Park. At this level it would be easy for one or two neurotic souls to pull us all down into grumbling and quarrelling. No one did. We had a tolerance, which I think it would not be so easy to find today. We did not expect too much of each other and we supported each other's weaknesses. When we had a corporal who knelt by his bed and said his prayers every night, nobody made fun of him; they went on talking in quiet tones and they respected his space. Giving everyone his appropriate area is another very important social rule when space is at a premium. It was not true to say that we all came from a common background or even country. But we were all doing the same thing – we were all plotters in the same Filter Room. In the much larger unit I was going into – an airfield – ranks, jobs, rewards, ages, everything was different. We were living for some time under canvas, but there were still profound differences in our lifestyle.

So three cheers for Hut 50; for me it has stood the test of time. If 137 Wing – the airfield I was going to be with for the next year and more – was like a miniature city, so Hut 50 was a monastery where we all lived in real harmony. I think we were luckier than we knew.

10

SCRAMBLING FOR ORDERS

I

'Did you hear that, sor,' the sergeant wheezed into my ear. 'They are going to attack us from the hill on the other side of the valley. If we go through the river we should short-circuit them and get the advantage of the high ground. Have to put the skates on though.'

'I'm sure you're right, Sarge,' I murmured. I had quickly learned to trust his judgement, even though I knew he was there to report on my conduct. That meant, I thought, that I had to do some daft things especially to catch the eye of authority when the staff officers were around. At the moment I was wriggling backwards through a snowy wood trying to avoid being trapped by gorse bushes and fallen tree trunks. Following the sergeant's advice, he and I had crept into the wood and actually overheard the 'enemy' platoon discussing its plan of attack. If we could get back to our own chaps quickly we should have a decisive advantage in the coming 'battle'. The wood thinned as the slope got steeper. Just as it turned into a cliff about twenty feet high, I saw beyond it on the next hill a cluster of the top brass, including the CO with his binoculars on me. With a wild whoop I leapt into space. I had seen there was what appeared to be a drift of snow at the bottom of the cliff and I remembered to hold my rifle stiffly out to one side. I was not completely daft.

Just beyond the cliff the rest of my platoon were waiting in the last clump of trees.

'Come on chaps,' I shouted. 'Sarge and I overheard their plans. We've got to ford the stream. They won't expect us to come this way.' (Not unless their sergeant is being as helpful to them as ours is to us, I thought with a tinge of gloom.)

'Who else would be so silly as to go into a hill stream in mid-February,' said Lofty, the big New Zealander. Holding his rifle above his head he ran straight into the water. (As the leader I should have been first in, but I couldn't catch up with Lofty.) I expected the water to be about two feet deep, but Lofty stumbled and completely disappeared. He came up spluttering and frozen blue with cold. Wading carefully, I found the stream came up to mid-chest. It *was* unbelievably cold. Climbing out on the other side was like struggling through rapidly hardening concrete. You could feel the water turning to ice on your clothes.

'C'mon you buggers! Run, damn you, run!' I shouted. My shouts were echoed by the sergeant, who had gone to the far end of the valley where there was a wooden footbridge. His job was to invigilate our progress, not to take part in it. What was he shouting? '. . . Keep doubled up! . . . Live ammo!'

Two starshells burst overhead, a sign that we had been spotted by the rival platoon. 'Run, but keep down. They'll be using live ammunition,' I screamed.

In confirmation, several whiplike cracks of rifle fire came from the woods ahead. Was it my imagination or could I hear the whistle of bullets? Now was the time to run all out. We could see the thin line of the enemy crouching on the edge of the trees. They looked somewhat upset by the sight of us, as well they might. 'Wha . . . what do we do now, Gilly?' said Simonds. He ran a catering business in real life.

'Into them with the bayonet,' I shouted. 'Don't actually kill 'em. Scare 'em to death.'

Somewhat surprisingly the only real casualties were the oldest member of the rival platoon (his nose was broken when Simonds fired a blank at him at too close range), and one of my chaps who put his foot in a rabbit hole and broke his ankle. Of course, we all had severe colds the whole month of the battle school. It was amazing we did not get pneumonia.

'Battle school,' do I hear you saying? What has that to do with RAF Intelligence? You might well ask. You will remember that Too Too and I were left alone over Christmas in Hut 50. I began to think I had been forgotten when suddenly a movement order was dropped in on me, telling me to report to the officers' training college at Cosford, near Wolverhampton, the very next day. English-centred RAF Admin always forgot that Stormont was on a different island from Britain.

So I arrived two days late on 12 January 1944. Not that it mattered. The course was just another round of square-bashing, made worse in that we had to take it in turns to be the officer in charge. I was, without question, the most physically unsuited, the most inept and the most immature of all the cadets. The drill sergeants thought I was a hopeless case. If it had been up to them I would have been returned to Northern Ireland after the first day. Quite right, because I didn't get any better. Just as the officers in charge of training us were beginning to think on the same lines as the sergeants, along came a piece of written work and I would easily get top marks. That put the officers in a quandary. After all, I was going to Intelligence was I not? There was a well-known respect for independent cranky brilliance in the RAF, like Barnes Wallis and his bouncing bomb. I might hope to render some small service to the state in that line, might I not?

This idea depended on my maintaining my mental mastery, and here, I am afraid, my vanity sometimes let me down. The last and most important section of written work on the course was a piece of dogma masquerading as a question. It went something like this: 'On a fighter sweep over enemy territory you shoot down an enemy fighter. The pilot bails out. What do you do?'

Well, you might think this was a moral question. We were not going to descend to the murderous behaviour of the Blitzkrieg and the Nazi labour camp, were we? But that was not the way Air Ministry looked at it. True, this enemy plane had just been destroyed, but the pilot could be flying another one tomorrow. He could be in a position to exact vengeance on an Allied plane. After all, just a few minutes before I had endeavoured to destroy him, so why should I spare him now? As I knew, once we were fighting on enemy soil everything, and every person on it, was classified a foe. We had a specific order not to bring bombs back from abortive raids on Germany, but to drop them on any habitable farmhouse, rail junction or village that we were passing over.

In the end, for me it was an aesthetic decision. Nothing would make me, from the safety of my Spitfire, blow to pieces another human being floating unarmed in space. Knowing this, and knowing there was a tough attitude fashionable among the older regular officers, personified in such phrases as 'the only good German is a dead one', it was self-indulgent to take a high moral tone, as I did, quoting the League of Nations and George Bernard Shaw.

Apparently that was the last red flag. The CO was all for sending me to the nastiest outpost of Empire that could be found. Luckily, his junior officers thought privately much as I did. They told me that whatever the CO said I must agree to with enthusiasm. So when he asked me whether I was man enough to go on the toughest battle school yet created, I assured him there was nothing I would like better. Actually, much of the battle school was cleverly thought out and more enjoyable than the pointless drill of the main course. It certainly made me appreciate the clean sheets and numerous coffee breaks of the Intelligence School at Highgate, which was my next port of call.

II

A tall Victorian building on the very brow of Highgate Hill, creeper on the redbrick and a neglected garden rambling off into clumps of laurel: that was the Intelligence School. We were there for only a week. Its purpose was to fit square pegs into square holes. Various psychological tests filled the main periods. There were twenty of us, including several household names – a radio announcer and another frequent broadcaster. This time I was not the first in written work, but fluctuated between third and sixth. I was still the youngest by six or seven years.

The chief lecturer put pressure on me to volunteer for Air Ministry. I would probably have agreed had I not fallen under the influence of the next youngest inmate. He, like me, had failed to get into air crew and was looking for an active substitute. He had discovered that an American plane, the North American Mitchell (B-25), was being flown by the RAF in the American manner: that was in a tight wingtip-to-wingtip group of six planes, an attack of three above and three below. This box of six flew in tight formation all the way to the target. The Americans flew each plane with pilot and co-pilot, navigator and bomb-aimer, mid-gunner/wireless operator and rear gunner, a total crew of six. The short-of-manpower RAF flew on missions with a crew of four: pilot, navigator/bomb-aimer, wireless op/mid-gunner, rear gunner. That was fine, except that the leading plane had to dictate the responses of the other five so that they all bombed together. This meant that the leading bomb-aimer was for some vital minutes unable to keep the navigational side of his work going. He had crawled forward into the plastic nose of the plane and was taking all the other navigators through the coordinated disciplines of the bombing run. So a supernumerary navigator was apparently carried in the front plane. Frank Watson, my new friend at Highgate, believed that if we could get on the right side of the local commanding officer we would probably be welcomed to assist in providing an extra body in the front flight.

We all knew that the Second Tactical Air Force was being built up for the forthcoming invasion of Europe by the Allies. It would be the biggest land battle since the First World War, and the operations/intelligence officers would have a front-line view. There were two close support bomber wings, each with three squadrons. Of these, 137 Wing operated from Hartford Bridge in Hampshire. Its Mitchell squadron was 226. Its 88 and 342 (French) Squadrons were still flying the elegant, but smaller Boston, where there was no room for an additional bomb-aimer. Operating from Dunsfold in Surrey, 139 Wing was completely converted to Mitchells. 98 and 180 Squadrons were RAF; 320 Squadron was Dutch. Watson had already had some flying experience with 139 Wing. He told me about it in graphic detail. He had arranged to go back to Dunsfold once this course was over. If I was to have the sort of grandstand view of the climax of the war that I now desperately wanted, I must get myself attached to 226 Squadron at Hartford Bridge. I explained this at length to the people at Highgate. They were famous for their string-pulling. I got my attachment to 137 Wing – at least temporarily.

My feeling of elation lasted only twenty-four hours. A crowded train journey, standing up all the way, took me to Wallingford in Berkshire. From there RAF transport carried me to an imposing eighteenth-century country mansion, Mongewell Park. It might have been built to house Pitt and his War Cabinet, mulling over their plans to defeat Napoleon. In fact, it was now the headquarters of the Second Tactical Air Force, planning a new invasion of Europe. I had never seen so many circles of braid, so many ribbons and decorations, or heard so many booming voices and hectoring laughter. Though you might have thought that conversation was pitched so high to command attention, no one seemed to wait for an answer. They also had the unnerving aptitude of looking straight through you without seeing you.

I made the foolish mistake of going into the bar at lunchtime. I knew it would be open to all officers irrespective of rank. I had not yet learned that many social rules in the forces were more honoured in the breach than in the event. If a junior officer wandered into such a high-powered gathering as this bar, he would simply be frozen out, ignored, talked through. No one below the rank of a group-captain (a full colonel in the Army or a Naval captain) would be served – unless he was decorated. That immediately changed the rules. A year or so later I was in a British

Army bar in Germany, where the corporal behind the counter had the Victoria Cross. He was often drawn into the conversation by the officers he was serving.

I was on the brink of giving up the attempt to catch the barman's eye when I bumped into a short, dark and slightly built Squadron Leader. He was wearing the blue and white ribbon of the Distinguished Flying Cross below his pilot's wings. To my surprise he smiled and asked if I was the new operations officer for Hartford Bridge. I said I thought I was, but how could he know? He pointed to the mirror behind the bar. 'Don't you look the part?' Tall, gangling and uneasy, I certainly was. 'No, it's not that I've got the second sight. I'm your opposite number up here. I'm Bill Edrich.'

Bill Edrich! I was too flummoxed for words. W.J. Edrich had gone in number three for England through the summer of 1938 when we were playing Australia and I was first getting deeply involved in the drama of cricket – a drama, like war, full of unexpected reverses. Edrich played in all five test matches in 1938 and failed in every one. Then, in the winter of 1938–9, he went with the England team to play a series against South Africa and in the very last match made the record-breaking score of 219. In 1940 he led a brilliant attack at low level on the docks at Rotterdam, which must have influenced the Nazi war machine in abandoning its plans to invade England and turn instead eastwards to the flat plains of Russia. I would have loved to talk to Bill Edrich about the rival conflicts of sport and war. A book by a famous cricket writer, Sir Pelham Warner, which my parents sent me for Christmas 1942 when I was in hospital in Ireland, summed up Edrich's character very well: 'When one realised the rough seas he had encountered for so long, his coming into his own again was a rare tribute to his courage, a courage so fully demonstrated subsequently in the grimmest of all wars.' I was too much in awe of this almost legendary character to approach him socially, though we had a most amicable relationship on those many nights when we shared opposite ends of the scrambler telephone.

There was little time on those occasions for a general chat. Nor was there on this first meeting. The bar was completely packed, distinguished elbow rubbing elbow. Edrich pointed out two tall blond figures at the far end of the counter: they were the Atcherley twins, famous for their exploits in 1920s aviation, at a time when hardly a week seemed to pass without some new flight being celebrated. Looking goggle-eyed at these figures from a past almost as distant as the Trojan War caused me to miss the opening gambit at the bar, unnatural squeals and yelps drawing my attention back. The line of drinkers was swaying from side to side. One portly figure was flat on his back. Others, bent double, were clutching their trousers and shouting imprecations.

'I'm afraid that's Basil, our CO. He thinks that from time to time we all need livening up.' Edrich shook his head ruefully.

I had heard of Air Vice-Marshal Embry and his bloody exploits. Shot down over France in 1940, he had escaped, been recaptured and escaped again, killing three of his captives with his bare hands. There was an echo here of my essay subject on morality in war. Embry had asked for a glass of water and killed the man who brought it. No doubt he would have shot to pieces the parachuting enemy without compunction. I looked at him with a repugnant interest. Small, with twinkly eyes and a quick birdlike glance, there was nothing to suggest a sadistic monster. He was helping up the winded officer who had fallen on his back.

The prank he had played on the bar loungers depended on surprise and speed. Coming in unobserved, he ran along the bent backs thrusting his hand into each trouser pocket in turn and giving the pendulous private parts a sharp tweak. The object was to get as far along the line as possible before being spotted. In this case he had tweaked four out of seven.

This was only an extreme example of the violent horseplay that broke out from time to time in all the RAF stations to which I belonged. My last commanding officer had an even more spectacular and dangerous party trick. He would inhale a mouthful of lighter fuel, light it and exhale it at the same moment. The more sharply he blew, the further the tongue of fire would curve across the mess.

When we left Hartford Bridge for France in October 1944, the damage to the Officers' Mess reached epic proportions. Plunged in a pungent mixture of soot and black paint, the bare bottoms of all the station wing commanders were imprinted above the fireplace. Naked sooty feet wandered over the ceiling, meeting other parts of the human anatomy here and there. In this case we all had to pay for the redecoration. In general, the authorities took a surprisingly relaxed view of such boisterous antics. Virtually all senior RAF officers had been in air crew at one stage of their careers and knew the pressures and tensions that went with it.

III

The next day an RAF truck brought me to Hartford Bridge. After more than eighteen months in the Air Force I was at last going to be working among aircraft. Hartford Bridge looked the very prototype of an airfield. Built among meandering lanes, gorse bushes and sandy dunes, the concrete works of man rose to a crescendo around the broad crossing of the two great runways – like a royal parade ground dedicated not to Apollo, the god of pomp and circumstance, but to Mars, the god of war, and his noisy brother, Vulcan. And indeed the clattering and hammering of repair work seemed never to cease on the clover leaves of lesser runways where the aircraft themselves clustered.

Boston and Mitchell seemed to express entirely different temperaments, rapier against battleaxe. In fact, the Mitchell, with its two powerful Wright Cyclone 1250hp engines, could carry twice the bomb load of the slightly more streamlined Boston. I already felt an affinity for the Mitchell. On this, my first sight of one, I got my driver to wait while I ran across and laid my hands on its metal sides. The smell of high octane fuel and hot metal was as intoxicating as sniffing glue to an addict. The two fitters tinkering with the starboard engine must have thought me crazy when, my voice cracking with emotion, I asked if I could climb on board.

'Help yourself laddie,' said the senior.

A perpendicular ladder with some three or four rungs carried me up to the navigational table in the central section of plane. In this compressed space the observer had to carry out the calculations that would confirm the pilot's view of their position. A squeeze past the radar and a couple of climbing steps took me to the pilot's seat, confronting a dense array of dials and gauges. Sure enough, next to it was the empty co-pilot's seat. I patted it affectionately. It seemed characteristically well made in the heavy American style with plenty of protective metal around the seat.

I had little opportunity to explore it any further in the next few days. I had joined an airfield at war, where I had a specific role which within a week I would be expected to fulfil. Much of this was left to me to find out for myself. I talked to armourers and engineers, to wireless operators and gunners; I went up into the control tower and watched how the aircraft were brought in by radio link; I flew on low-level training trips; I helped the photo-interpreter who taught me how to diagnose from shadows and patches of dust the mysteries of seeing the world from 10,000 feet (our average bombing height). Most important of all, I sat in the control room and helped Flight Lieutenant Hovendon carry out the preparation for a couple of raids: the job I was to take over.

Altogether there were seven intelligence officers in the Wing (at twenty, I was by some thirteen years the most junior). Squadron Leader Walkerdene was by a long way the most senior. Now in his late forties, he had flown above the trenches in the First World War. Small, energetic, impetuous and nervy, he was not a deep thinker, but made up in words what he lacked in profundity. He had been appropriately christened (without his knowing) as Squadron Leader Walkie-Talkerdene. His number two was also just over forty. Connie Constant had been in oil between the wars, spoke several European languages and was a thoughtful, sophisticated man. He was much nearer to the intelligence officer of my imagination than Squadron Leader Walkerdene; yet the senior flying officers clearly thought more highly of the squadron leader's garrulous advice in briefing for raids than the terse comments of Flight Lieutenant Constant.

Each squadron has its own intelligence officer. With 226 it was a Scots lawyer. Bob Laurie came from Edinburgh and had something of the sententious air that went with that windy city. It did not stop his rough and tough Dominion crews adoring him. The intelligence officer in a squadron had to be a favoured uncle, someone to be trusted to give you true advice in difficult circumstances. It was no good the intelligence officer pretending there was going to be no opposition in a raid which last time had cost us two planes. What you wanted to hear were words of wisdom and advice on how to get out of it alive, making clear in the briefing where the enemy flak was placed and which way to turn off the bombing run in order to avoid it.

Flight Lieutenant Hovendon had that sort of seamy battered face and heavy moustache you might have encountered on a race course. He would give you an unexpected tip in that gravelly voice that had experienced too many cigars and late nights. Predominantly English, 88 Squadron took to Hovers as a wily bird, as British as Lieutenant Leger was French. It would not have been just to have an English intelligence officer for 342, a totally French squadron. It was hard to pin down what made them as French as they were. It was not simply the language (mostly from the French colonies, they virtually all spoke colloquial English). No, it was something in the way they slung their flak-jackets over the shoulder, a certain panache. Though we all inhabited the same Officers' Mess, French and British didn't fraternise all that much.

Finally, there were the three operations officers, of whom I was the most junior. It was our job to receive the battle orders from 2 Group, and to transmit them to all the appropriate people from the commanding officer to the warrant officer in charge of the riggers. My best friend was

Leslie Rates, the senior flying officer operations. In peacetime he was something in the City. About six feet two inches tall with a face that looked carved in granite, he seemed like one of those minor faithful friends that you often encounter in Dickens. It was he who had christened our chief intelligence officer 'Walkie-Talkerdene'. There was a trace of the cockney in Rates's appropriately cynical reactions, whereas Flying Officer Robertson-Williams had clearly been to a minor public school. His heavy moustache did not completely conceal some anxious preoccupation. He had been with 137 Wing only a few weeks longer than me, and just before that he had married. He wrote his new wife a long letter every day. ''E's proper lovesick, 'e is,' said one of our sergeants. That did not explain why, coming into his billet to wake him up when he was late on duty, I saw a heavy automatic under his pillow.

One of the three of us was always on duty, from 8 a.m. to 8 a.m. the following morning. There was a barnlike Operations Room with a raised dais on one side facing across a big map table to the blackboard on the wall opposite, where there was space to fill in every aircraft and its crew and its present condition, down to the terse 'missing', or even more conclusive 'shot down' or 'crashed'. It was the duty of the Operations Sergeant to keep this board up to date under the jurisdiction of the ops officer. Besides him there was a switchboard and a WAAF operator with a direct line to everyone of importance on the airfield.

Just within the entrance was a small anteroom with a camp bed for the duty officer, a bathroom and shower. Not that there was over-much time for such luxuries. Usually, the day began about 2 a.m. with a telephone call. The time told you it was going to be the group operations officer (who else would ring at such an hour?). The thought of that cleared the voice remarkably:

'Hullo, this is 137 Wing, Pilot Officer Gill.'

'Hullo Mike, Two Group, Edrich here, ready to scramble?'

'Scrambling.' This was the remarkable device which meant that while the line remained clear for us any snooper would hear only a ululating mush. The fact that we were using the scrambler meant that a number of people had to be informed: the Commanding Officer (Group Captain MacDonald), the Wing Commander Operations (Jack Adams), the Wing Commander Flying (Ian Spencer), the Squadron Leader Navigation (Gerry Baker), the Squadron Leader Intelligence, and so on down to the Met Officer and the Armaments Officer. Everything that could be quantified, the number of bombs to be dropped, the type of bomb, the hour and minute of take-off, the time of arrival over target, the number of aircraft taking part, the fighter cover (if any): all possible information was dictated by Edrich against a standardised form on which I was writing it down. Once the order was completed I had to see that it was carried out, beginning with personally informing the commanding officer. This led me into trouble on my very first lone night of responsibility.

Group Captain MacDonald was a strikingly handsome man, probably in his late thirties. I could see that he might have quite a temper if roused. He was a career officer, who, I believe, had flown battle bombers (often called 'flying coffins') in the Phoney War and the subsequent battle for France. I also understood that it was his squadron that was asked to provide six planes to bomb the bridge at Maastricht on 12 May 1940. The whole squadron volunteered, so the first six on the duty roster were taken. Only one plane came back, but the bridge was partially destroyed. The leading pilot and navigator were posthumously awarded the Victoria Cross.

Now, almost exactly four years later, the group captain was awaiting another summons over which he had no control. His wife was expecting their first child. There had been complications and a history of earlier difficulties. Only the previous day the CO had announced to my telephonist that he did not want any duty calls put through to his house.

In the wee small hours the bell rang. It was Edrich with details of an air strike, which was called for very early in the morning. Even if I left telling the CO until the last possible moment I would still have to call him at 5.30 a.m. What should I do? On my instructions it said quite clearly that the commanding officer was the first person to be informed of any planned bombing raid. Yet only the day before he had said no duty calls to be put through to his house.

It was a crisis on my very first day in charge. What a stinker! What to do? I rang the Wing Commander Flying. He was the next in the chain of command, another career officer and reassuringly steady. Normally I would not make this call myself, but leave it to my sergeant while I personally dealt with the detailed fusing instructions on the bomb load, but I needed his advice. Considering that I had woken him at 3.30 a.m., Wing Commander Spencer was remarkably unruffled. 'Crew briefing at six? I'll be in by five-thirty. Let the old boy have a good night's rest.'

At 5 a.m. he was on the phone again. 'Had a look at the weather? It's pretty thick down here. Tell you what. I'll take Samson for a stroll down by the Met Office.' Samson was his bull terrier.

I took a look outside. Fog was rolling up from the narrow valleys like dry ice in a theatre production of *Macbeth*. In the meantime, the 500lb bombs that the battle order demanded were being loaded, eight to each Mitchell. I could hear the clanking of the bomb trolleys going round the dispersal, and the testing of engines like the tuning of a theatre orchestra.

By 5.30 a.m. the squadron intelligence officers had delivered the battle order of the individual planes and their crews to the Operations Room while, bleary-eyed and tousled, the men themselves were having the ops breakfast of orange juice, coffee, bacon and a couple of fried eggs. At 6 a.m. they were crowded into the briefing room. The 226 Squadron commander (Wing Commander Dennis Mitchell) described the target and the plan of attack. The Wing Commander Flying and Squadron Leader Navigation went into landmarks along the route and 'hot' areas to be avoided, because they were particularly well protected by enemy ack ack. The Met Officer described the weather potential. There was still an alarming amount of ground mist but the Met man was reassuring (as Met men tend to be).

Neither I nor my sergeant would be at the briefing. The battle orders transmitted to me by Bill Edrich over the scrambler telephone were being confirmed at this time by a coded repetition sent on ticker tape. We had to check these blocks of four figures against the volumes of decoding instructions which were stored in a safe in the Operations Room. It could be opened only by a combination of numbers known partly by the Duty Operations Officer and partly by his sergeant.

Officially, everything that I had scribbled down at Edrich's dictation should have been checked against the decoded tape before the planes took off. It was a devil of a job to carry this out satisfactorily. There were always a dozen unique crises to solve, eating into the time we needed on the coding. By the very definition of the job it could not be delegated to anyone else. Group HQ had the nasty trick of slipping into the coded tape a new instruction or piece of fresh information that had not been available or thought of when Edrich was dictating the battle order, so you could not afford to skip through the decoding. This was, after all, at that moment a linchpin of the war. Any slackness or failure on the part of the Operations Room could lead to the death of comrades, even a shift in the course of battle.

By 6.15 a.m. the briefing was over. The last observer had pushed his charts and notes into his navigation bag and scuttled through the ground mist after his impatient pilot. The revving of seventy-two engines reached a crescendo. Like impatient war horses, the planes were bouncing and slurping along the dispersal roads and getting into the right order for take-off. Take-off itself was at 6.40 a.m. and was a breathtaking sight. As it got under way there were two aircraft just leaving the ground at the far end of the runway, two more going full belt down the middle of the field and two more just starting off at the near end. All three squadrons – thirty-six aircraft – would be airborne in two-and-a-half minutes. The whole field rang and danced to the thunder of engine power precisely as it reached its apogee.

Now, I thought, I must tell the commanding officer. I didn't need to. There was a snarl of brakes outside the Operations Room. The door swung open with a crash. Framed in it was Group Captain MacDonald. He advanced to the edge of the dais, and pitched his voice across the twenty feet that separated us.

'Do you realise that you are responsible for sending thirty-six aircraft on a suicidal mission?' His voice had the cutting edge of a handsaw. There seemed no adequate reply.

Fortunately there was a diversion. Samson came in noisily and slumped down on the edge of the dais. Wing Commander Spencer was behind him.

'Ah, Neil, forecast is that this will all burn off in an hour, and then it's going to be another hot, dry day. I told Gill not to bother you.'

Another piece of luck for me was that Group Captain and Wing Commander had been friends since school days.

IV

For once the Met Officer was right. The ground mist cleared well before the return of our squadrons. It was the harbinger of a splendid month of May. Day after day dawned to brilliant sunshine. The Australian crews played poker dice in the dust of their dispersal area, stripped down to their underpants. They organised shooting contests with our issue .38 revolvers in the scrubland beyond the end of the runway. When going on an operation they would strap the six-shooter to their sides Western style. Hillaby, the laconic Met Officer, complained that it was more dangerous to visit 226 Squadron than to fly a mission over Berlin.

Not everyone was pleased with the long continued heat wave. 'We need this weather next month, not now,' grumbled Gerry Baker to Jack Adams. June was the month when we expected the invasion of Europe to take place. Bad weather was unlikely to hinder the ground fighting, but it could make a vital difference to air support. On the Western Front we knew that our biggest advantage was in the air, while on the Eastern Front it was the almost unlimited manpower of Russia.

What about the Germans? What were their advantages? Well, now they were fighting for the defence of their homeland – just as we had been four years before in the Battle of Britain. We had no reason to doubt their ruthless and brutal ability in war, and their ingenuity in developing arms that were second to none, like the 88mm gun that could be used against tanks or infantry or elevated into an anti-aircraft weapon. The Tiger Tank was probably better than any we had. Even the Spitfire was surpassed by the Me 109 at certain heights. Then, they were clearly developing something new. All over Western Europe, but particularly facing London and the south coast of Britain, were clusters of concrete platforms, not very large, but heavily defended from aerial attack and enormously reinforced to withstand the largest bombs. We knew all that well, but junior officers like me had not the faintest idea of their purpose.

The most alarming aspect was the speed with which they were being built. Some intelligence reports suggested they might simply be decoys intended to divert us into wasting time, air crews and bombs on something that was nothing more than what they appeared: a whole lot of concrete boxes. But would they have gone to such immense trouble to make them almost impregnable if there was nothing else? Throughout the month of May they were our chief targets, yet dozens of 1,000lb bombs hardly raised a pimple on their concrete surfaces.

My first few weeks in 137 Wing seemed like a prelude, a hush before the storm. In the whole of this time we had no aircraft losses. Every day the squadrons would take off, circling above the airfield to gain height, then fifteen minutes across the Channel, five or ten minutes to identify the target, drop the bombs and head for home. Probably there would be a repeat performance in the afternoon. From 10,000 feet, the whole of the Pas de Calais resembled a patient with a bad case of acne. Near the mysterious concrete caves the pock marks were almost continuous. An area as big as Kent looked as though it was being pulverised into a replica of the First World War trenches.

Just as the early scenes in a Shakespearian tragedy set up the action and introduce the central players, so within five days of my arrival at Hartford Bridge I had been ordered with some other junior Air Force officers to attend the passing-out parade of the Army cadets at Sandhurst. An annual event, this ceremony in spring 1944 could not have had a more appropriate presiding officer. It was Montgomery, whose victories in North Africa and Sicily had probably led to his replacing Rommel in British esteem. As I wrote to my mother: 'It was a delightful day, the band playing, the large crowd of assorted uniforms, doting parents and pretty girls – the whole thing had more the atmosphere of a garden party.' Except for Monty. 'What a rat-trap of a man he is! He looks made up of sand and grit. With all the flashing spurs and knee boots, red-tabbed tunics and fancy hats of the various high-ranking and Allied officers around him, he looked almost insignificant, small and slightly stooped in plain battle dress and beret. But one felt looking at his beaky nose and ferrety sharp eyes that he was the keenest person there.'

It was, of course, as well to think so, as Monty was to be in direct command of the largest invasion force that had ever left our shores. Now that invasion has the inevitability of history, but then there were many hazards. In order to learn more about them I had myself locked in with 'Overlord'. This was the multi-volume planning document on all aspects of the invasion (code name Overlord). Only the senior wing commanders and the intelligence officers were allowed to peruse these dense, unrewarding pages. They were a big disappointment. I liked the idea of being locked up with a set of volumes as dangerous as a pride of lions. Of course, what Hitler would have wanted to know was where the invading forces were going to land, how many battalions, where were the reserves . . . All these useful facts were heavily disguised behind fancy names and deliberately falsified numbers. It was bad enough working through the numerological code, the correct translation of which was my chief duty in laying out all aspects of our next bombing raid. Of course, I was only an intermediary. It surprised me how much the spearhead of these raids was pointed and carried through at the group level. That was the level of the dynamic Air Vice-Marshal Basil Embry and his advisers, like the Atcherly brothers. Very rarely do I recall our wing commanders of flying and operations sending up a suggested operation. Such suggestions were more likely to come from the Army, wanting, for instance, a German gun battery which was holding up our advance bombed out of the way. This was the correct line of the command, because we were the Second Tactical Air Force, brought into being to be a direct right arm for the Army.

All that would apply once we were in the fair land of France. Yet, as the fateful month of June unfurled, Gerry Baker's gloomy prognostications began to come true. It had been so dry and hot that I had been on a low-level flight in a Boston in late May when our principal task had been to plot the position of the numerous forest fires that danced through the greenwood verge of the New Forest. Very fearful these sudden blazes looked when viewed from directly above through the transparent bubble of the navigator's position. I had already decided that I should try to make my first operational flight the first that the Mitchells of 226 Squadron undertook after the invasion of Europe had begun. I had formed a friendship with a youthful sergeant, pilot George Sims, and his navigating officer, Peter Martin. Peter and I were the two youngest of the eighty or so officers in 137 Wing. George and Peter readily agreed to take me as a supernumerary on this trip whenever it should occur.

The timing of the invasion became hourly more difficult to predict. The Prime Minister wrote: 'June 3 brought little encouragement. A rising westerly wind was whipping up a moderate sea. There was heavy cloud and a towering cloud base. Predictions for June 5 were gloomy.' After many of the invasion forces had been at sea for hours in horrible conditions they were recalled, but kept on board their cramped, pitching and wallowing landing craft. The invasion was delayed a day.

At Hartford Bridge we knew something was going wrong and that it was an effect of the weather. On 5 June, the original D-Day, we were confined to the camp. Most of the officers trooped into the camp cinema in the evening. The film, as I recall, was one of those busty Regency romances with Margaret Lockwood, probably *The Man in Grey*. As the film ended, a scrawled notice was projected requesting all officers to report to the Officers' Mess. Splashing through the puddles, we wondered what the verdict was. The sky still looked stormy, yet it would be almost impossible to keep the element of surprise going if we had to land our seasick troops back in England . . . The bar was a large Nissen hut, already crowded with most of the French officers, who were apparently unmoved by Margaret Lockwood's upholstery.

The CO was in command, looking much more benign than usual. 'Come on chaps, what will you have? The drinks are on the house tonight. The invasion is tomorrow.' We all joined in toasting the great adventure. I had a large gin and tonic and thought I was living a piece of history.

11

FIRE ON THE RUNWAY

I

Later that night I was running, running, running, along a wide flat highway under a sky that was broadening with pre-dawn light. I was going to miss something if I did not run fast enough to catch it up. What could it be? The noise was so deafening it blotted out all thought. It was coming up behind me. That was it – I was running on the runway, the planes were taking off, they were coming up behind me. They were going to obliterate me with that fearsome noise. I sat up in bed. The whole hut rang and trembled with the sound of the engines. *They were really taking off into the lightening sky. It was the first operation after D-Day and I was not on it.* I scrambled into clothes and flying boots – I had inherited them from someone who had not been wearing them when he went missing – and really ran up the hill to the airfield. It was too late. The sound of the engines faded southwards.

I sat down heavily on a loading tender. That was strange. I was surrounded by Mitchells in varying stages of repair. For D-Day each squadron was committed to put fifteen planes at readiness instead of the usual twelve. That accounted for the fact that there was hardly a Boston in sight. It was their taking off that had woken me. They had gone to lay smoke in front of the landing beaches. There was no room for any additional passengers in the Boston, so I had not missed being on our first Mitchell operation after invasion.

I interrogated some of the crews on their return. It must have been a heart-wrenching mission. The Bostons flew just above the water, leaving long streamers of smoke to blind the defenders. In these opening moments of the battle there was little sign of a German response. We lost only one Boston, shot down by mistake by our own battleship, *Warspite*. The British Navy was notoriously trigger-happy when approached by a plane from an unusual angle.

We expected that the Mitchells would be in the next wave of attack, bombing the German shore defences and gun emplacements, but the weather proved even worse than the forecast. For four days we were grounded. Four crucial days, while the greatest armada in history was struggling to gain a foothold on the steep tidal beaches, and the Germans were rushing up their reinforcements.

Compared with the terrible losses of the First World War, the casualties on D-Day were not enormous, but they were not insignificant either. I don't remember them ever being published. On that first, longest, day, the assault on the beaches saw more than ten-and-a-half thousand casualties. It proved far harder to dislodge the defenders than we had expected. Why should the Germans prove so stubborn, when they were bound to lose anyway? We were expecting to take the local town of Caen on the morning of 7 June. A month later we had still not taken it.

The infantry would find itself pinned down between the hedges, ditches and narrow fields of Normandy. There was a fatalism often experienced by those battle-hardened troops. Many had been in the Western Desert battles against Rommel. They were not anxious to risk themselves unduly in these last struggles of the war. Later that summer our maid Dorothy told me that her only brother, brought back from Africa to contribute the tough capability of the hardened warrior, was convinced that he would not survive this last ordeal. He didn't.

It was quite different for air crews taking part in these short bombing raids aimed at the German defenders. Our crews felt humiliated that they could not contribute more to the battle. In those first days after D-Day they were not able to prove their mettle, pinned down, rendered impotent and unable to operate by mere fog and rain, while the poor bloody infantry was expected to slog away without any assistance from its namby-pamby partner in the air. What was the good of relying on an ally who gave up once there was a change in the weather? It was easy to envisage how the British Tommy and American GI would see it.

Each day was no better than the last. We would go through all the rigours and tensions of a briefing which would then be cancelled. It gave me an insight into the moody temperament that afflicted most air crew. I felt so jumpy that I wondered whether I should abandon my plan to take an observer's eye view of the final themes of the war. But on the fourth morning there were some breaks in the cloud.

The fallibility of the weather was an additional psychological strain for the airmen. Days passed and we had not even been allocated a specific target. Then, on 10 June two events hinted at change. The code breakers had discovered that a Panzer group headquarters had been set up to run the battle of Normandy from an orchard twelve miles south of the main battle area at Caen. At the same time, the weather showed signs of a change, but only in a meagre way. All day we waited for it to get just a little bit brighter.

'We really need it this time,' said Squadron Leader Walkerdene. I went through the briefing in a terrified dream. 'Cheer up,' twinkled the real navigator, Pilot Officer Martin, pinching my knee. 'It's well known that intelligence officers always keep out of trouble,' grinned Sergeant Sims.

The exhilaration of the mass take-off lifted the spirits. What did I write in my observer's log book at the time? 'Immense activity both in air and in Channel. Two large fires on Cherbourg peninsula. Meagre, inaccurate heavy flak from Caen area. Weather: clear patches over France. 9/10 strato-cn. en route.'

The area round the Mulberry mobile harbours was so densely active that, as Sergeant Sims said, we didn't need a plane, we could have walked across the Channel on the piled-up shipping. By contrast, the Norman countryside on a midsummer evening seemed far from the turmoil of war. I watched as we put an end to that. On the bombing run the bombs rolled out horizontally like a series of extra-large French loaves. I followed them down through my field-glasses as they straightened into the vertical just before the moment of impact. Dense smoke shot back towards us and was quickly followed by the contributions of the other squadrons. At 12,000 feet we were too distant to see human detail, but that pile of mounting explosive looked conclusive. Indeed, two months later, when the Allies finally fought the seven miles down from Caen, they found the mass graves that replaced their last supper for many of the Panzer group that evening. The general himself and nineteen staff officers were among the German losses.

I didn't know it at the time, of course, but I was more interested in discovering what detail the waning sun revealed to us from 12,000 feet. Most elegant of all were the long avenues of poplar trees near a church in the Caen area. These might have been carved by an industrious craftsman in memory of the nineteen staff officers.

The flight back to base was like the return from some particularly splendid theatre performance which we had all been witnessing. Flight discipline was rigorously maintained – it had to be when all six planes in an individual box were flying wingtip to wingtip, not more than a few feet apart – but this didn't stop the humming of a familiar song or recounting a well-known tale. Adrenaline carried us along in a glow of self-regard.

The same mood elevated the debriefing back at the squadron dispersal. We all felt sure we had been on target and had in some way atoned for the wasted days that had perforce preceded them. There was a section in Siegfried Sassoon's First World War memories that caught this same lyrical self-regard: 'What I felt was a sort of personal manifesto of being intensely alive – a sense of physical adventure and improvident jubilation . . .'.

Across the splatter of the champagne corks in the debriefing room Squadron Leader Walkerdene beckoned.

'How was it then?'

'Some marvellous views, especially coming back.'

'I'm glad I was able to get you that trip,' said the self-regarding squadron leader. He had done nothing to encourage my efforts. Now he was waving a piece of paper at me.

'I'm sorry Gill, they want you at Air Ministry. As from tomorrow. They're on the track of those concrete platforms. There's a lot of additional ciphering to be done.'

Seeing my disappointment he added, 'You can make a personal appeal. It's in your rights. I was sure you would want to do that. I've fixed you an appointment with Personnel for tomorrow morning.'

So perhaps he wasn't so bad after all.

He was certainly right that the rumours of a new weapon had put the planners at Air Ministry in a jitter. But the thought of spending months, perhaps years, pouring over dreary blocks of codified numbers was beyond bearing. They surely didn't need me or my friend Frank Watson from the Intelligence course – the brainy boys had already acquired what appeared to be half of All Souls College, Oxford.

Frank was in the waiting room. I was very pleased to see him. Five or six years older than me, he was infinitely more sophisticated. At my request we went into the interview together. The Personnel Officer was very friendly. He explained that the Air Ministry believed these pilotless planes to be Hitler's last desperate gamble. They would put as many in the battle as they could. Hence the RAF would want every officer who could fly to counter them . . . Ah, but we were not pilots. That was a point on our side. The Personnel Officer could not envisage what we wanted to do if we didn't fly. At this point I joined in and explained that I wanted to make a record of the experiences of war.

'How come?' asked the bewildered Personnel Officer. I wasn't very good at explaining but, as it happened, I had been on that important raid the evening before, and the leading plane in a box of six Mitchells had to carry an additional navigator . . .

At this point the Personnel Officer picked up one of his many phones. 'You better come in Charlie,' he said in the tone of one who had seen everything. We got our permission to fly in a Mitchell on a bombing raid when it did not interfere with normal duties . . . and when the squadron commander endorsed it.

II

My meeting at the Air Ministry occurred on the morning of Monday 12 June 1944. The intelligence offices were crowded with energetic young men, feverishly passing each other short memos on unlikely defence tactics to use against pilotless bombs. That night the first four buzz bombs landed in southern England. In the next three months literally thousands fell on London and the small towns and villages of the south. There was an unlikely rumour that we might be forced to do a deal with the Nazis. Hitler would surely never have abandoned this singularly nasty weapon. Moreover, it glossed over the Nazis' weakest point – the shortage of manpower. Nor were we likely to start negotiating at this late hour.

I had discovered that when my day off came round, I could take the local train into London and meet my father for a meal and a movie or a musical show. We would still have time to catch our respective last trains to Canterbury and Hartford Bridge. It was a pleasure for both of us. My father had taken my mother back to Yorkshire. Quite rightly he thought it was putting too much stress on her fragile nerves for her to stay in Bomb Alley. Life in bomb-battered Canterbury cannot have been any fun for him either.

So, at 11 a.m. on Tuesday 13 June, we met in Piccadilly Circus. Our intention was to stroll past Trafalgar Square, down to the Mall, to Buckingham Palace and so past Hyde Park Corner under the protection of another great war leader, the Duke of Wellington, on to the Hyde Park Hotel for lunch. But things didn't work out that way.

We had only just ceased admiring the window-dressing of Fortnum and Mason and its clock chiming the hours, when a sudden absence of sound caused us to lose our breath. It was the chug-a-way chug-a-lug of Hitler's new weapon. It caught our attention because it wasn't like any other sudden silence. This one was literally a messenger of death. When it stopped it meant the engine had cut off and this crude mechanical device was falling – falling for ten seconds on average and then exploding with the fire power of a 500lb bomb. The dive-bombers at Canterbury had screeched to terrorise; the buzz-bomber left it to your imagination.

What we had not worked out was that at any moment when the chug-a-lug was in the air we needed to know what we were going to do if it stopped. Because it did not fly very high – mostly about 2,000 feet – it was unlikely that we should get a siting on it during its rapid fall. In this first experience we followed instinct and fell flat in the gutter. At the explosion, little whorls of dust rose with the debris of the pavement. The bomb had gone off somewhere north of us, in Soho.

Perversely, we walked down to Jermyn Street, parallel to Piccadilly, but a good deal narrower. We thought we would be safer surrounded by solid early Victorian terraces. We had not got far before the tell-tale chuntering was heard coming up from the river. Now we saw it, our view unobstructed across Green Park, a little spurt of flame coming out of its backside, veering and lurching, presumably to put off the anti-aircraft fire. It looked like a child's mechanical toy. Just before it got overhead, the engine cut out and it dived out of sight.

This time we had thought out our response. This part of London had not only imposing flights of entrance steps, but other narrower steps down which the tradesmen would deliver their crates of wine and assorted goodies. Open to the sky, readily accessible, an ideal buffer for everything, but the direct hit.

Twice more that morning we needed to prepare a defence at short notice. We survived, but the pleasure of the morning constitutional was quite lost. We didn't try it again.

III

Hartford Bridge fell only just within the range of the buzz bomb. I don't remember any blasts disrupting the endless toil of the fitters and riggers. One of the first things I had to master was the geography of the airfield – no small order as I was told it was the fifth largest in Britain. I needed to be able to get in touch immediately with any section of it, and also to understand the relative responsibilities of armourers and radar observers, and where the emergency field dressing was kept.

In some ways it was like being the latest arrival at a traditional public school. The air crews steadily played down their responsibilities, but they expected the newcomer to play the game without being taught. Breakfast for officers was in a big tent from 7 to 8 a.m. There was little difference in food and general amenities between the Officers' Mess and airmen's canteen. After breakfast everyone who could went up to the airfield. Some toiled up the steep little lanes on ramshackle old bicycles or hitched a trip on a lorry-load of incendiary bombs, or managed to get onto the neat little Jeeps (each squadron had recently been allocated one of these quintessentially Yankee inventions). Rough-riding, versatile, amenable and hard to beat, they must have been one of the most popular personifications of Western ingenuity and the value of Lend Lease.

However, they were of no use to Pilot Officer A.M. Gill. As the most junior officer on the field, he was the bottom of the list in getting a ride. Even then he would have to have a driver. Pilot Officer Gill might have aspirations to see the end of the war from close-up, but he would not be driving to the scene: he couldn't drive.

All this sounds a serious disability in getting around a network of Nissen huts, partially disembowelled aeroplanes, stacks of bombs and radio operators trying out their wavelengths. The first thing I noticed was how helpful individuals were. And the second – and perhaps it linked with the first – was how superstitious the air crews were. I suppose this comes out of their inability to control their own destiny. There was also the increasing tension, which went with each further successful completion of a mission. I witnessed this at close quarters when I became friendly with a New Zealand crew. They were only a few months older than me and had that quiet reserve of manner that often seemed to distinguish the people of the far dominion from their brasher neighbours in Australia.

When I knew the Kiwis, they were already halfway through the fatal forties. At this stage of the war a tour (the allocated number of missions that had to be flown before a crew could be withdrawn for a spell in training) that had begun as thirty-five bombing missions had risen to fifty missions. Superstition made a particular hazard of the last half-dozen missions. In fact, the New Zealanders' engines had been playing up, something that was most exasperating to pilot and crew. As with all of us, the New Zealanders had been waiting impatiently for the weather to improve. In a few weeks it became patchier, but it was too late for the Kiwis. They did not return from their forty-eighth mission.

The Mitchells flew wingtip to wingtip and on this particular trip were only briefly under fire on the bombing run itself. The box leader's navigator tried to keep the planes on course while continually altering height and veering from side to side. He needed to hold the bomber on the straight and narrow when the air was in tumult with the bursting of hostile flak all around. For a few minutes, the other pilots agreed, everything was pretty hot – bursting anti-aircraft shells, planes going in all directions, following the box leader's evasive rising and falling. Then suddenly they were out of it, out of Jerry's flak range, bombs dropped and setting course for England.

They could sit back and count their blessings. But, hold on, one was missing. How could that be? It was the Kiwis. Somewhere in the minutes of maximum confusion they had slipped away. Must have gone down low, probably hedge-hopping back to base. But they didn't come back to Hartford Bridge or any other RAF base. After a couple of days they were left on the operations blackboard: 'missing'.

In the mid-years of the war, the centre of aerial conflict was with the daylight bombers and their main targets were support for the Army in its tank battles in the Western Desert. There was another use for these day-time marauders: propaganda. Low-level missions produced some spectacular footage in which tanks, artillery, armoured patrols and refuelling tankers seemed from the air like animated toy soldiers.

The two film photographers Ted Moore and Chuck Evans had joined 137 Wing at a time late in 1943 when the Germans were making attacks on shipping; these destroyed such large numbers of vital oil and food reserves that some economists believed the Germans could win the war by starving us out. Ted Moore had told me he had decided to ask for a transfer to another front – probably in the Far East. The unique role of the cameraman-cum-pilot gave Moore and Evans more authority than their actual rank as flight lieutenants suggested.

Ted Moore was a small compact person from South Africa. Before the war he had been a news cameraman on Pathé Pictorial. Chuck Evans had been his assistant. Tall, with dark wavy hair and an open cheerful expression, he usually accepted Ted's opinion, but now his wife was expecting their first child. Not surprisingly, she hoped to persuade Chuck to stay on the European front. Our CO was likely to view Chuck's attitude with favour. As you will remember, *his* wife was expecting their first child.

Ted had told me all this over a late evening drink in the Officers' Mess tent at Hartford Bridge. He felt his view of the war had reached the limits that could be shown from the somewhat cumbersome spare seat of the Mitchell.

Now, for some reason, he called me over. As I often did, I was walking from breakfast in the cluster of bell tents in the valley to the 226 admin office on the far ledge of the airfield itself. I had only just become aware

that the figure pacing up and down the puddle of dirty oil on the middle
of the now empty dispersal area was the man I had talked with a couple
of nights before.

He looked at me absently and asked what I was doing on the edge of
the runway.

I explained this was a short cut from breakfast to a view of the
squadrons coming back.

'That's it, you don't want to get in their way. Someone might be
injured.' He fumbled in his pocket and brought out a filthy rag. He
looked at it with surprising intensity, then said, 'He left this behind.'

It was an extremely tattered miniature woollen teddy bear. Apparently
Evans never went on a mission without it. This morning, over-sleeping,
in the bustle to get off, he had mislaid the bear. Ted had found it and was
waiting to give it back to its owner just as soon as he physically could. It
wasn't long before we heard the preliminary tremble in the air that spelt
the approach of thirty-six bombers in close formation. Wait, in the
second box of six there was a gap, there was one plane missing. If we had
been waiting in the flying control tower we could have been in
communication with the squadron commander and we would have
known what had happened and which plane was missing. But now we
had to wait for the planes to lose height, to land and come taxiing over to
their individual dispersal bay. By that time we had identified by its
absence which plane was missing. It was indeed the Mitchell that Chuck
Evans had been flying in. No one had seen it go down.

Years later Ted Moore achieved fame with the top cinematography
award of the year for *A Man for All Seasons*.

Long before that had happened a whole lot of medals and citations
were presented to us on the airfield itself by the King and Queen. I had
heard that the King could be frightfully shirty if things didn't work out
the way he had expected. Something certainly went wrong that afternoon.

Virtually the entire personnel of 137 Wing were formed up into a
hollow square. Junior officers formed a guard of honour. I was both the

youngest and one of the tallest so was in a position to hear the row. Something had delayed the royal party. Standing to attention for over an hour might be all right for a Guards regiment, but it made the mixed company of RAF, French and Dutch crews very restive.

All the decorations were carefully laid out. The adjutant, responding to a crib taped to his wrist, picked up the appropriate medal and placed it on a brocaded pillow. This was handed to one of the top RAF brass, I think it was Sir Trafford Leigh-Mallory. He held the cushion out for the King, who had to pick up the medal and stick it onto the recipient's chest. No doubt this wasn't as easy as it should have looked. But the King made it impossibly difficult. He wanted all the trestle tables rearranged, but there were no airmen to do the rearranging. They had been standing to attention for over an hour and were in no mood to be helpful; and the top brass had been wining and dining too indulgently: that was why they were late for their own parade. Trestle tables are all right if you have at least four handlers per table. Unfortunately there weren't that many air vice-marshals to go round. I wrote to my mother: 'If the pictures get on the newsreel, you will probably see me – looking an excellent imitation of a lamp-post! The King disappointed me by being in a bad temper and displaying very poor manners, but I thought the Queen was very charming and much prettier than I had expected.'

She had looked me in the eye and said how youthful many of the air crews looked.

IV

A few days later we had some more distinguished guests, this time from across the Atlantic. Squadron Leader Walkerdene looked more than usually excited. He asked me to stay on duty in case the Yanks wanted to have anything explained to them. There were at least a dozen of them and not one less than a full colonel.

It was the suggestion that they might need something explained that grabbed my attention. Hartford Bridge did indeed harbour an exciting modern invention that none of us had seen in action. Squadron Leader Walkie-Talkerdene ushered us all into the crowded control tower. He explained that one of the hazards of flying from Britain was the way the weather could change in a minute or two. He reminded the American Army men how they had had to make the invasions of Europe without the support of the Mitchells, Bostons and Mosquitoes of 2 Group. 'Much help they would have been,' muttered one of the American generals. 'All that has changed now,' Walkie-Talkerdene went on impetuously. 'What we're about to see has never been seen before. Observe, gentlemen, we are on a hilltop and there is quite a thick mist gathering in the hollows – enough to stop us flying, but no longer, thanks to the wonders of Fido. Switch on Fido.' He gave me a meaningful nudge.

For a few awkward seconds nothing happened. Then there was a dazzling flash that lit up every corner of the control tower, a shrill hissing like the threat of a dozen monster snakes, a powerful smell of petrol. It was all coming from the main runway. As we watched, flames raced forwards leaping like an athlete of fire down the concrete runway. The height of the flames seemed to vary, but to be around eighty feet.

It was a barbaric sight and demanded that the viewer did not take too strong a breath of the tormented air in case the heat overwhelmed us and drew us into the magnet of fire, as was said to happen in the bombed German cities when the RAF inflicted a firestorm on them. Perhaps it was the memory of the dreadful torments that both the RAF and the Luftwaffe had launched on its enemy that made one of the senior American generals turn somewhat impatiently to Squadron Leader Walkerdene, who was just getting into his stride.

'How much does this cost a minute?' It was the sort of question that our squadron leader should have been able to answer, but, of course, he didn't have a clue (nor did anyone else). We could only respond rather lamely that we would forward the figures to him, General Eisenhower, in his London headquarters. 'In the meantime, it's costing too much for a demonstration. Switch it off.' In photographs for which he was prepared, Ike always looked jovial, but there was a tough side to his character.

As for Fido, it was in practical use within a week and was, on the larger airfields such as Hartford Bridge, a valuable method of clearing the foggy air.

It was just about this time that I began to realise how much I was enjoying myself. Within my first five weeks on an active service station I had met at close quarters the Supreme Allied Commander, General Eisenhower; the top fighting general, Montgomery; and the King and Queen at an unguarded moment. This was exactly the way I had daydreamed my war might be. Only one extra touch was needed: it was time to go on another mission.

Once it seemed that it was time to put on my crash hat, there was no point in dawdling. The previous day, 16 July, the Mitchells had attempted to bomb a fuel dump south of Caen. Enemy defensive fire was so strong that we had failed to hit the target and we were briefed to return to it. There was no time to find the best available crew. I scrambled in with a non-commissioned outfit. They didn't mind taking me, and that was it.

The weather was still tricky. After spending twenty minutes circling the airfield looking for a gap in the clouds we were recalled. These sudden changes in plan and enforced idleness were undoubtedly the hardest things to bear. Unexpectedly, in the early afternoon the Met Officer spotted a wider break and the chance that it was going to spread eastwards carried us hopefully into the air again. I was more scared than I had been the first time. But once over the beaches there was so much to see that the immediate action carried me along. The beach was much changed in the five weeks since I had last been there. It seemed the whole of the Normandy coast had been chewed over by some monster and then spat out.

The attractive little town of Lisieux was a mass of sandy-coloured rubble. We were returning the invasion that we had had to endure so many hundred years ago from the Normans. Enemy anti-aircraft fire grew in intensity once we were above the valley of the Seine. The air was dense with ugly black smudges. Death might be in any of them. The crew sang 'Coming in on a Wing and a Prayer'.

Suddenly, the hostile flak intensified before it was expected. We were on the bombing run. The plane shot sideways and upwards. 'Bombs gone,' shouted the navigator (a bit late in the day). Everything this crew did was a bit slow in happening. 'Where's the bloody box?' shouted the pilot. 'Go on, find it for us. Anybody got any suggestions?' A box, you will remember, was a flight formation of six aircraft. Flying so close together was supposed to give us safety in numbers. It was quite terrifying. One moment we were in a mill of thirty-six aircraft, narrowly missing collisions; now there wasn't a plane in the sky. What was worse, there wasn't a cloud either. 'Don't know about you fellows, but I'm going home,' said the pilot. 'You better hurry up,' said Mac the navigator, 'there's a gun battery loading up down there. Start taking evasive action *now*.'

Four puffs, well away to the left, seemed less dangerous than the flying bomb in Piccadilly. Fifty seconds later the next round of four shells had cut the difference between us by half. The pilot cursed and waited for the navigator to give him a warning. 'Off to the right now.' There seemed nothing in the world except the toiling gunners below and the sweating quintet in the plane above. Now I understood what was meant by 'ageing in a moment'. Everything seemed to rest on the mysterious symbiosis that linked the warriors on the ground to the lurching, zigzagging men in the air. Would it never stop? Just off to the left the shell bursts were getting closer and made the air tremble. That was the last chance for the German gunners. We were out of their range from then on.

When we got back to Hartford Bridge (we were the last crew in) I got as fierce a drubbing from old Walky T. as if I had been caught climbing back into school. I listened carefully to what was said. A bombing raid was not a joy ride. If we had been hit by that aggressive gun battery, it was unlikely that I, as the unknown factor, would have had the opportunity to try to get out: that would have fallen to the pilot and navigator. They would probably not have made it either. In my year or so of active service I never knew anybody who escaped by parachute from a falling plane. It was better to suppose that you wouldn't, or not to think about it at all.

The fact that one lone British bomber had lost its way flying over Normandy and was able to get back to base without the appearance of a single Messerschmitt was another symptom of Germany's loss of grip on the war. Once this begins to happen it is hard to stop.

It would be wrong to suggest that the three Mitchell squadrons covered the range of activities going on at this very large airfield. No doubt there were more totally unwarlike men in raincoats sitting in a corner of the bar than I noticed. They tended to keep themselves to themselves. As one of them said to me, it would be better to know as little as possible. If you were caught you would be bound to be tortured. Better to know the minimum so you couldn't betray your friends. These men were the exact opposite of the brash Aussies or introspective New Zealanders of 137 Wing. They waited only till the sky was right. That meant a pile of cumulus to dim the light of the moon. Then the clumsy old Lysander aircraft would be wheeled out to the end of the runway. The plane took off in the middle of the night as silently as possible. The two or three crews on this regular dropping run did their job well. One of their passengers even appeared back in his old seat at the end of the bar – for a few days at any rate. The conventions of war made the spy's lot, even at this gathering place, somehow outside the comradeship that had evolved over the centuries in barracks and parade grounds.

There was another advantage to this rolling heathland. It was quite near London and yet relatively desolate. That brought another distinguished guest to see us in the early autumn. He had with him no petulant team of generals, only a small lapdog, but the guest merited a considerable amount of attention. Prince Bernhard of the Netherlands might have passed for a playboy with the amount of care he lavished on his small canine. He demanded that his dog be given the seat next to him at lunch and fed him special titbits. I'm not sure that the dog didn't accompany the Prince on the mission that had brought him to Hartford Bridge, but he might have found the Spitfire Mark IX noisy and frightening. The Prince was a skilled pilot and had come to see how this new version of our favourite plane was operating. The Mark IX Spitfire could manoeuvre at 39,000 feet, they said, but how adeptly? It was unlikely that the lapdog would help the Prince make up his mind. Before he left, he was fulsome in the plane's praises. He had that characteristic Dutch mixture of hardheaded realism and a streak of disarming erotic fantasy.

I should know. I was now sharing a cabin with a philosophical Norwegian. He had many of the same fey characteristics that went with the northern temperament. As I may not have explained adequately, the whole of 137 Wing was put under canvas in late April. This was to acclimatise us to work in difficult and alien conditions. It did indeed show that work in such conditions was difficult and alien. The powers-that-be quickly agreed that we needed the best possible conditions when fighting the Germans, so we were moved back into the Nissen huts that the Wing had occupied before its brief experiment into Boy Scoutery. Besides the orderly rows of huts, like lines of metal mushrooms, there were a few of a more substantial nature, usually shared between two or three admin officers. I was put in with Captain Torgelson, late of the Norwegian Flying Corps and now the senior flying control officer on the airfield.

I cannot believe that it was mere coincidence that the oldest and youngest officers were put together. It was the sort of tease that gave Squadron Leader Walkerdene his twinkle. It also gave me an insight into a lifetime of daring and adventure. Captain Torgelson had flown with

Nansen in the far north. After the Norwegian resistance crumbled in spring 1940, before the Blitzkrieg, Captain Torgelson went back to his post as headmaster of a senior secondary school in Narvik. He noted that the Germans had left a number of twin-engined sea planes anchored in Narvik harbour. They had sufficient fuel, Captain Torgelson reckoned, to reach the Shetlands. There was no time for checking the engines or studying a map. He had to go or stay. He went, without even saying goodbye to his wife.

With no fuel to spare, he landed on Shetland sands. If I was shocked by his apparent indifference to the fate of his Nordic family, he maintained he was horrified by my lack of sexual experience. Arguments about Nietzsche and Kierkegaard were soon bouncing around that sturdy little hut.

This serious Norseman even found me a book in English to read, *Human Sexual Energy*, by Van Der Velde. It occurs to me now, did he carry this weighty tome with him in his escape from the Germans? It hardly seems likely.

In the meantime, we had a new squadron commander. It was his first flight with us in late July. Bald-headed and sturdily built, he had a navigator who was the exact opposite in build and temperament: lanky, bony and hollow-eyed. He had the Distinguished Service Order and, at the age of twenty-six, had learnt how to handle a tough yet hard-working ground crew almost twice his age. How this team would respond to the wing's new commanding officer remained to be seen.

Every morning those who could find an excuse to go up to the airfield did so. After all, the airfield was the reason why we were there. It was also the carriageway that brought news from the wider battlefront. This morning there was something extra, something dynamic in the air. I tried to prise information from the excited ground crew. All they could say was that something had happened to our new wing commander. We should soon know; we could hear the vibrant power of the returning squadrons. I put on an extra spurt, running up the last steep slope, and saw the whole plateau bisected by the wide sweep of the runway in front of me.

I nearly jumped out of my skin when our new toy, the squadron Jeep, drew up alongside.

'Hop in,' shouted Bob Laurie, looking much less like a careful Scottish Writer to the Signet. 'They've lost an engine.'

Right on cue an amazing spectacle reared up on the opposite side of the airfield. It could have been a crazy artistic vision of Frankenstein, the dying moments of a metal monster. Even as we watched, the whole right-hand side of the monster peeled off and went cart-wheeling across the airfield to a scattering of bicycles, airmen, back-up planes and ambulances.

'He hasn't got control,' shouted Bob. 'Any moment he's going to blow up!' As if in answer, the monster ground a supply hut to powdered concrete. A wild figure leapt out of the top hatch to shouts of applause. It was the Wing Commander's long-limbed navigator, waving his arms and dancing over the tangle of junk which had once been a bomber. He was shouting some long and complex message. What was it? 'Friends, Romans, countrymen . . .'

The Wing Commander shimmied his considerable bulk through the ruins of the fuselage. We agreed that it was a more decorous way to arrive than coming through the ceiling like the navigator. But what had happened to all that high octane fuel?

'We dumped it in the North Sea,' said the navigator. 'Think I would have danced on top of full tanks?'

After a bitterly contested summer the German discipline began to crack. For a few heady days it seemed the war might end that autumn. But it proved indeed a bridge too far, though all 137 Wing's resources were marshalled to bomb together – forty-eight Mitchells and thirty Bostons. This was to break up German troop concentrations in the woods south of Caen. Appallingly bad weather held up the Air Force's chief duties – to act as the spearhead for the Army. The airfield became a monument to lost friends.

Early in October we took over the German airfield of Vitry-en-Artois in northern France. It was better maintained than Hartford Bridge. What struck us all were the pads of matching grey leather above the urinals. Intensive research revealed that these were for the foreheads of the impressive young airmen who would regularly drink themselves insensible. Our French interpreter and guide was surprised that the pragmatic British had not worked out a similar device . . . Thinking it over forced us to admit that our drinking bouts tended to go on haphazardly until a quick dash for the outside door was necessary. Yet there also seemed something unwholesome in such excess as the Germans anticipated.

It all came down to customs that had been established long before the Wright Brothers took off in their skinny little concoctions of wire, string and sails. Only three weeks before, German fighter planes had taken off regularly from the concrete runways. Now it was our turn to savour the amenities.

Now that we were based on French soil, and here to liberate this ancient enemy, 342 Squadron sounded a fresh note of cheerful optimism and comradeship. Moreover, it was clear that the German pilots had done themselves well. An eighteenth-century chateaux was our new headquarters. It seemed the right place and the right time to celebrate the return of the native – a lorryload of champagne, more little tins of caviar than I had believed were still in existence and, of course, an adequate show of beautiful women. It was mid-October and getting a little late to celebrate the victory of the Battle for Normandy in secluded bowers in the frosty garden. Moreover, there was something unbalanced in the revellers. It was not only differences of ages and languages, there was something else. I realised that behind the music in the Glenn Miller style there was a continual droning. It was not in English or French. Could it be? It could. I remembered there was a Scots officer who, in times of stress (like now), resorted to the bagpipes.

I was curious to see who the bagpipes were summoning forth. It wasn't difficult. Once I was inside the French windows, the corridors acted as resonators. I turned a corner, and it was the close-up of the crew of the disintegrating Mitchell back at Hartford Bridge. But there was a different plot. My arrival was the cue for a rearrangement of the scene. The piper slung his pipes under his arm and went off to deafen another part of the chateau. The navigator piled two chairs on top of each other. The wireless operator took up his position by a small barrel. Beside the bed there was a splendid black-haired temptress. There was something irresistibly comic about the scene: the plump and middle-aged Wing Commander, comfortably wrapped in his somewhat tattered silk dressing-gown, dividing his attention between the oysters in their barrels (specially flown up from Whitstable the day before) and the glamorous serving maid. It might have been a scene recorded by Hogarth. The wireless operator dug out an oyster from his small barrel. The navigator cracked open the oyster and sprinkled it with fresh lemon juice. The dark lady took it between her teeth and transferred it to the Wing Commander's mouth.

12

A COTTAGE IN THE WOODS

I

Not all of the half-dozen bombing raids I took part in were particularly eventful. I made the mistake of assuming that geographical variety would show up from 10,000 feet, which often it didn't. I was disappointed by my first view of Holland. Our mission was to destroy the raised causeway between Zuid Beveland Island and the Dutch mainland. We achieved our objective. I wrote in my log book: 'Belgium and Holland appeared dead countries, much inundated with flooding; dull country, dull weather, dull trip.'

This was in the autumn of 1944. The British and American armies were slugging their way slowly to the Rhine, but for the supporting Second Tactical Air Force, stuck in the mud of northern France, there was little to occupy the dreary days. Recognising this, the powers-that-be instigated a series of forty-eight-hour leave passes to the newly liberated city of Paris. Being democratic, there had to be equivalent proportions of airmen, NCOs and officers. Lots were cast to make the final choice truly impartial. Human nature then took a hand.

One of the first of the officers to draw lucky was Wing Commander Operations, Jack Adams. Stockily built with a briskly dark moustache, he looked far from the romantic self-sacrificing war pilot immortalised by Richard Hillary in the *The Last Enemy*. But appearances can be misleading. Jack must have had a romantic streak in his nature. He discovered that this first Paris trip coincided with my twenty-first birthday. He had seen Paris many times in the peaceful days before the Second World War, I never. Jack bequeathed his leave ticket to me on the condition that I used it to behave in a thoroughly reprehensible manner. I was not at all sure what Jack meant, but he said I was not to worry, I would know when it was happening.

My first impression of the romantic capital of art, music and *joie de vivre* was that it badly needed a fresh coat of paint. I was not in a position to come to any strong judgement, as it was the first foreign city I had seen. The journey from 137 Wing had been in the back of a three-ton truck crowded with airmen who were, like myself, steadily getting soaked in the freezing fog of northern France.

When we were deposited at our modest hotel on the Left Bank, we were delighted to discover that every room had a private bath or shower, by no means common on the Continent at this time. Common or unique, I didn't care. The hot bath followed by the embrace of freshly laundered sheets took charge of the next twelve hours. The next day was much the same. Most impressive was being saluted by the policemen on point duty – much smarter than our West End bobbies, I decided.

I chummed up with a British Army captain. He had gone straight from public school to Spain, as a Roman Catholic volunteer fighting for Franco – the only Englishman I ever met who supported the Nationalists to the point of fighting for them. Otherwise, there seemed nothing particularly odd about him. We went to the Folies-Bergères and afterwards invited two of the 'girls' out for supper. They had remarkably sharklike teeth and made it quite clear that they meant only to eat with them. Some time around two in the morning, with Trevor my Army friend, I found myself in a basement nightclub. Two French companies had made a merger and were celebrating by taking out the wives of the directors. We were invited to join the party. That suited everyone. The wives were in their early forties and enjoyed flirting with these foreign officers. They were more interesting than the voracious Folies girls and they came with free champagne. This is perhaps what won the day.

Returning from a trip to the *Hommes*, I saw Trevor spread-eagled on the floor of a small cubicle and looking decidedly green. The flutter of bar girls promised to look after him. I expect they did; I never saw him again. I had other things to occupy my attention.

I had collected my overcoat and was trying to work out where this insignificant side street led. The nightclub was clearly closing down. At the entrance I bumped into someone whose perfume was familiar. She had sung a French version of the blues, not very well. But under the flashing lights, with the sparkling wine and heavy perfume, she had been part of the show. That was it – part of the show. We looked at each other. At that moment the rain came on with renewed vigour. One of those rickety French taxis squealed to a stop, the driver leant out and after a short argument we bundled inside. The taxi drove off and the argument in French continued fiercely. She explained that if I paid double the taxi would take me home later. That seemed an unlikely proposition, even after several glasses of champagne. I put the extra money down as a hostage to fortune – then there was my promise to Jack Adams. Nothing so far seemed to have matched his expectations for me. The street resembled a set for *Les Miserables*. The rain had stopped and the gaunt women on the corners seemed to be waiting for betrayal.

The war was still on. I had a reminder of this when, later in the night, my partner stirred next to me in her sleep. What long sentences. It wasn't English, but it wasn't French either. It had to be German. While I was wondering whether to wake her – she sounded so unhappy – I reminded myself that the Germans had been occupying Paris for four years. It would have been odd if there hadn't been a few wartime romances, and with that consoling thought I dropped off to sleep in her arms.

When I woke the light was changing. I turned and reached for my bedfellow. She wasn't there. I felt a sudden pang of loneliness. She was standing naked in the window, eating an apple with the first rays of sunlight gleaming on her skin. She turned and laughed at me. Now I knew what the Wing Commander meant. On my return I didn't need to give Wing Commander Adams a complete account of my stolen weekend. He took one close look at my careworn features and burst into applause. 'What, didn't I tell you? Connie, come over here!' They thought the bags under my eyes were a symptom of debauchery. What a thing to think.

Shortly afterwards I clinched a rare opportunity to go on operations with the dandy of the Wing, Tony Parsons. Parsons had deeply impressed me a few weeks previously when, having returned with a badly wounded rear gunner, he carefully brushed off his hat and executed a salute while coming down a collapsible ladder butt-end first. Having personally overseen the careful removal of the unlucky rear gunner, he took us on a tour of the fuselage. It was an impressive collection of jagged holes of every size and shape. It was difficult to imagine that anyone had survived that storm of shot and shell. For the first time we were to bomb Germany itself.

The target was a concentration of troops defending the Ruhr village of Udem. At the time I wrote: 'Concentration of bombs across the village which disappeared under smoke and flame. Some accurate heavy flak from Goch. Fine cloudless weather and immense air activity over Germany – heavies going out to the Ruhr, rocket phoons diving on the Goch area. Heavy German artillery barrage west of Goch.'

We expected to return to the attack the next day, but at the last minute Army Intelligence discovered the enemy had withdrawn. Some weeks later I was being driven to our new airfield, Gilze Rijen in southern Holland. I saw a signpost to Udem and, seized by the mood of the moment, got my driver (under duress) to make a diversion. It looked as though the whole main street had been bulldozed into an enormous dust heap. Two towers were all that was left of the church, the school, the old cattle market. Clearing up was a massive task, but everyone took part. Many of the citizens were injured and there was no compensation for those who had lost arms and legs. A blinded musician sat on the rubble and added a note of defiance to the sorting of the broken bricks and stones. It was a daunting sight – yet it was being tackled with such energy and discipline that, paradoxically, we left Udem with a feeling of being uplifted, a feeling which often came to me later in my position of disarmament officer on the North Rhine Province.

My feelings about the enemy were hard to analyse. All my life my reaction to change has been aversion, an instinctive feeling of fright. This feeling never predominates for long, and underneath is excitement and, in this case, curiosity. There was also trepidation. How could the Germans do other than hate us, after six years of war? Did we not hate them? Plenty of things had been revealed in the last few months that gave me cause: the awful photographs of the shambling ghouls in the concentration camps, the naked corpses being shovelled into mass graves, Richard Dimbleby's radio account of entering Belsen. We had known about the Nazi atrocities, but the occupation of Germany had revealed them to be on a scale that dwarfed the barbarities of Attila and Nero.

The mounting pressure and anticipation of the last days and weeks of the war were a considerable strain. It was only a matter of time. Yet the Germans went on fighting with that single-minded brutal energy that had supported them against the combined forces of Britain, North America, Australia and most of Europe. We knew that their available manpower was not unlimited. What we did not know was how determined the Americans were to fight the Nazi system to the bitter end. As we believed we were. We were lucky that our secret weapon (the atom bomb) was just a few months more developed than the German rocketry. Had the situation been reversed, as it might easily have been, the whole course of human history could have been quite different and that was impossible to imagine.

Instead, we were able to treat the end of the war as a sort of jape, a time for comic relief.

In April 1945 we moved north. One evening, one of our most experienced pilots came into the dormitory and announced that he had commandeered a jeep and was going to have a look at the enemy, who were a few miles away where the front line was an intermesh of canals and flat fields. Stocked with supplies of Stein Hagen, I and some half-dozen others jumped on board.

We had begun by looking somewhat apprehensively for the enemy. We didn't see one German. They had sensibly tucked themselves away somewhere. They weren't missed. As the night wore on, more and more often we were stunned by our pilot's brilliance in driving. There was one moment when I noticed the source of that brilliance . . . no one was driving the jeep. Somehow, in our drunken state, we were making our relatively slow progress alongside the dykes, illuminated by fantastic fireworks displays, with only the occasional zigzag keeping us from sudden death. During a detonation of fireworks I decided to find out how many of us there were taking the jeep ride. Normally, jeeps, being open-sided vehicles, carry about eight people, double the specified workload of four. Well, we were more than I expected – twenty-six.

The so-called driver slapped me on the back. 'You'll not forget this night, boy,' he said, misty-eyed with Stein Hagen. I suppose that was true. By this time I was heartily sick of the war. I wanted to get on with what was going to be the rest of my life.

The disarmament wing, to which I was posted on the break-up of 137 Wing in the autumn of 1945, saw the most unhappy period of my RAF career. Allocated a jeep, a sergeant interpreter, a driver, and lists of enemy war equipment that it was my job to track down and destroy, I found myself sandwiched between two unpleasant types of human being. The sergeant interpreters were mostly young men whose parents had sacrificed themselves in order to get their favoured sons to the relative safety of Britain in the 1930s. They themselves had vanished into the Nazi death camps. The bitter hatred of these young men for anything German was understandable but deeply depressing. On my other side were the officers, many of whom had served in the Military Police in Palestine before the war. They were adept at finding ways to cheat the Germans out of whatever they had left from the tattered remains of their homes. Characteristic of their approach was to declare that all the watches and clocks in a tenement block had been confiscated by order of the British Luftwaffe. The unfortunate German householders knew this was unlikely to be true, but what could they do? The sight of a brandished Mauser was a potent persuader.

The war began with Hitler's defeat of Poland in less than a month, as he established the success of a new form of war, the Blitzkrieg. As the war continued its ruthless course, more and more of the vanquished enemy were needed to assemble Hitler's own guns, tanks and submarines. Thus when I came to sort out one of the largest of Hitler's war factories, Krupp's works at Essen on the Rhine, I found out that the German involvement was fewer than three thousand workers against eleven thousand slave labourers imported from Russia, Poland and the Baltic. Now these starving scraps of humanity had been left with no hope except vengeance and a need to get back to their homeland.

We were living in the small village of Wülfrath, in the Ruhr, based in a former Nazi Brown House. One afternoon I glimpsed through the window three German civilian policemen stumbling and falling in the winding cobbled street outside. I'd heard about local robber gangs and I assumed the policemen had been involved in some kind of gang battle. The local Polish gangs were shifting further north looking for articles to loot. These policemen had not been armed and now appeared to be seriously injured. I ran upstairs to fetch my .38 revolver. I shared a comfortable room with Flight Lieutenant Jenkins, a radar expert. He was lying on his bed smoking a pipe. He was unmoved by the plight of the policemen, and made no answer when I asked him to accompany me. He was due to be demobbed in a couple of weeks and back to running his local cinema in Kent before Christmas.

The two German girls who kept the house neat for us had managed to get the policemen inside. Two of the policemen had passed out. The third was still conscious. He had a dark welt across his midriff. I tried to telephone the first-aid centre at the bottom of the street that had been set up next to an RAF military centre and was run by a WAAF medical orderly. There, some three hundred yards away, were order, discipline and help. But all lines seemed to be down. Unfortunately, Jenkins, the radar expert upstairs, was also our communications man.

Meanwhile the policemen needed immediate medical attention. I made sure again that all six chambers of my service revolver were loaded. I was not a good shot, but how was the enemy going to know that?

I set off down the hill, my shoes making a great clatter on the cobbles. Turning a corner, a black cat darted across the road directly in front of me. If I hadn't got my pistol jammed in its holster I would probably have fired a couple of rounds to encourage myself. It was a bendy road and I was conscious of prying eyes peeping round the old lace curtains.

The last corner took me directly into the entrance of the RAF regiment's quarters. As soon as I saw the sentry's broad Yorkshire back I felt a great rush of confidence. I doubt that my fluty tones had the same effect on him. His sergeant, hearing the shooting, had already sent British soldiers to boost up the German police. The telephone breakdown was soon put right. The bandit was found on the edge of the village. He had lost his gun in the tussle with the police. For their courage the policemen were promoted. They all survived. The bandit was tried by a military tribunal in Mettmann and executed.

II

After Christmas 1945 I was posted to Bad Godesberg. This was to allow me to take a three-month course in physics and chemistry. What had this to do with tidying up the Ruhr? Or capturing Polish bandits? More than you might expect. The British government had set up a scheme that allowed servicemen to take useful courses in subjects that would extend their potential capacity when they were demobilised. I was going to spend six or seven years learning to be a doctor. The first two years were purely school subjects: physics and chemistry. They could be taught in any technical school which had the appropriate facilities and a teacher whose basic language was English. The Germans provided the laboratory, the RAF the teacher.

This was one of the most useful courses I ever took. Within three weeks of the impact of H_2O on my ill-trained mind I knew I would never be a doctor. I could never, never, NEVER learn all those boring formulas. I continued the course. It gave me three months to think seriously about what path I might take. It also gave me time to think about how I was to break the news to my father.

Journalism? My six months on the local Canterbury paper had been an enjoyable interlude, but could I see myself thirty years on, wreathed in stale tobacco and old jokes?

I had just won a local RAF award for creative writing. Effectively, this was a short story in which I imagined the narrator had just been given the order to shoot someone and shoot to kill. Clearly my experience walking down the village street, not knowing when I was going to be shot at, had some influence on my choice of subject. At a deeper level, living among the terrible destruction we had wrought on the conquered enemy posed implicit problems. Curiously, losing did not stir up the individual conscience to the same degree.

The Bad Godesberg Officers' Mess was comfortable and modern. The RAF had clearly chosen it because the destruction close by was relatively acceptable. It was enough to look at the patient lined face of Maria, the German house administrator. It called for sympathy and a dignified distance. It was a silent reminder of the horrors of war.

I persuaded Maria to allow me to escort her to her home among the birches. Walking through the snow-crusted woods, she seemed to have little to say until we reached a small chalet-like cottage. Here she barred the door, but not very effectively. Inside, her room was crammed with objects from the first few months of life, all of the best quality: a shiny pram, a carrycot, rattles, woolly toys and party clothes. Everything just as it should be. Except there was no occupant. I looked up with a question, but anticipated the answer. The child had died of starvation in the winter of 1943–4. I took her hand and spoke some words of sympathy. She had been living with these overwhelming reminders of her loss for two years. In search of consolation, I pointed at a photograph of a handsome, thoughtful-looking young man. Yes, he was the father, but he would not be returning: he had been killed at Stalingrad.

One of the service duties that I still had to carry out was that of Orderly Officer. They were nothing like as hair-raising as my close encounter with the banditry. Mostly it was a case of enforcing closing times. By 10 o'clock there were few people about so it was quite a surprise to hear someone playing the piano. It seemed to be coming from the NAAFI, the only centre for the airmen to meet the former enemy.

The lights were low; the keys of the piano were being struck with more feeling than accuracy.

> We'll meet again . . .
> Don't know where
> Don't know when . . .

The voice sounded familiar.

'Come on, break it up now.' The Orderly Sergeant strode forward with the voice of authority.

'Just a minute, Sarge. I think I recognise that voice.'

I did. It was Wyndham Davidson. He was deeply sun-tanned and lined, but I would never have failed to recognise those precise tones. It turned out that he had been posted to Nigeria when I went to Northern Ireland. He had been back only a month or so. I considered him a kind person and introduced him to Maria. We must have seemed an odd three-some as we walked together in the woods. However, war is no protector of human needs and in the autumn I was posted back to the Ruhr.

Years later I received a long letter from Wyndham. I was flying to the States with my wife Georgina the very next morning, so I'd had no time to follow it up. At about half-past eleven our front door bell rang. He announced himself on the speaker-phone.

I walked on to the landing, and coming up the stairs was an old man. His hair, which used to be such a romantic black, was now a tousled grey. He intercepted my look of surprise.

'It happens to us all,' he grunted.

III

My last position in the RAF became in many ways the most interesting. The German airfield at Wahn, near Cologne, was being expanded under RAF supervision to fit the needs of a rapidly growing civilian air centre. It was the RAF's job to ensure that while all the latest equipment was made available, we should still keep an eye on this formidable ex-enemy. We were attempting to repair shattered Germany, though we had no clear vision of the world we were building. When we met someone who did, it was a genuine shock. One of the most exciting was Group Captain Cheshire. He was the most highly decorated airman on the Allied side. The British Labour Government gave him a Mosquito in which to travel around the world to assess its wants. In the autumn of 1946 he landed at Wahn. It was my task to entertain him until our senior officer had ascertained the official line on Cheshire. The man who had marshalled the most terrible air raids ever carried out and had seen the atom bomb drop on Nagasaki was unperturbed. He looked remarkably fresh and lively.

Tentatively I tried to probe his attitude. He seemed to think that the world could be of one mind. One country would follow another. When the Allies – USA, UK, Russia and the as yet uncommitted China – saw the cost of war, they would hold off. In this he reminded me of the older masters of games at school: some boys, of course, always cheat, but they would be in the minority. It seemed hard to believe that was all we had learned. I reserved my judgement and hoped for the best.

Group Captain Cheshire's optimism reminded me of one of the parties that I attended in the last days of the war. I had chummed up with our new squadron leader's navigator. We had strolled round the fading magnificence of the north German schloss that had become our officers' quarters. It was strangely sentimental of Germany, we both thought, to want to preserve this decayed nineteenth-century palace. We agreed that it was an incongrous memorial to the Third Reich.

My newfound friend told me that, having spent five years destroying every aspect of Hitler's omnivorous greed, he wanted his peacetime career to be that of architect, in some recompense for all the works of destruction that he had participated in.

The following day 137 Wing tried once more to destroy the bridge over the River Meuse. The raid was not a success. Among others we lost the Wing Commander and my friend his navigator. Two or three days later the British army had taken the bridge. We discovered that the Germans had dragged the corpses out of the debris of their aeroplanes and hung them on scaffolding at the approach to the bridge. They hung placards around their necks with an epitaph: 'These are the British airmen who sought to kill you.'

So much for my friend's plans to build new bridges.

> Not marble, nor the gilded monuments
> Of princes, shall outlive this powerful rhyme;
> But you shall shine more bright in these contents
> Than unswept stone, besmeared with sluttish time.
> When wasteful war shall statues overturn,
> And broils root out the work of masonry
> Nor Mars his sword nor war's quick fire shall burn
> The living record of your memory.

Afterword

ANTS ON SNOW

Georgina Gill

Michael never went to Guy's Hospital. Wanting to understand what had turned the ordered world of his childhood into turmoil, and perhaps to change things, he decided to study philosophy and psychology at university. Edinburgh accepted him, but before he went he followed his uncles to America. He went to stay with his charismatic Uncle Clifford, sophisticated Aunt Harriet and cousin Carolyn, who had so impacted on his twelfth year. She was now a full-grown beauty, with a trail of suitable admirers. Michael enjoyed summer on the Great Lakes, cocktail parties, much driving about in fast cars and a thoroughly hedonistic contrast to England and the war years. But he returned, and spent four years at Edinburgh University, making friends who have lasted a lifetime, and meeting Yvonne Gilan, the beautiful actress who was to become his wife.

Michael continued to write, short stories for little magazines, and, on graduation in 1951, he took a job on the *Scotsman* as a sub-editor and arts reviewer. In 1954 Adrian was born. Shortly afterwards a colleague of Michael's on the *Scotsman* persuaded him to apply for a job at the BBC, mainly so that he'd have a companion for the journey to London. Michael got the job.

Michael's BBC career started in radio, working on the North American Service. This meant compiling programmes for America which would portray life in Britain. They were almost a reverse angle of Alistair Cooke's *Letter from America*, which had been running since the war years.

It gave him a wonderful introduction to London; a brief to cover arts and politics meant a chance to interview practically anyone and honed his ability to find the point of every story and to present it with simplicity and style. In 1955 his work won him the English-Speaking Union Award for an outstanding contribution to Anglo–US understanding.

In 1958 Michael moved to television. He became an Arts Producer in BBC TV Schools Programmes, creating the first British educational art programming on television. He worked on the arts magazine *Monitor*, with Huw Wheldon as editor, a nursery for so many talents, from Melvyn Bragg, Patrick Garland and Jonathan Miller to Ken Russell and John Schlesinger. Michael introduced John Berger to the programme, and over the next five years they made many television programmes together for adults and children. As Michael wrote later:

> We became friends. I stayed with him and his second wife in their large, quiet house in the Forest of Dean, rode round London on the back of his motor-bike, argued with him in Soho restaurants. . . . Films, whether for the cinema or television, were created out of a dialogue between writer and director; I could not imagine working in any other way.

In 1963 Michael obtained a grant from the British Film Institute to make *The Peaches*. This was a short fantasy film, written by his wife Yvonne, starring Juliet Harmer (with a cameo role for Adrian as a small bespectacled chess player) and shot partly in the grounds of their family house in Stanmore, just north of London. It has a wonderful early sixties exuberance, as a beautiful young woman is pursued along the River Thames by sinister bowler-hatted young men, in a kind of fairy tale of Beauty and the City Beasts. It became the British choice for the Cannes Film Festival in 1964, and won several international awards.

Pondering Hollywood, Michael remained with the BBC and created the first British adult educational arts series. In 1966 he made *Giacometti*, a film about the sculptor, with the art critic David Sylvester. The black-and-white film was shown more recently in connection with a Giacometti exhibition, and has worn well.

In 1967 the BBC was to launch colour television on BBC 2. David Attenborough, the channel Controller, thought that a major series on art would be an appropriate way to celebrate the event. He invited Kenneth Clark, former Director of the National Gallery and author of many books, popular and scholarly, on art and artists, to write the series. Michael was asked to produce and direct it. Michael was not initially enthusiastic. He wrote later:

Glittering, self-possessed, armed with precise certainties, Clark seemed to epitomise attitudes the opposite of those of my friends and myself . . . On the other hand, at this very moment . . . I was involved in a film which I believed was going to be a disaster. It had seemed a clever idea to get three bright young foreign journalists – a Frenchman, an Australian and a Zulu – to wander through the swinging London scene, both participating and commenting. But Olivier Todd, Robert Hughes and Lewis Nkosi had little to say to each other; instead of being witty and innovative, the shooting, which was still in progress, showed the concept to be terribly contrived. I was sure the critics were going to pan it. (They did). Nor was it likely that the audience would like it any better. (They didn't).

Naturally, Humphrey Burton (Head of the BBC Music and Arts Department), when he approached me, knew nothing of this future shock. If he had, would he be offering me the most prestigious series at his disposal? Experience taught that such opportunities were rarely given twice. Television was a competitive trade; moreover there was a tide in the affairs of men. . . .

All these contrary currents, rushing through my head like a flood, allowed me to reply with instant enthusiasm, almost before

Burton had finished speaking. Energetic enthusiasm was something Heads of Department responded to gratefully, in a world full of difficult, self-regarding geniuses.

A few days later I had my first meeting with Clark, though it could hardly be called face to face. He had been lunching in a private dining-room in the BBC Television Centre with the Controller of Channel Two, David Attenborough, Humphrey Burton and Stephen Hearst, Head of Arts Department. I was brought in at the coffee stage. The three officials greeted me cheerfully. Clark loitered behind, half turned away. His manner might be termed self-effacing; to me it suggested disdain. His greeting, though perfectly civil, was distinctly chilly. While Attenborough who, as he often demonstrated on film, would find it impossible to be other than warm even to a boa-constrictor, explained the pleasure he felt at the prospect of Clark working with the BBC and the others detailed the resources that would be put at our disposal, Clark and I hardly exchanged a word.

When we had our private meeting, a week or so later, things were no better. Clark produced a small piece of paper on which he had jotted down in his microscopic handwriting the twelve subjects of his programmes. They seemed a very banal list; Raphael, Durer, Rembrandt . . . all the old war horses; and to lump them all into one series would mean there would be little time to say anything profound or original about any of them. Implying this caused Clark's smile to grow even frostier. He envisaged, he said, sitting at a desk in the television studio from which he could cue in the marvellous film I would have taken; it would appear behind his head, in colour. I explained that in my films I tried to make every frame appropriate to the style of the artist concerned; a film was not a superior form of lecture, it was a different entity altogether. Ah, said Clark, but I *am* a lecturer, it is what I know about; I am not a film star. We parted at an impasse.

In the spring of that year I had been the producer of a film about the painter Graham Sutherland. It had been photographed at his home in Menton and also at Nîmes, where the critic Douglas Cooper lived. Sutherland came to London to dub the commentary. I told him about my meeting with Clark. Sutherland nodded. 'I've known K over thirty years, and in all that time I suppose I've had five minutes of intimacy with him.' David Sylvester had also worked with Clark, and advised me not to. 'When you are looking over a script together, he will make you aware that he has noticed that your fingernails are dirty.' A pipe-smoker, my fingernails were always dirty.

I reported to Humphrey Burton that I had probably better be taken off the project. I felt that Clark was too senior and inflexible in his ways to make our partnership possible. Clark clearly felt the same. He wrote to Humphrey suggesting that he was afraid he could not come up to my requirements for a writer. Slightly waspishly, he added that I would probably be happier with a younger, more radical figure, like John Berger.

Humphrey persisted. 'Give it one more try. Show him your Bacon.' In fact this film on the painter, with its staccato cutting and harsh slaughterhouse scenes, could have little direct relevance for the project on high art which we were contemplating. But we must have both approached the viewing in a mood of conciliation. Clark said if I would bear with the efforts of a tyro, he would agree to come to as many of the locations as I required: there should be no lecture desk. I said he should write his scripts as he had always done, as complete entities, and I would turn them, without appreciable alteration, into film scripts.

This was the summer when London and Moscow zoos were co-operating to try and produce a baby panda. The world's press reported every stage of the difficult, and ultimately sterile, courtship. Humphrey Burton was so delighted with our agreement that, as he wrote in a memo, he felt as though he had brought about the mating of Chi Chi and An An.

The first film shoot was less than auspicious.

Very early in our planning we had decided to begin, not with the first film, but one from the middle of the series. In this way any early errors in style would be cushioned by being surrounded by the more confident presentation of later filming.

They decided to start with the Renaissance, Programme Four in the series, very much Clark's period, and with a wealth of beauty to show.

But while our planning was going on, in November 1966, an unprecedented catastrophe occurred in Florence. The Arno flooded, burst its banks, and inundated all the lower city. At first the extent of the disaster was not apparent from London. Few lives were lost and floods subsided within thirty-six hours. But they left a terrible trail of damage; not only from the mud and refuse of the Arno. Many Florentines heated their homes and shops with oil which they kept stored in their cellars. Mixed with the flood, the oil was carried into churches and libraries and cloisters, seeping into the stone, staining the paintings, gumming together the pages of illuminated manuscripts. Not even the war had caused so much destruction. My friend Robert Hughes came back from making a TV report on the damage with a startling account of seeing the great Cimabue crucifix broken and lying in the mud, of the stench, and of the devoted labours of volunteer helpers from all over Europe.

Still, there were nearly six months to go before filming in Florence in April, and they decided to keep their first location.

It was much worse than I could have believed. I had first visited Florence soon after the war when the banks of the Arno were a confusion of noise and dust and rebuilding. Now the area of disaster was larger, the amount to be restored greater, the damage more complex and difficult to repair. In every cloister and chapel powerful heaters whirred, but hideous brown stains disfigured most of the places in which Clark wished to appear.

They discussed alternative locations, not as appropriate as those originally chosen by Clark. They could not afford to delay the filming, as this would put all later plans back.

Two alternatives suggested themselves: re-writing the present script to fit what was still available in Florence, or for Sir Kenneth to write another programme quickly enough for us to be able to arrange filming in a completely different place within a month. Neither option seemed very palatable. I asked Clark if he would like a day to think about it. The answer came at once and briskly.

'Oh no, I'll write Number Five. It's got the advantage of keeping us in Italy. The Accademia's all right, you said? Most of the rest is set in Rome. You're travelling back on Tuesday? I'll have it ready for you when you arrive.'

Tuesday was three days away. Normally, a writer would take at least two to three weeks for a six-thousand-word script.

The second script read better than the first, though 'the sections on individual artists simply followed each other like separate railway carriages. And they still centred on art history, though it was implied that they were about something else.'

Michael had invited Peter Montagnon, who had made a number of distinguished programmes on the arts, to be his co-producer. Discussing the script problem after the speedy arrival of the second unsatisfactory script, Peter made a momentous suggestion, which Michael noted.

'He's obviously getting better, and he clearly responds well to pressure. Why don't we ask him to write the other Italian script, the one on Baroque Rome, right away? If he could do it in two weeks, we could film it on the same trip. That would be a big budget saving and we'd have two in the bag.'

That was characteristic of Peter. Very small, with fragile wrists and an intelligent aesthetic face, his quiet manner concealed a dynamo of tough professional thinking. It was just this sort of ginger that I had hoped for when I asked him to join the team. . . .

So it was that I read Clark's first draft of Programme Seven over lunch on a terrace in Fiesole. I had gone there to see if there was a distant view of Florence that was better as an approach shot than any of the others I had seen. (There was not.) As I was leaving my hotel the London post had arrived and I had stuffed the script unopened in my briefcase. Now I took it down in one long gulp through the white wine and the coffee. It was not their influence, nor the ambrosial air, that made it an experience of a quite different order from reading the first two. Suddenly there was a unifying theme that laced its way through the pages and the theme was not art, but Rome. Rome at a certain moment in her history. Artists and architects (and popes) were the foreground that illuminated the theme, but the whole had an invigorating sweep that carried you from start to finish. The writing was fresh, caustic and pithy, totally unlike the well-worked caution of Clark's earlier efforts. It was one of the best scripts I had read.

So filming was about to begin, in Florence.

I was preoccupied with the imminent arrival of Clark and the film unit. It would be the first time we had all worked together. Lady Clark was coming too. Here was one of the radical social adjustments which give a film-maker's life such variety. For the last few days I had led a studious existence, walking the streets of Florence alone, or in the company of our local researcher, a charming and witty German art historian, spending hours looking in detail at every object and location we were going to film, reading the background texts. It was a quiet, concentrated period that I very much enjoyed, reminding me of the academic life I had nearly chosen on leaving university. Now I had to marshal a different set of skills, to pass on my conclusions to writer, cameraman and recordist with such energy and enthusiasm that they would adjust *their* vision towards the one I had arrived at. There was never very much time to do it, and simultaneously I needed to be aware of the intricate social balances that were developing between twelve diverse temperaments thrown together on the road. They demanded adjustment and tact from the director; leadership at the platoon level, as an old war-hand said.

The first day's filming was a silent shoot at the Accademia.

The six unfinished sculptures by Michelangelo, known as the Prisoners, suggested exciting possibilities for filming. By moving the camera in close-up over the roughly worked stone, to where the finished portion of the torso jutted forth and then sank back into the rock, and continuing with similar explorations on the other figures I hoped to create a simile for the imagination of the artist. As was so often to happen, the unit grasped the idea and excelled it. Tubby (Englander, lighting cameraman) accentuated the effect by powerful raking side-lighting, and Ken (MacMillan, camera-operator), on the tracking camera, provided some ingeniously slow and sinuous movements. We spent a happy and absorbed day under the cynical eye of the museum guards. We were the third unit to film the sculptures in a month. The Germans, we were told, had worked everything out in advance and were able to carry through the most complex moves with hardly a word spoken; the American cameraman quarrelled continuously with his director; we, on the other hand, spent more time discussing what to do than actually filming.

'You see,' whispered Erhardt, our twinkly German fixer, 'these guardians are all Fascisti at heart. They prefer the military precision of my countrymen to your democracy.'

To be able to talk things through in the unhurried atmosphere of the museum was a valuable introduction to each other's style of work. We settled down with remarkable ease; the filming on the Prisoners was technically as complex as most of what we were to achieve in the next two years. No sequence I worked on gave me greater pleasure.

The next day began less auspiciously. Back again in the Accademia at 8.30 we were to concentrate on the David. Later in the morning Clark was to speak two important sections in front of it. There seemed nothing particularly difficult about that. From the museum entrance there was an unhampered view of the statue, bathed in natural light against the far wall. All we had to do was place the camera inside the swing doors and position Clark in the foreground. Both Tubby and Ken demurred. It would be a terribly boring shot, they thought. Once they had the camera in position they proved it. The distant David towered over the stand-in speaker's shoulder with all the impact of a postage stamp. On the other hand, if we got closer nothing was visible except David's knees, feet and the enormous plinth on which he stood. Perhaps we could angle the camera to look up at the statue, suggested Ken. Foreshortening had the unfortunate effect of increasing the prominence of David's already well-developed manhood. Each suggestion involved lugging the heavy 35mm camera on its gyro-mount into a new position. Our voices rose in urgency as the time for Clark's arrival drew closer. The guards snickered together. The Inglesi were at it again.

They were still at it when, precisely at 10.30, the time for which he was called, Sir Kenneth entered with Lady Clark. He was dressed immaculately in cool grey with a touch of cambric at the breast pocket, but at first I didn't notice. I was lying sweating on the marble floor locked in argument with the equally prostrate Ken. A discreet cough from Tubby brought me to my feet.

Clark asked me dryly if I thought he had dressed correctly for this particular sequence. I can see now that what to wear when posed in front of a naked man does present interesting problems, but at the time it seemed a matter of supreme indifference. Hardly looking at him, I explained that we were having some difficulties; would he and Lady Clark like to go away for an hour and do some shopping? His eyes seemed to recede to grey points, but he remained as courteous as usual. No, no, it would be interesting for them to watch us at work . . . He retired with Lady Clark to the thronelike chairs the guards had brought up, and crossed his elegant knees. Here was the long-awaited crunch and I was grovelling at his feet, cheek on the dusty marble, squinting up through Ken's viewfinder.

Clark's ironic gaze, boring into the back of my neck, told me I was an incompetent loon, and every unavailing minute increased the weight of the charge. For the truth was there was no easy answer. If you envisage that the dimensions of the television screen are roughly 3 × 4, where height precedes breadth; that the David on its plinth is a narrow twenty feet high; and Sir Kenneth Clark was probably about five foot ten, you begin to see the nature of the problem. Why had I not foreseen it? Because the perfect proportions of Michelangelo's carving deceives the eye as to its true size even when you are in its presence.

Yet within minutes I had an inadvertent revenge. Anyone who from below has tried to focus on the top of a tall object while interposing a smaller object in the foreground will recognise the only solution: to get the camera as low as possible and bring the foreground object as close as possible. If the two objects are still not in alignment there is no alternative except to lower the background or raise the foreground. I could not do anything to the sculpture, so I would have to raise Clark. It was a prospect I had been struggling against for some time, because I knew he would not like it – I would not have liked on my first exposure to the group of technicians I was going to be working with for the next couple of years to be stuck high on a box in an empty museum where every other natural alternative – leaning against pillars, sitting on chairs, walking about – *seemed* available.

Actually two metal camera boxes were needed . . . the second box made the perch quite rickety. Clark watched these feverish but largely silent preparations inscrutably from the sidelines, rather as an aristocrat might have observed the erection of the guillotine meant for him. When the moment of trial came he refused the offer of my supporting hand. A man with plenty of reason for personal vanity, he must have know the camera angle would be the least flattering to his uneven top teeth and the beginning of middle-aged flab around his jowls. It accentuated his unfortunate tendency to look down his nose . . .

Yet art . . . also provides unexpected recompense. The realisation of the ambiguous visual response that the perfect proportions of the David evoked led me to persuade Clark to stay on and shelter behind the plinth, while we set up the camera for a long shot. The revelation of the true size of Michelangelo's masterpiece when the diminutive figure of Clark walked into view created a memorable *frisson* in the completed film.

The Roman shoot in May continued uneasily. The Vatican, wrote Michael, insisted on the delivery by my own hand of enormous amounts of Italian lire (in cash) before they would allow the filming of the Sistine Chapel that they had agreed to in principle months before. A transaction that did not prevent the arrest, by a clanking platoon of the Swiss Guard, of Peter Montagnon while filming in St. Peter's Square a few days later.

Back in London, editing Programme 5, Michael remained unsure of its quality.

The film seemed an uncertain mixture of standard art criticism and social history, requiring more knowledge of the fifteenth-century background than we could expect from a television audience. Nor did the three giant stars of our show – Leonardo, Michelangelo and Raphael – get along very well together. There seemed nothing really to unite them except their proximity – a state of affairs that was mirrored by our own relations with the Clarks. These reached their nadir in a lunch laid on at their home, Saltwood Castle in Kent. Peter, Ann Turner, our head of research and a programme director, Tubby Englander and I had gone down for a reconnaissance. After a distinctly meagre meal, Lady Clark said she expected us to leave a token of our gratitude for the cook. When asked what would be appropriate, she said she assumed we did not want to be outdone by the Queen Mother, who the week before had left £20 (in those days a good meal could be had in the West End for £2). Our combined resources did not reach the required amount, but Peter suggested writing a cheque. 'Careful, K, it might bounce,' called Lady Clark across the table.

Relations improved as K continued to respond with flexibility and brilliance to the demands of film. Michael particularly enjoyed working with him on the film about the Dutch Golden Age.

I had been stationed in Holland at the end of the war and retained the happiest memories of it. I liked Dutch art and the practical humanism of Dutch society; an appreciation I was surprised to find Clark shared.

Our days in Amsterdam and the Hague were much more relaxed than the summer trip to Italy had been. Lady Clark was with us, but so was their friend, the actress Irene Worth, adding a touch of mature glamour to our filming on the canals. It was as though the soft clear light of that rational man-made landscape entered into our own relations with each other. I persuaded Clark to let us start the film with a dawn sequence on the polders north of Amsterdam, where Rembrandt had done some of his most memorable drawings, and suggested the title for the programme: The Light of Experience.

We were guided, in a breathtakingly rushed night journey to reach the location before the sun, by an old friend, Friso ten Holt, the Dutch painter. This led to the revelation of another side of Clark's character. I told him the story of Friso's brief television fame and its unhappy aftermath. K visited his studio on the Prinsengracht, liked his pictures, and put him in touch with a London gallery that subsequently mounted a successful show of his work.

Filming at Greenwich showed another endearing trait.

I was filming the exterior of the Royal Naval College when he appeared round a corner, moving with considerable haste. 'I know you're busy,' he murmured, 'but just come and look at this'. He took my hand (*he took my hand*, this man who never touched anybody) and rushed me into the chapel. Under the pulpit he stopped and gestured at the asymmetrical sweep of the stairs. 'Aren't those the most perfect curves you've ever seen,' he whispered. He was trembling with excitement. Now I knew why he was so successful as a lecturer. He was really passionate about aesthetics.

The next big filming stint carried the crew through Europe on a five-month trip which would give them the first four films. Michael's home in Stanmore provided the first location.

> 'Just do that again, Nicholas', I demanded. My ten-year-old son crawled carefully through the icy fronds of the giant thistles. Above his head the camera panned with him, recording the stirring of the spiky tops. With added huffs and puffs on the sound track I hoped this would suggest the passage of some nameless Dark Age beast in the first programme.

Filming Kenneth Clark in the Baptistery at Poitiers turned out to be a crucial hinge of the whole series.

> Its very dreariness, its glum seediness, was part of Clark's theme. Insignificance is exceptionally hard to put over on television – an aggressive medium that bombards the eye far more than it persuades it. We are accustomed to such cajolery and are liable to switch over or switch off attention as soon as we are no longer gripped by the metaphorical lapel . . .
>
> Despite the awful weather half a dozen people huddled outside, drawn by the unprecedented light we had been pouring into this corner of the Dark Ages. They turned out to be foreign students. When in answer to their questions I told them we were filming because Poitiers had been a bastion of civilisation in the Dark Ages, I aroused an immediate response. 'This dump?' scoffed one young black American. 'Man, they shouldn't have bothered.'

Later in the shoot they reached Paris as planned in May – May 1968.

The next seven days were some of the most remarkable in my working career. We were filming the opening sequences of the series in a city in turmoil. When Clark on the Left Bank of the Seine just beyond Notre Dame said: 'What is civilisation? I can't define it – yet. But I think I can recognise it when I see it; and I am looking at it now', what he was actually looking at were the menacing groups of fifty armed riot police who stood on every street corner. I and two others were gassed the next day when we were involved in a full-scale confrontation on the Boulevard Saint-Germain. I sat in a box with taxi drivers and advocates at the Odeon Theatre while the students discussed philosophical issues and the police massed outside. As the week progressed and we continued our film-making, the spasmodic strikes in sympathy hardened into a nationwide stoppage. How were we going to leave Paris and fulfil the complex schedule that lay before us? On the black market Peter acquired just enough cans of petrol to carry our convoy with care to the German border. Early on Saturday 18 May we fled the riot-torn site of civilisation for the barbarian north.

They filmed in Germany and Norway, and then followed the Viking route to Iona.

It took longer to reach – by ferry, aeroplane, car, steamer, and ultimately a small boat – than any other location in the entire series. It was worth it. . . .

The sand glowed against the dark sea, the seals came up around the rowing boat on which I had Clark land in the wake of St Columba (characteristically of film-making we had to carry the boat on our shoulders across the island to achieve this sequence). Certain places do seem to generate an aura beyond the explicable combinations of geography and climate; I think of Delphi in Greece and Ise in Japan. Neither for me has quite the power of Iona. Yet even here while we were filming Clark beside the celtic cross, a priest came running out of the cathedral with the news that Robert Kennedy had been assassinated. . . .

Iona was in many ways a culmination of everything I felt about *Civilisation*. The journey of St Columba was an affirmation of confidence in the Christian message against all the perils of the Dark Ages; it led to Iona becoming a haven of art and scholarship (the Book of Kells was probably written there); as such it was recognised as a founding stone of western civilisation, hence the tombs of many Scottish kings; yet it was totally destroyed by the pagan Vikings early in the tenth century. This seemed proof of the fragility of human aspirations and society, rising and falling and rising again as Iona had done in the teeth of the new barbarian menace of Hitler – the centre of the rebuilt cathedral contained a sculpture by Lipschitz, a Jew who had escaped the Holocaust. But beyond the brevity of human life Iona embodied the effortless continuity of nature. On that speck of sand in the shining light of air and ocean it was as though one were looking straight into the eye of God.

Though the BBC was confident about the quality of *Civilisation*, some early reviews were less sure. By the end of the three months of weekly broadcasts, most had been won over, and the day after the final broadcast in May 1969 *The Times* devoted its main leader to the series under the heading *How Like an Angel*, a unique recognition for a television series. Clark was made a lord.

The series had difficulty in finding a home on US television, but the administrator of the National Gallery of Art in Washington, Howard Adams, put it on at lunchtime in the gallery theatre. This seated three hundred people but on the first day twenty-four thousand turned up. *The New York Times* printed on its front page a

photograph of a long queue, which included Jackie Onassis and half
the members of the Nixon administration.

The most extraordinary scene occurred two years later when the
Gallery gave Clark a special award. People were packed throughout
the gallery: Clark had to progress slowly from room to room to
reach the podium; the dense crowds rose to their feet at his passing
so that he was like a surfer borne forward on a rising surge of
adulation. I have never experienced such an intensely emotional and
adoring crowd except at the appearance of the Pope at St. Peter's.

Before the series was completed Michael came to believe that the kind
of extended personal essay that *Civilisation* had become would be a new
form of broadcasting. He went to see Huw Wheldon, by then Director of
BBC Television, to suggest that they look for possible candidates for
further series. Michael decided that the country which had so attracted
his family and himself would be his next subject: America.

Michael described the search for the ideal storyteller for America in an
article for *The Listener* in April 1976.

The trouble was – I thought to myself for the thousandth time, as I
settled down in the tube train on my way to the Television Centre
and absently opened my copy of *The Listener* – the trouble was I
needed an impossible combination of talents: someone who knew the
whole of the States intimately, and yet had preserved the fresh vision
of the immigrant, a brilliant storyteller with a balanced sense of
history, a seasoned performer who could write for film, an extrovert
who was also a bibliophile, a man generous enough to take the cut
and thrust of team work, a pleasant companion, witty as well as
clever . . . impossible! My eye fell on an exceptionally well-turned
paragraph – funny, it was about America, too: the reprint of a
radio talk on the funeral of Eisenhower. Who could have written it?
(This is absolutely true.) I turned the page to look for the author.

That afternoon (it was 8 May 1969), I met Alistair Cooke for the first time over tea at the Dorchester. And the next morning, it was all settled – except for three-and–a-half years' hard work, thousands of words, millions of feet of film, and over 150,000 miles of travel.

The article also contains a vivid description of the visits from the American uncle, Clifford, and the extraordinary story of the earlier American uncles.

Our family connections with the United States began in 1830, when a great-great-great-uncle emigrated from Southowram in Yorkshire. Later, he became one of the Forty-Niners, and, on failing to find gold, set up a grocery business in San Francisco. A great-great-uncle was for many years paymaster on the Grand Trunk Railway. A lively artist, he sketched scenes in the Civil War, edited a comic magazine called *Froth*, wrote and performed in a number of operettas in Detroit in the 1860s and 1870s, and despite his mutton-chop whiskers, was famous for his female impersonations. One of his sons absconded at the age of nineteen with two beautiful teenaged actresses, and was arrested in the Far West for passing dud cheques. The other, who was secretary of the Detroit Stock Exchange, maintained that he was the Earl of Scarthmore in Yorkshire, England, and ended up in an asylum.

Another ancestor, Bethel Aspinall of Minneapolis, inherited a fortune in middle age and set off to see the world. He got only as far as Memphis, Tennessee, where he fell down a lift-shaft, leaving all his money to his English nephews. Young men of nineteen and twenty-one, they had a heady season in London with their own hansom cabs and a box at the opera, and then decided to breed English bloodstock in the West. Their idea was to cross the thoroughbreds they shipped out with them with the tough wild horse that they would catch on the open range.

But the ranch they started in Colorado in 1883 was not a success, despite the advice of Buffalo Bill Cody, a neighbour. The horses were rustled, and while gambling in a saloon in Denver, the younger brother, Will, accused his opponent of cheating. The next day, his brother Fred went looking for him and saw his boot sticking out of a rubbish dump. Will was on the end of it, miraculously not dead, though he had been hit on the head and robbed. He survived to see, thirty years later, on a bartender who was serving him in New York, the pearl-monogrammed tiepin which he had lost in that Denver saloon.

Such stories were fortified by old letters describing breakneck moonlight rides across the prairies; sepia photographs of young men sporting long moustaches, bandoliers and pistols; and the huge head of a buffalo in the Batley museum, which my great-grandfather had shot while on a visit to Colorado. They strengthened a romantic vision of America already fed on Zane Grey, Mayne Reid and R. M. Ballantyne. . . .

Fred and Will gave up the ranch and retired to Detroit, where, in the course of time, they prospered and married. But neither had a son, and so they invited their nephew, my uncle Clifford, to join them in their brick manufacturing business. It was 1904; he was sixteen, and had spent all his life on the farm in Yorkshire. When he went, his mother and his younger sister went with him to settle him in. It was a trip my mother, who was twelve, has never forgotten.

She stayed in an Indian village on the shore of Lake Huron, drove in horse-drawn sleighs across the snow, was entranced by the warmth, wealth and size of America. When it was time to return, Fred drove her and her mother from Detroit to Quebec in a newfangled open car. The journey took a week. The ladies were swathed in veils against the dust of the dirt roads, and it was my mother's job to sit at the back and jump out with a brick to put under the rear wheel, if the uncertain engine faltered on a hill.

Following the success of *Alistair Cooke's America*, in 1973 Michael was invited to join an Anglo-French delegation to China to arrange a major exhibition of Chinese archaeological treasures which would travel Europe and the United States. He returned to make two films there, and was fascinated and impressed by the country, then hard to visit for non-Communist foreigners. In an article for *The Listener* he wrote:

Everywhere the food was delicious, varied and exotic. Some things like sea slugs were almost too exotic. They are considered a great delicacy and are usually encountered floating in a sort of broth. They look a cross between a distended snail and a jellyfish and the first hazard is to capture them with the chopsticks. Then you seize one end with the teeth and suck in the rest of the warm glutinous mass. They are clearly an acquired taste, like oysters, which they somewhat resemble with their faint flavour of the sea. . . .

In the big cities of China, there are few policemen visible except those on traffic duty. I learnt not to bother to lock my hotel room, to be confidently careless with money and private possessions. I was told opium smoking had been eliminated, I never saw a drunk or a prostitute. Cigarettes are everywhere, and on the long-distance trains there is a good deal of card-playing: that seems almost the limit of indulgence. There are few cinemas and fewer films; there are no dance-halls, no magazines of entertainment, not many new books; television is rudimentary and virtually restricted to public places; radio is largely instructional or devoted to the music of the revolutionary operas; there are no privately owned motor-cars. In these circumstances pleasures become as personal and simple as observing the bloom on a single flower or the polish on a stone. I once saw from my hotel window my middle-aged interpreter stand for half an hour alone watching the changing colours of the sunset over a lake. . . .

At the end of a long evening's discussion in Peking a highly intelligent man said: 'perhaps the greatest gift we can offer the

West is our optimism'. This man, a middle-rank cadre in government, bicycled to the office, probably earned about £12 a month, probably paid about 60p in rent for his three-roomed apartment, worked six days a week, and, in common with his fellows, had no time off beyond the seventh day. 'China is too poor yet to allow us holidays,' the man explained.

The hopes of intellectuals seem based on faith in the potential of the 80 per cent peasant population. This made more sense each time we went to a country commune. I had asked to be allowed to visit one of the self-help projects, but I wasn't prepared for what I saw when I climbed to the top of a large earth mound in Shensi Province. Two thousand men and women from fourteen villages were toiling resolutely with the simplest tools to build a vast reservoir to improve their water supply. Red flags fluttered and patriotic music echoed tinnily from the amplifiers. The sight of so much organised energy seemed the true apotheosis of Communism.

In 1976 Michael made *Royal Heritage* for the BBC, to mark the Queen's Silver Jubilee. No royalist at the outset, he became increasingly impressed by the Queen, the Duke of Edinburgh and Prince Charles. Michael and I had just met, and I would lose him for weekends to Balmoral or Sandringham. He would return with tales of the Queen's talent for mimicry, or a brace of pheasants from a Sandringham shoot.

Windsor was our favourite palace. It seems to express the genius of the British and their peculiar conception of monarchy in the way that Versailles formulates the rational intellect of the French. Rambling, old, enduring, full of surprising beauty and some ugliness, added to and modified through a thousand years, Windsor is built into the landscape, so as to seem an essential and enhancing part of it. It speaks for a noble past yet is quite well adapted for modern living. It stirs you more than you expected.

What could follow *Royal Heritage*? Michael and I were living together, Michael's sons were growing up, and he was beginning, at 53, to think about changes to his life.

Adrian Malone, producer of *The Ascent of Man*, had just finished a series on economics with J. K. Galbraith, *The Age of Uncertainty*. Filming in the United States with the great economist, he had seen that Americans might like to make their own major documentary series. The commercial nature of the networks, and the fragmented and underfunded status of the Public Broadcasting Service, had so far precluded this. Adrian believed he might find funding to start a centre of excellence, a Bauhaus as he put it, which would provide the expertise to make these major series.

While the BBC had been able to fund *Civilisation* on its own as a special expenditure (Michael's initial request had been for £9,000 a programme, since production costs in those days were calculated only on the actual money that had to be paid out in fees and travel expenses; only a little more than this took a twelve-person film unit travelling with a 35mm camera, tracks and lights all over Europe for nearly two years), costs had risen sharply through the 1970s and *Alistair Cooke's America* had been made possible by the support of Time-Life. So the money for these series was increasingly going to come from America; why not set up a production base there? Adrian initially invited Michael to contribute, as a kind of visiting producer or professor. Michael, feeling changes around him, thought that he might at last follow the uncles and emigrate. A friend of J.K. Galbraith's, Stanley Weiss, loaned Adrian the money to move his family to the States. Michael found work with *American Heritage* magazine, who thought they might make films based on their magazine's rich knowledge base and talented stable of writers, rather like the enduring *National Geographic* films. One of these was made, *An American Christmas*, produced with WGBH, the Boston public broadcasting station. It took us on some wonderful trips across the United States, from the Navajo mid-winter in Arizona's Canyon de

Chelly, to recollections of snow-bound winters in Iowa, and the dropping of Christmas parcels by helicopter to the isolated lighthouses of New England.

The next film project drew Michael back to London. He'd spent so much of his childhood near the sea, and his love of history constantly reminded him of the importance of the sea's role in our island story. So when he was approached to make a series about the sea, he agreed immediately. The Thomson Organisation, noting the sales of the books associated with television series, and contemplating the advance of the home video system, with the possibility of similar sales of video tapes for the home market, offered finance for the series.

Clare Francis had twice sailed the Atlantic single-handed and written a successful book, *Come Hell or High Water*, about her adventures. Would she, could she, present a major television series? Michael invited her to lunch on her return from skippering ADC *Accutrac*'s bid to win the Round the World Trophy. She was small, blonde, and very good-looking, with a fragile air that concealed the strength of the ballet dancer she had trained to be. She was elegantly dressed and very feminine, but Michael was transfixed by a glimpse of her hands on the tablecloth, scarred with the marks of wind, water and rope. He was delighted with her, and she agreed to present the series, though she was anxious that it not begin too soon. 'Something rather exciting may happen.' It did: her son Tom was born just a few months before the television series went into production, carrying Clare into the pressured schedules of television all over the world for the next two years. Michael filmed the oldest boat in the world, Pharoah Cheop's funeral boat, the wooden planks and the ropes which bound them still perfectly sound; he sailed with Clare and the film unit on the replica of Sir Francis Drake's ship the *Golden Hinde*, on her voyage around the world. They travelled with her through the South China Sea, where the chief hazard was once again piracy. Powerful small boats roamed the waters, looking for rich pickings from private yachts. The *Golden Hinde* was a very visible and not a very fast target.

One of Michael's most vivid filming trips was to the Louisiades, a group of islands off the coast of Papua New Guinea, thought to be one of the most untouched fishing communities in the world. It seemed an earthly paradise of grass-skirted women, palm trees and ritual, marred only by giant land crabs. Missionaries had been there, so the islanders were nominally Christian, and one anthropologist had worked there. She guided the unit through the mazes of appropriate behaviour.

Most of the islanders can build sea-going boats and sail them, swim underwater and catch fish, grow crops and skin a pig; they can sing, play musical instruments and are clever storytellers; they can build a house and furnish it; they know something of herbal medicines. Their lives demand many skills, daring and initiative. The benefits of civilisation – wider horizons, more complex pleasure, a longer life-expectancy – seem increasingly passive in contrast. Something like the island way of life was the common lot of mankind for thousands of centuries. Now it has almost vanished everywhere.

One of Michael's most enjoyable experiences of later years was the making of *Vintage: A History of Wine by Hugh Johnson*. Michael had been initially concerned about the visual potential of the subject (it's either red or white) but was rapidly won over by Hugh's enthusiasm and knowledge, and their shared love of history. Quickly their approach to wine became the story of its close entanglement, over thousands of years, with the culture and history of Europe. In Babylon, Ur and Sumer they had drunk wine imported from the north, carried down the Euphrates on rafts. Romans planted their vines up the Rhone valley and northwards throughout Europe, and now the making of fine wine has followed money and power to the New World. Interesting locations, from the Caucasus to Japan, and winemakers who epitomised Hugh's description – 'Farmer and artist, drudge and dreamer, hedonist and masochist, alchemist and accountant – the winegrower is all these things, and has been since the flood' – all contributed to a series which brought depth and illumination to what might have been considered a slight subject.

Working with the Mexican novelist Carlos Fuentes and American historian Peggy Liss on *The Buried Mirror: Reflections on Spain and the New World* brought new challenges and rewards, from running with the wetbacks through an illegal border crossing from Mexico, to making artistic amends for Spain's absence from *Civilisation*.

Highlanders was a project which had grown from *Royal Heritage* days, when Michael, happy to be in Scotland again, though in rather grander circles than during his student days, mentioned to the then Lord Chamberlain, Lord Maclean, that he would love to make a series about Scotland, and particularly the Highlands. Lord Maclean responded immediately: 'You must meet my cousin Fitzroy.' The meeting was arranged for a day when Lord Maclean, as clan chief, honoured Sir Fitzroy Maclean for reclaiming his hereditary territory of the island of Dunconnel. Of Fitzroy's many daring military exploits, this was the most recent, though no battles were involved. He had rowed out to the small uninhabited island off the west coast of Scotland and planted the Maclean standard, unopposed. Fitzroy was enthusiastic about television, and delighted to collaborate with Michael on the making of a series about the Highland clans. Collaboration began with enjoyable lunches and visits to the Macleans' beautiful Adam house on the edge of Loch Fyne. Commissioning editors were less enthusiastic, and at one of our meetings the subject matter swerved to another passion of Fitzroy's, Russia. He felt it important to bring to general attention the many nations and cultures which coexisted under the banner of the then monolithic-seeming Soviet Union. Michael, Fitzroy and Jerome Gary, a young American producer who had joined the team, made a far-reaching reconnaissance trip over all the Russias, and beyond. It was at the furthest point of this journey, in the Ferghana valley on the borders of China, that Michael felt an overwhelming urge to come home. It was 1981 and I was nine months pregnant with our daughter Chloe. Fitzroy and Jerome waved Michael off, and without a ticket, and without any Russian, miming imminent fatherhood, Michael managed to board plane after plane through a very long day, until he arrived at our home unannounced at midnight.

The Russian series was made, but not by us. Michael's old collaborator Peter Montagnon had started his own independent production company, Antelope (fast on its feet and smells good). Ted Turner had taken an interest in the company, and Fitzroy had persuaded Turner that his series on Russia should be made.

Later Fitzroy suggested a short series on Yugoslavia, where he had spent so much of the Second World War fighting with Tito's partisans. It was ten years after Tito's death, and the strains which eventually blasted Yugoslavia apart were beginning to show. Fitzroy was deeply attached to the country, and was the only foreigner at the time to have obtained permission to buy a house there. He owned a small palace on the island of Korcula, where we took Chloe for her first foreign holiday. Visiting Yugoslavia with Fitzroy was rather like being involved in a royal progress, though with real affection from the people. If we ever went out without Fitzroy, we found that six-month-old Chloe was quite a good substitute crowd-pleaser, babies also being warmly welcomed everywhere in Yugoslavia.

Eventually *Highlanders* was made, commissioned by ITV to mark the two hundred-and-fiftieth anniversary of the return of Bonnie Prince Charlie. For a man who had named his two sons Charles and James, it wasn't a bad pretext. As Michael had noted about Iona, many of the locations were harder to reach than anywhere else in the world. Seas and mountains made short journeys full of complications. I was producing another series for our company at the same time; *Nomads*, which looked at the lives of travelling people in Mauritania, Mongolia, Siberia and Kenya. Though by definition the nomads were hard to reach, I often thought that the logistics of our series were proving much less complicated than Michael's *Highlanders*.

The last film that Michael directed was very close to his heart, a film about Vermeer. It was made for Melvyn Bragg's *South Bank Show*, the first time that Melvyn and Michael had worked together since the *Monitor* days of the early 1960s, and the impetus was given by the international Vermeer exhibition in 1996. Michael had always loved Vermeer's work, and the chance to spend months examining the paintings, teasing out their meanings, and using the buildings and landscapes of Holland to evoke the age was a pleasure indeed, as was working again with Dutch art historians, fixers and scientists.

Michael explored other projects in the years that followed; a film about Matisse based upon Hilary Spurling's biography, films about China, changing so rapidly from the closed society he had visited in 1973; but the last series he was to produce was *The Face of Russia*, written and presented by James Billington, the Librarian of Congress. It had started life as a ten-part series, an acknowledgement of all that Russia had brought culturally to the world, at a moment when Russian turmoil was exporting mainly mafiosi and millionaires. Michael didn't direct any of them; instead they were made with flair by Murray Grigor, a friend and colleague of long standing. The programmes dwindled to three, cramming in Russia's journey from religious art to modernism, its unique architecture and the literature which sprang into being fully-formed in the nineteenth century, perhaps, it has been said, following the building of the European, classically inspired St Petersburg, which could allow Russians to step outside themselves, at least theoretically, and to look back, to examine themselves and their world. The last programme dealt with the equally extraordinary birth of Russian music, also in the nineteenth century, and with Russia's influential twentieth-century cinema.

At the end of these films, in 1998, Michael seemed tired. He was 75, and, though he had never envisaged retirement (he told me early in our relationship that he would like to go like Humphrey Jennings, the brilliant documentary director of the 1940s, who went over a cliff backwards while making a film, framing with his hands a 'marvellous shot'; that sounded good, until I learned that Jennings was only 42 at the time), it began to seem unlikely that Michael would make another film.

He worked on his memoir, recalling his early childhood and the war years. He admired our teenage daughter, in her last years at school and soon to go to his old university, Edinburgh. Thinking that deafness played its part in his gradually increasing absence from the life around him, I started on a round of doctors and therapists. He was diagnosed with Alzheimer's Disease in 2000. Since then the scope of his life has quietly diminished. Age Concern has helped, as have sensitive and thoughtful carers, doctors and specialists. A talented artist visitor from Age Concern, David Clegg, helped Michael to finish this memoir. David then set up an art project, working with artists Becky Shaw and Eric Fong, who collaborated with five of Age Concern's dementia clients to create some impressive and extraordinary works of art. Over a period of several months Becky and David visited Michael. They taped a continuing conversation with him, from which Becky drew complex coloured diagrams of the ebbs and flows of the conversation. These mind maps were studded with the images that Michael had described, from grass-skirted Julia in the Louisiades, to horses from cave paintings, to the Mitchell bombers of the war years. Becky compared Michael's mind to a museum, in which much of value was hidden, but many things could not be retrieved. She constructed, from the mind maps, a large perspex structure, a kind of three-dimensional maze, in which were embedded these icons of Michael's life. It was displayed at the Serpentine Gallery in 2003, as part of *Remembering the Present*, the Age Concern project. Family and many friends came, some of whom could find the episodes in which they figured frozen in the perspex museum. It seemed that creativity hadn't ended after all.

Conversation with Michael becomes increasingly surreal, but bears rewards. The title of this afterword comes from a conversation he had recently with Wendy Ewald, the photographer daughter of Michael's beautiful cousin Carolyn. She was discussing the pleasures and pains of writing down memories, and he spoke of his increasing difficulty in capturing the words. 'Yes,' he said, 'they're like ants on snow'.

INDEX